Practical Succession Management

Dedicated to
Ruth Munro and Bruce Douglas-Mann. We need more of these characters in our
next generation of organisational leadership.

Practical Succession Management

How to Future-proof Your Organisation

ANDREW MUNRO

GOWER

Published by
Gower Publishing Limited
Gower House
Croft Road
Aldershot
Hants GU11 3HR
England

Gower Publishing Company
Suite 420
101 Cherry Street
Burlington,
VT 05401-4405
USA

Andrew Munro has asserted his right under the Copyright, Designs and Patents Act 1988 to be identified as the author of this work.

British Library Cataloguing in Publication Data
Munro, Andrew
    Practical succession management : how to future-proof your
    organisation
    1. Executive succession 2. Executive succession - Planning
    3. Industrial management
    I. Title
    658.4'07128

    ISBN 0 566 08570 4

Library of Congress Cataloging-in-Publication Data
Munro, Andrew.
    Practical succession management : how to future-proof your organization / by Andrew Munro.
        p. cm.
    ISBN: 0-566-08570-4
    1. Executive succession -- Planning. I. Title
    HD38.2.M864 2004
    658.4'0711--dc22

                                                                        2004017180

Typeset by Bournemouth Colour Press, Parkstone, Poole.
Printed in Great Britain by T.J. International Ltd, Padstow.

Contents

List of Figures

Preface

I fell into this project by accident. Although succession management has been a major theme within our consultancy for over ten years now and, going further back, a focus of my professional interest for almost 20 years, my approach has been low profile, working for our clients "behind the scenes". Succession management is not the kind of consulting activity that lends itself to high-profile conference presentations or articles in the professional press. In 2002 Gower contacted one of our clients to work on a book on succession management. He pointed them in our direction and I was happy to meet the publishing team to share my views about what a practical book on succession management should look like. It was one of those sunny summer afternoons that bring out the best in everyone. Encouraged by an attentive group, I attempted to summarise the key issues we were picking up from workshop delegates and our clients in our own research programmes on how to make succession work. I outlined the kind of book I would want to read. It should be practical, but not a simplistic check-list of the blindingly obvious. It should help readers think about the fundamental issues, not recycle old conference notes. It should see succession management as a solution to business problems, not as a set of personnel policies. Here I outlined the concept of "future-proofing", an idea which Sun Microsystems had introduced to help it think about what needs to be done to build organisational resilience.[1] The book should highlight the need for flexibility and responsiveness to organisational uncertainty and change, not provide a standard fixed recipe. And I continued in this vein, attempting to reflect the feedback from those we had come into contact with, who were grappling with the difficult issues of succession.

Gower called my bluff and suggested I should write it. After a period of reflection and discussion with my colleagues I thought, why not? At this point it was a combination of arrogance (after all, I knew a lot about succession) and naïvety (succession can't be that difficult to write about). Wrong and wrong!

In planning this book my initial thought was to distil the learning from our own consultancy projects, resource material and support documentation. I wanted to stand back and rethink the many assignments we'd been involved in over the last 12 years. I also planned to collate existing material from the research literature and from "best-in-class" organisations which had a tradition and track record of managing succession. At the time it seemed a relatively straightforward task to summarise a set of guidelines and best practices and I was confident the book would be written well ahead of the agreed deadline. That was the plan!

In any event, with a number of colleagues we undertook a series of fact-finding interviews and focus groups during the course of 2002–2003, involving over one hundred organisations. Typically these interviews were with senior HR professionals. They also incorporated meetings with a number of consultancies operating across different succession-related activities. In addition we met with executives to review their own personal experiences of succession, as senior managers involved in planning succession processes or as younger managers experiencing the "sharp end". These provided stimulating meetings, generating fresh insights and, above all, new questions that began to challenge many assumptions and beliefs about what succession management might involve.

Secondly, we accessed the research literature that was available in the area of succession management to review what was known about the range and variety of succession practice and outcomes. In fact the available research literature was fragmentary to say the least, described in one definitive summary as "diffused and often chaotic....There is little we know conclusively, much we do not know because of mixed results and even more we have not yet studied."[2] Not a promising start. We also reviewed specific case studies of "best practice" and organisational innovation. No doubt we have missed many significant developments; if so, please email us and let us know. But on closer examination the "best practice" organisations proved quite elusive. Particular organisations, the kind which feature in the business press and prominent at professional conferences, could be admired for specific initiatives and imaginative practices. However, finding organisations that were willing to "put themselves on the line" and say that what they were doing was outstandingly successful and driving the business forward proved more problematic. Indeed the so-called "best-in-class" companies were more likely to be praised by outside observers than to congratulate themselves on the ingenuity or business impact of their succession practices.[3] "Cause-and-consequence" proved a difficult theme. Did the presence of specific activities in successful organisations highlight promising initiatives driving their success? Or was the appearance of such initiatives a consequence of their success? We have therefore, except in a handful of instances, deliberately avoided attributing succession practices to specific organisations. There is a well-established "best-in-class" grouping of famous companies[4] but I was determined to avoid what could be called the "Enron factor". In the two or three year run-up to its demise, Enron appeared in many best-in-class publications. Enron was lauded as the new business model, the pioneer of innovative practice and the exemplar of the future. Researchers and consultants practically fell over each other in the rush to tell the world about Enron's strategic brilliance, organisational ingenuity and leading-edge management practice.

Thirdly, we drew on our own consultancy experience over the past decade. Along with my colleagues we have run a series of public and in-company programmes, attended by over 1200 delegates from a wide spectrum of organisations, from the public and private sectors, large and medium-sized firms. For the past eight years we have also coordinated a consortium of organisations, the Strategic Resourcing and Succession Network, to provide a forum for the frank exchange of experiences. This group of companies has been an invaluable source of feedback about the realities of what is and isn't working in implementing succession processes. For our part, working with the 70 or so organisations that have been part of this network gave us the opportunity to experiment with new concepts and approaches in a way that is difficult when grappling with the priorities of day-to-day consultancy assignments. Some of these ideas fell by the wayside; others provided a platform to move the succession agenda forward.

As part of this experience of working with organisations tackling succession, a series of preliminary "dos" and "don'ts" became apparent. "Dos" are the kind of ideas and innovations about succession practice that appear in professional publications and conference presentations, and are seized on and imitated quickly. But in our research it was not so much the tangible practice that made the difference. Instead it was the thinking and spirit behind it that helped the organisation move forward. The existence of a talent review mechanism across business units may or may not be useful. But the quality of dialogue between participating managers and the types of decisions and agreed actions stemming from this debate will make the difference. "Don'ts", far from closing down options, provide valuable insights. Organisations are good at introducing initiatives, at starting new things. In some cases, it may be far better to stop doing things. In the experience of our network of organisations, too much time and effort have been wasted on the trivial, irrelevant and at times the simply absurd. "Fire-walking" on hot coals as part of a team-building event may motivate your workforce; it may also hurt the feet of your executives. If specific initiatives are not followed through with real and genuine change, they will create cynicism. Organisations would benefit from a full and frank review of the "don'ts".[5]

We have been actively engaged in working closely with organisations to support the design and implementation of succession management processes. We have had the good fortune to work with some extraordinarily innovative individuals whose motivation to make succession a force for business success has kept challenging us to rethink and recreate alternative strategies and tactics. Assignments have spread across a range of different industries, from leisure and entertainment, financial services and utilities to professional services and information technology. But the focus of this book is not to "package" best-in-class practice or prescribe an "A to Z" of succession management. This has been attempted and, in all candour, it simply does not work.[6] Rather, we want to highlight what we believe is a mix of tried-and-tested approaches, reflecting some disciplines that have stood the test of time while also identifying some interesting concepts and emerging practices which we see as representing the way ahead.

Who this book is for

If you are a CEO or aspiring CEO I hope you find much in this book to implement the right kind of succession process for your business to survive and endure for the long term. As Ron Dennis, current principal of the successful Formula 1 racing team, McLaren, said, "You are being a fool if you try to make yourself the beginning and end of the company. If you do not run it on the basis of being a chapter, your ego can run amok and your desire to be recognised will just get in the way."[7] If you are a CEO who wants to be the beginning and the end of the "book", then succession management will be of no relevance to you. If you want to be a chapter in a continuing successful narrative of "future-proofing" your organisation, then succession should be one of your key leadership priorities.

For those operating in a Human Resources role with responsibility for supporting the design and implementation of succession activity, this book will provide resource material to make your life easier. This book incorporates a series of templates, protocols and check-lists which you should adapt and customise according to the distinctive requirements of your organisation. I hope this book will also stimulate and challenge your thinking to advance in new directions. Succession management has for too long been associated with the routine annual chore of paper gathering and collation which eventually disappears into a corporate black hole, demotivating everyone involved in the entire experience. Succession management can be something very different, with the potential to shape your organisation's business destiny and be a critical dynamic in "future-proofing" your company in an intensely competitive world.

If you are a younger manager interested in the concept of succession management but unsure of what it is or involves, I congratulate you for your foresight. If you aspire to be a leader who wants to build a better organisation which makes a difference, this book will inform your thinking about organisational success, the kind of leadership that will be needed and your role in identifying, nurturing and developing talent. I sincerely hope that reflecting on these ideas will contribute to your own personal success and also help you build a better organisation. Aim to be the best chapter in the book, but make sure you have developed the management that will lead your company into another chapter.

Finally, for those working professionally in business and management education or research, I would emphasise that this is not an academic analysis of succession management. The thrust of this book has been informed by those active practitioners engaged in the hurly burly of making succession work in the face of business uncertainty and change. Nevertheless, I have added relevant endnotes for those who wish to follow up the material with a more comprehensive appreciation of the available research. Accessing the supporting research and wider literature will provide a much deeper analysis of succession management than is possible within the scope of this book. However, I do hope that this book's practitioner perspective will inform your thinking to find ways of connecting robust theory and imaginative research with the day-to-day challenges facing those involved directly in implementation.

There are hundreds of individuals who, as clients, workshop delegates, colleagues and associates, have contributed to this book by giving their experiences, ideas and suggestions. This book therefore is a summary of the collective wisdom of more than a thousand individuals who in different ways have applied their minds and energies to different facets of succession management. It goes without saying that while specific individuals can claim credit for many of the better insights and ideas throughout this book, no one should be blamed for any of the book's shortcomings. Those are mine alone.

Many thanks to my work colleagues and associates at Azure Consulting International, specifically Susanna Douglas-Mann, Michelle Jones, Ann Hartley and Alan Kitching, who shaped my initial material into something readable and, at Andrews Munro Ltd, most significantly Brendan Andrews for his encouragement of my efforts.

Tom Kennie at Ranmore Consulting, Professor Robin Middlehurst at Surrey University, John Beckett and Melinda Beckett Hughes of Portland International and Sandra Henson of Ascentia have pioneered some of our ideas in their work with clients in the area of leadership development and executive coaching, and I appreciate their support and willingness to test out some early concepts.

Over the last few years we have benefited from our contact with many highly insightful individuals. Specific thanks to the following who, in a variety of ways, have contributed ideas and thinking to this book: Sue Baker; Jane Basley of Rank Gaming; Robert Bolton of ATOSKPMG; Barbara Busby of The Environment Agency; Denice Cording at Cable & Wireless; Mike Dunlop of Sun Microsystems; Jo Dunne of LendLease; Margaret Edge of Sainsburys; David Fisher at BDO Stoy Hayward; Barry Gipson of Bank of Ireland; Neil Hayward of Serco; Jim Horstead of Fairplace Consulting; Margaret Johnson of Bradford & Bingley; Steve Brown, Phil Langstaff, Alan McAvan, Jackie Moore, Pat O'Kane, Jill Wade and Martin West of HBOS; Jacky Kelly, now at Shell; Penny Lee of Thames Water; Peter Loe of Experian; Sarah Maggs of Orange; Graham Maundrell of De La Rue; Stephen McCafferty and Ian Miller of Standard Life; Christine Ray of Rank Group; Chris Rayner of Compass Group; Maggie Riley at MR Associates; Liz Taylor of Scottish & Newcastle International; Bob

Thompson of National Grid Transco; David Thompson of the Post Office; Lorraine Vaun Davis of Nationwide Building Society; Pavita Walker of Barclays; and Steve Yardley at ITNet.

Thanks also to Duncan Armitage, Paula Giles, Robyn Brown and their colleagues for providing an Australasian perspective, as well as a pleasant few days in Sydney.

Professor Peter Saville and Lisa Cramp gave me superb support and guidance at an early point in my career when I was coming to terms with organisational realities.

In reviewing literally thousands of articles, research reports and publications, three individuals stand out prominently: Warren Buffett, Peter Drucker and Jim Collins, individuals whose wisdom and common sense helped me make sense of what seemed at times a bewildering and confusing area. My sincere thanks to each of them for their insights.

Notes

1. Mike Dunlop at Sun Microsystems highlighted this powerful concept. In the mid-1990s Sun Microsystems was an organisation enjoying the momentum of rapid growth. Revenues were strong and rising. Somewhere, someone in Sun Microsystems asked the question "What do we need to do to 'future-proof' this organisation?" This question triggered a series of initiatives to ensure that succession and talent management became a greater priority.
2. I. Kesner and T. Sebora, "Executive Succession: Past, Present and Future", *Journal of Management*, vol. 20, no. 2 (1994), pp. 327–72. This is a good overview of the issues engaging research and a useful summary of emerging findings.
3. One of our best clients, a major player in the financial services sector, found itself in the embarrassing position of being acclaimed in various publications as a success story in its implementation of the Balanced Score Card concept; embarrassed, because at the same time it was dismantling formal measurement mechanics. It wasn't that the Balanced Score Card was a bad idea that hadn't worked. It advanced management thinking at a point in its evolution. But our client didn't want to be hailed as a "best-practice innovator". The organisation had assimilated the core philosophy and moved on to refocus and redirect its management efforts in another direction.
4. The listing of the "succession good and the great" includes General Electric for its consistent commitment to succession management, Motorola for using succession to catalyse organisational change, IBM for its leadership development programmes, BP Amoco for its leadership audits, Eli Lilley for its action-learning leadership sessions, Dow Chemical for its management development and so on.
5. "Don'ts" are the opposite of best practice. But it may be there is more to be learned from failure than success. This point came home to me on a benchmarking visit to a large manufacturing company in the UK. After listening to the problems the organisation was facing in making senior appointments, on the way out the HR Director pointed towards a colleague huddled over his PC, engrossed in manipulating a database, and said, "This is where we do our succession planning." Whatever that individual was doing it wasn't succession management. An easy "don't" may be holding back the implementation of a specialist software system in the expectation of making succession management happen. Smart technology to manage the information flow of succession is important. But it is a mistaken assumption that buying in "succession software" will make it happen.
6. "All prescriptions, old and new alike, have potential side effects if implemented poorly, too simplistically, or simply because circumstances have changed" (R. Eccles and N. Nohria, *Beyond the Hype*, 1992). Or for a more extreme view: "Once you find a management technique that works, give it up. Most prevent closer human relationships" (R. Farson, *Management of the Absurd: Paradoxes in Leadership*, 1996).
7. Russell Hotten, *Formula 1: The Business of Winning*, 1998.

1 An Overview of Succession Management

"Succession has always been the ultimate test of any top management and the ultimate test of any institution." Peter Drucker

"All in all we're prepared for the truck." Warren Buffett

> Succession management is moving up the corporate agenda but is proving increasingly difficult to implement. The forces for strong corporate governance, organisational stewardship and continuity of capable leadership are strong, but are competing with complex dynamics which make succession in practice a tough nut to crack. Organisations can either avoid the issue altogether, keep doing what they're currently doing but do it better and faster, or rethink the fundamentals of what succession in the twenty-first century might require.

New realities and preliminary themes

Succession, or, who moves into the positions of power, has been a "tipping point" throughout human history. It has triggered wars between nations, sparked political divisions, ignited family feuds, and it has led to the downfall of many businesses. Succession management, then, is no trivial affair; it has been and continues to be an important shaper and driver of political, economic, social and business events, affecting us all. But until about 20 years ago organisational succession was pretty much a non-event. Typically the CEO reviewed the potential list of insider candidates, all of whom were personally known, and recommended their choice of successor, which was rubber-stamped by the Board. Occasionally an external candidate would be sought, but this tended to be more the exception than the rule. In the early years of the twenty-first century we seem to be in a different era.

- Succession is now the focus of intensive media speculation and investor attention. Formerly the private domain of the executive suite, succession features daily in the press. Speculation about the position of top management and possible replacements make good media copy. Uncertainty about an organisation's succession plans is viewed unfavourably by shareholder groups and is likely to impact directly on its share price.
- Forced CEO succession is now the "new norm" and there is greater pressure to appoint an outsider, preferably the charismatic leader who will transform company fortunes. Expectations of leadership performance, no doubt coinciding with the massive increase in executive compensation over the last two decades, are high. Under-performing CEOs

are being ruthlessly despatched. And the assumption of succession from within is under attack as external hires are viewed as more likely to improve business performance.

- There is a growing concern, reflected in the drive towards better corporate governance and stewardship, that we have got leadership progression and succession wrong over the last few years. While senior executive compensation has rocketed, there is a growing unease about our business leadership. We feel we are being badly led, and there is a growing suspicion that classic succession, far from being part of the solution, may be part of the problem.

- Succession management isn't simply the passing of the baton to the next CEO. No doubt the CEO and senior team have a major impact in determining an organisation's fortunes. Increasingly, however, competitive success is shaped by the organisation's skill in utilising the talents and know-how of key technical and professional groups and its effectiveness in coordinating employee performance throughout its ranks. Succession management therefore becomes less about a handful of top team appointments and more about how the organisation thinks about and manages its talent. There is a shift in management mind-set, from "filling jobs" to constantly seeking out those individuals who can move the organisation forward. Succession, then, is not simply decision-making for top-level appointments. It is about performance management at all levels.

We seem to have arrived at a point where we don't quite know how to think about succession management or what to do about it. When Enron, the US utility company, could be named by *Fortune* magazine in 2000 as the top company for "Quality of Management", two years before its implosion brought on by a combination of arrogance and greed, we must begin to question the way in which we define managerial quality. When one of the UK's largest banks appoints a CEO who lasts all of one day in the job, and then takes another year to find a new CEO, we must wonder about the processes in which we screen and select our CEOs. And when media group BSkyB named James Murdoch, son of News Corp chairman, Rupert Murdoch, as its CEO after an extensive screening and selection process with a prestigious headhunter firm, we are bemused by the coincidence.

THE FAILED INSIDER COUP

In May 2000, Sir Rick Greenbury, chairman and chief executive of Marks & Spencer – the highly profitable UK food and fashion retailer – flew to India to meet suppliers. Although he was acutely aware of the challenges facing him and the organisation, he didn't appreciate the full force of those difficulties, for him personally and for M & S, until he heard the news of a boardroom coup to oust him, led by one of his "loyal" lieutenants. Less than two years before, M & S was the UK's favourite retailer, posting record tax profits of more than £1 billion. This was no one-off. For decades M & S had been a classic account of a well-run business with good management and a commitment to progression from within. Such consistent performance had made M & S feature in three Harvard Business School case studies.

The same year, things began to unravel. Profits fell, and M & S was accused of complacency and arrogance and losing touch with its customers; it became the target of intensive press criticism. By late 2000, the company was in trouble and Greenbury, formerly acclaimed as the most admired businessperson within his peer group, was under personal attack. The man who in 1998 had said "We thought we were geniuses" was now seen as overseeing a series of poor business decisions: the expensive purchase of Littlewoods stores, European expansion, and in the eyes of loyal M & S customers, committing the cardinal sin of getting its fashion range wrong. One insider commented, "The problem came when under years of success the company began to operate to please Rick [Greenbury], not the customer."

Having twice deferred his retirement, and faced with indecision from the non-executive Board, Greenbury embarked on a succession strategy which came back to haunt him. The plan was to create four new Managing Director roles for the potential succession candidates, and let them fight it out. Given new powers and responsibilities, whoever proved themselves most capable in their new roles would emerge as the successor. The reality was that this strategy forged tension and acrimony between the four, "distracting them from the primary purpose of running the business". The outcome was intense infighting and lobbying for position. Keith Oates, as deputy chairman, felt he was the heir apparent, and began a campaign of internal politicking and press briefings to promote himself as Greenbury's successor. But Oates, unable to command sufficient support, failed in his boardroom coup and departed. Greenbury agreed to split his position and gave Peter Salsbury, another of the contenders in the succession tournament, the CEO role, describing him as the "ideal man to lead M & S into the twenty-first century".

One non-executive director commented, "Peter changed dramatically from the day he was made chief executive. None of us were prepared for his behaviour." Despite the initial support of Greenbury, Salsbury, once appointed, made his contempt for his former boss clear. Embarking on a series of restructuring manoeuvres to cull the old guard, he distanced Greenbury from any strategic decision-making and influence. Isolated, Greenbury resigned. But Salsbury had his own business pressures. Profits were down, the share price was plummeting, customer satisfaction falling, and competitors such as Next, Gap and Matalan were in ascendance. Then came the unthinkable: stories of a hostile takeover. Although it didn't materialise, the Board appointed the Belgian Luc Vandevelde, who had steered the merger of French rivals, Promodes and Carrefour, as executive chairman in 2000; this was the first truly external appointment in M & S's history. Several months later Vandevelde had seen enough of Salsbury's leadership approach. A misjudged advertising campaign was the final blow and Salsbury left in September, eventually to be replaced by Roger Holmes of the Kingfisher group.

Three years later Marks & Spencer is still recovering from its succession bungle. It is showing few signs of regaining its momentum to be the major force in UK retailing; for many investment analysts the jury is still out.[1]

THE OUTSIDER REJECTED BY THE CULTURE

In the late 1990s Xerox looked like an organisation with a bright future. It had shown tremendous levels of corporate resilience in its response to both the expiry of its patents in the early 1970s and market share falling from 95 per cent to 13 per cent with the onslaught of cut-price Japanese competitors. It is true that it had

failed to exploit the sensational innovations coming from its Palo Alto Research Centre, most notably the personal computer. It is also true that it had underestimated the impact of the inkjet printer and lost out heavily to Hewlett Packard. But throughout the 1980s its CEO, David Kearns, a former IBM marketing executive, had driven through a series of change initiatives to improve product quality and reduce manufacturing costs. By 1999 earnings were rising and its share price hit a record high of $64.

This was a textbook example of corporate recovery, of an organisation reinventing itself to respond to new challenges. Moreover, Xerox was hailed as one of the "best-in-class" organisations that understood succession and knew how to manage its processes. "Every one of our upper level managers is supposed to be able to name two or three replacements on the spot. It comes with the territory." The appointment of Paul Allaire, a Xerox insider who had worked his way through the Xerox ranks to CEO in 1990, confirmed this was an organisation with the breadth and depth of talent to provide continuity from within. By 2000 Xerox posted a loss of $198 million and was struggling under a mountain of debt and investors were "deserting in droves". The loss of $38 billion in shareholder value qualified Xerox as "a catastrophe of the first order".

So what had happened? Allaire, following the Xerox model, had reviewed succession options with the Board since the early 1990s and, faced with the belief that Xerox needed to undergo another corporate reinvention to face the digital age, looked externally for the next CEO. Richard Thoman, the chief financial officer of IBM, looked the perfect match. With a business career spanning American Express, RJR Nabisco and the heavyweight consultancy firm of McKinsey & Co, and an armful of academic qualifications, his profile looked exactly right to embark on another round of corporate realignment and change. Joining the company as heir apparent in 1997, Thoman began to shake things up by pushing for more fundamental shifts in Xerox's strategy. The future lay in helping organisations find new ways to manage documentation more efficiently and imaginatively; it lay in moving the salesforce from "box sellers into systems consultants". Thoman embarked on a reorganisation of Xerox's vaunted salesforce, until that point the jewel in its business crown, rethinking how it was structured and compensated. He also began to question Xerox's financial controls and business metrics to ask difficult questions of its fundamental structure. Critics said that he was moving too quickly, taking on too much, too soon.

Thirteen months later Thoman received the news from Allaire that he had lost the confidence of the Board and would have to resign. In Thoman's version of events he argued that he never had the authority to impose his own leadership agenda because of the continued presence of Allaire. Allaire's account is that Thoman forced a pace of change that the Xerox culture, known for its bureaucracy as "Burox", couldn't accept. In addition, Thoman's leadership style was seen as intellectually blunt and abrasive and he found it difficult to connect with the Xerox staff. He couldn't "get a feel for what was going on in the company and what was and wasn't possible. To be successful at Xerox, you have to be liked." "The lesson of Xerox is that halfway measures don't work. If you bring in a change agent then let him make change or don't start," said one insider. Xerox's stock dropped by 72 per cent over a 12-month period and it was overwhelmed with rumours of bankruptcy.

What initial conclusions can we draw from these two organisations?

- Poorly managed succession can stall, if not completely derail, an organisation permanently. But "brilliance" in the formalities of succession management is no guarantee of business success either. Both Marks & Spencer and Xerox had a commitment to progression from within. Ed Lawler, analysing the succession problems of AT & T and IBM in the late 1990s, said that, despite these companies' considerable investment in management development, "They prepared a wonderful group of executives for yesterday's business. By being so good at narrowing the gene pool, they replicated people who would have been good leaders in the past but not the future."

- Succession one way or another will happen. It is an inevitable part of organisational life. It may happen after delay and disruption. It may result in the appointment of the wrong candidate who will trigger an irreversible decline in business fortunes. But it will happen. Rick Greenbury was not immortal. Marks & Spencer had to find a successor eventually. The issue then is not so much whether succession should be managed, but how it should happen to enhance and strengthen the organisation's competitive position. It is not just *who* is chosen as successor that makes a difference, but *how* the process operates.

- Bringing in a heavy-hitting player from outside with an impressive track record, breadth of business experience and intellectual prowess is not enough. Richard Thoman was not only incredibly intelligent; he had operated effectively as a leader at many extremely successful firms. He understood marketing, finance and manufacturing; he also knew from operating as number two at IBM how to turn around businesses in decline and reinvent a massive technology firm. Leadership succession, then, is more than individual capability. Succession needs to look beyond personal effectiveness to identify the fit between the individual and the organisation, its strategy, culture, and its politics.

- Succession management is not like other business processes, where a combination of rational analysis and process efficiency can deliver ongoing incremental improvements. Succession decisions and how they are arrived at generate an intensity of emotion, driven no doubt by personal ambition as well as fuelled by those very human feelings of envy and jealousy, which makes objective and cool-headed evaluation difficult. When personal reputations are at stake and management egos are on the line, succession has the potential to become a political struggle in pursuit of personal and factional interests rather than a mechanism to ensure long-term business success.

At first sight succession management should be a simple and straightforward affair. Business logic dictates that organisations should look ahead into the future and review their requirements for leadership and professional talent and expertise. It is an obvious discipline to anticipate and plan for the loss of key personnel and evaluate the effectiveness and impact of the current executive population. And of course firms should be proactive in developing those talented managers to prepare them for positions of greater responsibility. These activities, predictable and recurring time and time again within the organisational tide, should be part of a well-worked formula. But they are not. For the past six years we have conducted a series of benchmarking surveys, examining succession-related activity and outcomes across our database of over 300 organisations. The results, consistent with many other research programmes, indicate that for many organisations succession has been, is and continues to be a difficult and traumatic activity.

A SNAPSHOT OF SUCCESSION PRACTICE[2]

Sixteen per cent of organisations think that succession and resourcing is well integrated with the business planning process; more than 50 per cent perceive little link between them.

Only a third of organisations report that they have identified the roles that are critical to the organisation.

Eleven per cent of organisations have meaningful review processes in place to drive effective succession planning. Another 46 per cent of surveyed firms report that while there are occasional review processes they don't result in planned action.

Only 10 per cent of organisations perceive that the top management team commit significant time to succession and resourcing priorities; over a half of surveyed firms think minimal time and effort is invested.

Seventeen per cent of organisations report that their processes for identifying potential are well integrated based on different sources of information; 40 per cent either do nothing or rely on management discretion and judgement.

Three per cent of firms report that they make good use of information technology in support of succession processes; 83 per cent make little or no use of IT in this way.

What is driving the succession agenda?

THE "NASTY, BRUTISH AND SHORT LIFE OF CEOS"

In the early 1980s the average tenure of CEOs was around 12–15 years. Now it is less than three years. Succession, an organisational event that used to happen relatively infrequently, is now becoming a familiar feature of the corporate landscape. One survey concluded that forced CEO succession has become the new norm in the US and this trend of "deliver or depart" is seen to be emerging throughout the rest of the world. Certainly a record number of CEOs worldwide have been sacked for performance reasons in the last two to three years. "The professional life of a large company's chief executive increasingly resembles that of the Hobbesian man: it is nasty, brutish and short."[3] It is not surprising therefore that a half of senior executives surveyed said they would turn down the CEO role.[4]

Two interpretations are possible. One view is that we are seeing a fundamental shift in business leadership brought on by increased stake-holder impatience. Top executive positions in the twenty-first century are now so demanding and complex and the pressures from shareholders for immediate profitability so intense, that no one can be expected to be successful for more than three or four years. It is unrealistic for one individual to continue to lead the organisation beyond that time scale. Almost 50 years ago, Peter Drucker, that most penetrating thinker of management practice, made the point that a business reliant on one individual would not grow and prosper.[5] No one individual can ever execute the full range of responsibilities of the CEO role. Clearly, few were listening to that message. Over the past two decades the "celebrity CEO" has emerged, the one-man/woman band who will single-handedly transform an organisation's fortunes. Certainly the belief that business leadership has become more demanding might go some way towards explaining the massive increase in CEO remuneration over the last 20 years. According to *Business Week*, in 1980 the average CEO in the US made 42 times the average hourly worker's pay. By 2000, it was 531 times the hourly worker's pay.

Alternatively, a more candid analysis might conclude that the current generation of CEOs are simply not up to the task. We are removing our business leaders more quickly than ever because, quite frankly, they are not delivering what they promised. It is not that business life has suddenly become so much more demanding and challenging in the last decade. (Has there ever been a period in human history when leadership has been easy?) The harsh reality is that our business leaders have got a lot worse. Is it possible that succession processes dating back to the last 10–15 years have been responsible for a number of ill-judged appointments? If so, a number of CEOs are just not ready for the job when they get it. Some leadership attributes and qualities have been overplayed at the expense of others. We have focused on the obvious appeal of "charismatic outsiders", short-listed from a narrow pool of "credible candidates" presented by the headhunters,[6] and we have overlooked those individuals with the character and capability to advance a long-term leadership agenda.

Whatever interpretation we make (both views incorporate important truths), the immediate pressures on our current generation of business leaders suggest that succession is going to become an increasingly common activity at least for the next few years until we establish a more effective process for producing better leadership. And because CEO succession typically triggers a whole series of other organisational changes, such as restructuring and the bringing in of former colleagues which in turn trigger additional appointments, there will be more succession activity in the future. If this is so, we'd better improve how we manage succession; we are certainly going to get more opportunity to practise. Organisations that lack the infrastructure and the commitment to get to grips with resourcing and succession are going to be penalised. In a business world where speed of execution is a key driver of success, delays and disruptions in filling key roles will be heavily punished.

THE IMPETUS FOR BETTER CORPORATE GOVERNANCE AND STEWARDSHIP IN A POST-ENRON WORLD

The business period from the late 1990s up to the present day was and is likely to continue to be a traumatic and painful time for many organisations and their shareholders. Dot coms, which had promised so much to transform business economics, mostly fizzled out in disillusionment. The global economy was stalling. And more worryingly, the outbreak of corporate scandals and fiascos (for example, Enron and WorldCom in the US; Barings, Equitable Life and Marconi in the UK; and Elf, Vivendi and Parmalat on the Continent, to name but a few) shook fundamental confidence in our business enterprises and the way they were being managed. It wasn't simply the stories of individual deceit and greed, the accounting irregularities or the conflicts of interest with professional advisors that were the problem, bad though they were. It was the sheer cynicism of the whole period. During the Senate hearings investigating the Enron debacle, one senator observed to Jeff Skilling, the former CEO of Enron, that "Enron looks to me like the captain of the Titanic who gave himself a bonus, then lowered himself and the top folks down in the life boat and then hollered up and said, 'By the way everything's going to be just fine'." Skilling's response: "I think it's a pretty bad analogy, Senator, because I wasn't on the Titanic. I got off in Ireland."[7] For chutzpah, maximum points. For leadership character and integrity, a zero.

Jim Collins, putting this business period into broader perspective, identified the "built-to-flip" factor: the opportunism which sacrifices long-term value in search of short-term reward. Rather than representing the greatest period of wealth *creation* in history, he argues that this phase saw the largest *transfer* of wealth. It was a massive transfer of wealth to "those in the know" (those who knew the entire business edifice was built on sand and "cashed out" before the waves of economic reality crashed in) from those out of the loop who saw their investments disappear. This is a business world in which levels of trust in our corporations are plummeting. Peter Drucker remarks, "Don't be surprised that morale is low. The contempt for top management is dreadful. And the present generation of management is not going to regain the trust of their people...don't believe in your capability to restore morale. Just try to build a little trust...it will take years."[8]

"The institutional mechanisms we use for choosing our corporate leaders...are deeply flawed."[9] Government and regulatory agencies, the media, pension fund managers, employees who had lost their jobs and their life savings began to ask some tough questions. What kinds of individuals are running our business enterprises? How are these individuals selected? How are they being rewarded? Who is making these decisions? What controls and checks are in place to ensure that the organisations we are investing in are being run properly? What accountabilities need to be defined to create better stewardship? In the UK, the Higgs code,[10] following the initiatives of Cadbury and Greenbury, was yet another attempt to establish better corporate governance, including recommendations for improving executive succession.

MANAGING SUPPLY AND DEMAND

At its most fundamental, succession management is the matching of supply and demand. Who do we need, when and where? Do we have the capability to meet this requirement? Succession management is the personalised version of corporate manpower planning. Businesses anticipate demand, and strategic forecasts inform workforce plans which translate into a view of the shape and size of the workforce and an assessment of management and leadership accountabilities. Supply is estimated through an analysis of the workforce profile, highlighting the flow of individuals in and out and up throughout the organisation. A resourcing plan is then designed to bridge the gap between demand and supply. If ever there was a time when this was a simple and straightforward exercise it certainly isn't now. Predicting demand has always been a problematic area and is becoming increasingly difficult. And in a world in which lifelong employment no longer represents the career norm, supply management is becoming equally problematic. As talented technicians, professionals and managers (the "knowledge workers") look to downshift and discover a better work–life balance or prefer the flexibility of portfolio careers, the expectation that conventional career progression will provide a predictable supply of the "leadership pipeline" looks unsustainable. We seem to be moving into a period when the flux of demographic, social and financial trends makes supply-side succession, at best, an informed guess, but more likely a leap of faith into the unknown.

But some events can be anticipated and planned for. A former economist, the head of management development in a UK utility company, said, "While there are many uncertainties in succession planning there are also some knowns. Good succession practices identify the knowns and manage them. And they should provide the flexibility to deal with the unknowns." Easier said than done! But the point is a good one; the assessment and management of business risk is perhaps the most critical of all corporate capabilities, and predicting supply and demand in an unpredictable world and developing imaginative responses to reconcile them may be one of the most important priorities for an organisation.

THE LEGACY OF DELAYERING AND DOWNSIZING

The current leadership crisis, as observed in the increasing despatch of under-performing executives, together with large holes in succession coverage, accelerating remuneration and falling levels of employee trust, did not come out of the blue. Our problems are a result of events that took place 10 to 15 years ago, a period in which the commercial pragmatism of cost reduction was made fashionable through business process re-engineering, outsourcing and new look organisational design. The conventional hierarchy was generally seen as a bad thing, adding unnecessary cost, slowing down the decision-making process and disempowering front-line staff. So companies hived off business activities and removed management layers to streamline organisations around a smaller and simpler set of work activities and levels.

Leaders are not born. But neither are they made overnight. Leadership, that is, genuine leadership with the capability to take on the big organisational challenges with the commitment to make a positive difference over the long term, takes time to develop and evolve. Those aspiring to leadership positions need to get to grips with a wide range of life and organisational challenges if they are to mature as leaders and understand and manage the full demands and complexities of the leadership role. The irony for organisations is that as the leadership requirement has risen they have made it more difficult to develop this capability. Minimalist "hub and spoke" organisations which have outsourced most functions and now operate around only a handful of activities will not find it easy to generate leadership capability from within. And "flattened firms", structured around five "work levels" with huge jumps in leadership scope from one level to the next, are finding it difficult to provide the range of opportunities to test and develop emerging leaders.

There is a "succession squeeze". On the one hand, dissatisfied with corporate leadership, fuelled by the lack of connection between shareholder return and executive remuneration, we are attempting to exert greater control over leadership selection and performance. But as the demand for better leadership is rising, we are less sure about the kind of leadership required to run our future enterprises. And despite the expansion in leadership training and business education we are finding it more difficult to develop and prepare emerging talent for leadership responsibility.[11]

Succession as a "tough nut to crack"

The drive towards better leadership and improved succession is gathering momentum. Organisations are acutely aware of the importance of planned leadership change. Yet succession continues to be a "tough nut to crack". Survey after survey indicates the gulf between succession as a priority in principle and a troublesome area in practice. (No doubt consultancy-driven surveys have an in-built bias. Has there ever been a survey led by a consultancy which says everything is fine, and concludes that things should be left as they are?) Nonetheless the evidence from different sources is consistent and compelling. At an anecdotal level, when we launched our first public programme in succession management we anticipated a modest response from a niche group of senior HR professionals. In fact, since its introduction six years ago, over 1200 delegates have attended this workshop. One recent survey found that only 7 per cent of 481 large companies judged their succession management programmes as excellent. Two thirds described them as fair or worse. In another study conducted by the Society of Human Resource Management, only 32 per cent of 473 organisations had any set of formal succession plans at all.

Of course in the old days, succession was a simple and straightforward affair. Succession was determined by birth order, a process in which leadership responsibility passed from father to son.[12] But we operate in an era in which who gets which job is not simply a matter of family connection — at least not much of the time (although, for example, Richard Branson, head of the Virgin Group, has expressed his intention to hand over his empire to his son).

A level-headed perspective might express utter bewilderment at this. After all, the last 20–30 years have seen a huge expansion in business education and leadership development. Globally this is now a billion-pound industry. Whatever the reasons for our failings to get on top of succession management it is not through a lack of effort and resource. We have invested in a massive research enterprise looking at leadership from every possible perspective, but we are still arguing about the causes and consequences of leadership. Organisational and occupational psychologists have armed us with an increasingly sophisticated set of assessment tools to provide more "scientific" evaluations to guide leadership progression. But there is still alarmingly little data about the predictive power of these new tools. The increase in information technology has been breathtaking. The average office PC kitted with standard software has the processing power to handle a trip to the moon. But somehow we still can't extract data about our people when we need it in a format that is both meaningful and informative.

So why, despite this concerted effort from academics, the consultancy sector and human resource professionals, have we so little to show for our efforts?[13]

THE FUTURE IS FAR AWAY

Succession management requires us to do two very difficult things. First, it asks us to think about the future and its uncertainties. At the heart of succession is a view about the future. Succession management requires us to think beyond short-term priorities and immediate pressures. Succession should be the process that helps us attain our future goals and identify who we need to help us reach that future. But faced with today's pressing operational realities, the future can look far away, so far away that no immediate action is required. Secondly, succession management asks us to accept that the future may be very different to the present. Whatever lies ahead it can be safely predicted it will be different from the current situation. We should *not* be equipping our next generation of managers and professionals for today's roles. Instead we should be preparing them for future roles with potentially very different requirements.

And herein lies the paradox at the heart of succession management. Because we know that our business will evolve and change, we can't predict the future. We don't know if we will be acquiring new businesses or fighting off a hostile takeover from a rival. We don't know if technological innovation will render our entire product range obsolete overnight or whether it will open up fantastic growth opportunities. We don't know if we will centralise or decentralise or if we will outsource functions or retain them. Because we don't know the future we can't specify our leadership requirements. Therefore it doesn't make much sense to plan and develop management capability for the future. But, and here is the paradox, if we don't plan and develop our management and leadership capability, we will lack the effectiveness to compete in the future.

As evolutionary psychologists remind us, our minds are not well adapted to long-term thinking about the unknown. Immediate and pressing problems, those issues impacting on us personally and directly, are much more engaging than those fuzzier problems of the distant future, where the issues and consequences are less clearly defined. Our mental software, our "Stone Age minds",[14] the culmination of evolutionary pressures on the African Savannah three thousand generations ago, help us survive for the moment and fight off impending danger. We are less well equipped, however, to marshal resources against threats we can't quite imagine, never mind anticipate. It is hardly surprising that getting succession management onto the corporate agenda is difficult.

SURFACING THE "SHADOW SIDE"

Succession management, which has been described as a "messy melodrama", opens up difficult issues which many organisations would rather keep within the organisational "shadow side".[15] In the official version of corporate events, ideas and proposals are aired and reviewed with full consideration. Decisions are made objectively and rationally, and resources and budgets are allocated fairly according to business requirements. In the public arena, succession plans are compiled thoughtfully and systematically based on an objective evaluation of the merits of different candidates. The review process to agree succession coverage is an insightful evaluation, coolly conducted in the best long-term interests of the organisation. On the "shadow side" is the real world in which things really get decided and get done. In this real world, succession decisions, decisions about appointments, progression and deployment bring emotional and political tensions to the surface, igniting intense feelings which create conflict:

- conflict about the future direction of the business
- conflict about organisational structures, role size and reporting lines and relationships
- conflict about values, culture and the kinds of leaders needed to move the organisation forward
- above all, conflict about the power dynamics within the organisation and who makes which decisions.[16]

In summary, succession management has the potential to raise issues which organisations would prefer to leave in the "shadow side". In the shadow side, outside the glare of public scrutiny and accountability, it is much easier to make decisions that are expedient and indefensible and put together short-term compromises which preserve the political dynamic. As one weary observer of succession processes commented, "Yes, the succession plan...that's where you look after your friends and settle old scores."

CONFLICTING STAKE-HOLDER DEMANDS

Another way of highlighting the difficulty of succession management is to examine the different groups and agencies that in some way or other have an involvement in succession activity and ask: who does and doesn't want succession management? In principle, leadership progression to ensure business continuity is seen as a "good thing". In practice, what is the perception of key stake-holder groups?

The Board

Faced with increasing share-holder activism, Boards are under pressure to make senior appointments from outside the organisation. External appointments are increasingly seen as the safe option, a way of signalling to the marketplace that organisational change and improvement are taken seriously. The merger of TV companies Granada and Carlton to create ITV plc led to investors demanding the removal of Carlton chief, Michael Green, as chairman and the appointment of a new face as his replacement. Associated with the fiasco of ITV Digital, and the loss of £1 billion of shareholder value, Green was seen as lacking the credibility to steer the merger towards the construction of a new enterprise.

Partly driven by city expectations that an outsider is best positioned to establish corporate reputation, the Board is also influenced by the ties that bind, the extensive network of connections running across boardrooms.[17] Non-executive directors, through their membership of several Boards, represent a "club" with a network of family, educational, social and business links. Like any club it owes its loyalties to current members and seeks to protect their interests. Through these "ties which bind" which span across different sectors and organisations, Board directors often have more personal knowledge of outside candidates than they do of internal candidates. It is hardly surprising, then, that succession triggers a telephone call to the headhunters rather than a serious and committed appraisal of the organisation's own pool of leadership talent. Warren Buffett is one of the few to buck the trend, "Our Board knows that the ultimate scorecard on its performance will be determined by the record of my successor."

The top team

If the CEO and senior team are a far-thinking group, displaying stewardship to build an organisation that will endure long after this top team has moved on or retired, then succession management will be a key priority. Not every CEO, however, has the leadership mind-set of Jack Welch of General Electric who, commenting on his succession, said, "From now on choosing my successor is the most important decision I'll make. It occupies a considerable amount of thought almost every day." If the top team is a paranoid collection of individuals, finding it difficult to work together as a unified decision-making team, fearful of the business challenges they face, focusing only on meeting expectations of next quarter's results, and looking only to secure their own personal financial position, then succession is unlikely to be a key priority. In this scenario, succession is an unwelcome distraction raising difficult issues the team would rather not address.

Investors, private equity and venture capitalists

The last decade or so has seen the growing influence of a range of different investor groups, some such as Warren Buffett of Berkshire Hathaway taking a long-term investment position and alert to the importance of well-managed succession; indeed, being prepared to act assertively if the current leadership is not seen as maximising shareholder return. Other groups have a shorter business horizon, looking, for example, for firms being mismanaged or where smart financial engineering can leverage under-exploited assets. The focus is to remove the current management and establish a new team with the aim of preparing the organisation quickly for a future sale. Here it is unlikely, particularly in the aggressive drive to reduce costs, that much effort will be directed around those resourcing and development practices that will build leadership capability from within.

The headhunters

Why would executive search firms want succession management? The economics of executive searches are best advanced, not through progression from within, but rather through a merry-go-round of job moves across organisations. The ties that bind also run from business leaders to the headhunters and back again. Many business leaders owe their position to the headhunters, and many headhunters owe their financial success to the business leader that they appointed. In this symbiotic relationship it is hardly surprising that top executives are often predisposed to turn to the executive search firms to fill senior positions rather than look internally to make appointments. It may be in their own personal interests if things go badly in their current role.

The management and professional population

Why is succession a good thing for the individual professional or manager? For the chosen few, succession management is no doubt a very good thing, providing additional opportunities for career development. Proactive grooming has many advantages: attending prestigious business school programmes, access to top executive mentoring and the ongoing support of a personal coach and counsellor. Importantly it also bestows the status of being seen as heading for the top. But for ambitious rivals, passed over for the "executive suite", succession management may be a bitter pill to swallow. Succession planning may be the outcome in which they, despite their suitability for a role, are turned down, and a less experienced colleague, but one with the badge of "high potential", is successful. Even more galling they may be asked to "ride shotgun" during the successor's six-month induction programme.

As a hard-working middle manager, succession management may appear to be the mechanism that removes your best people and replaces them with the "problem children" of other business units. Having worked hard to recruit good people, train and develop them, why should the middle manager feel good about losing key talent to an organisational fast track programme? When the next round of Head Office documentation arrives, it must therefore be tempting for middle managers to avoid ticking those boxes marked "high potential". Of course, at best, succession management widens the total pool of available leadership and professional capability to create a free trade of talent in which everyone wins. At least that's the theory. But as a manager under pressure to meet quarterly targets, succession management might represent another barrier to running a successful unit.

AVOIDING TOUGH PERFORMANCE ISSUES

Succession management is not simply replacement planning. Nor is it just about proactive development directed towards the talented few. It should be a resourcing game plan based on a fundamental analysis of future performance requirements. The starting point is today's performance and the gap between today and tomorrow. Succession management requires a challenging set of expectations to outline the kind of performance that is needed now in order to build for the future. It is therefore also about identifying and tackling those individuals whose impact and contribution are constraining the flow of talent within the "leadership pipeline".

Is it possible that some organisations tolerate succession exposure, preferring to operate with gaps in the ranks of the next generation of management? Yes, because the alternative might be too difficult to address. Effective succession management requires a willingness to confront those mediocre individuals who are holding back the development of their teams. At another level, succession exposure fills a psychological need for some managers. It allows them to believe in their own greatness and indispensability. After all, if no one is ready to progress to their level, they must be special. And it allows them to manage at the level below the one they should be operating at but a level at which they feel more comfortable. The absence of managers ready for progression and to take on greater responsibility allows executives to micro-manage and for decision-making to drop down a level. In this scenario the entire organisation becomes "pushed down". Front-line employees feel constrained by close supervision; first-line management feels disempowered, unable to make quick decisions without passing issues up to middle management; middle management experience a lack of strategic direction from senior executives; and senior executives feel uncertain and confused about their leadership responsibilities as the top team become embroiled in day-to-day operations.

Conversely, time and time again we have seen succession coverage create the presence of a generation of managers pushing ahead to drive organisational change and improvement. The stretch provided by managers ready to progress and to take on greater responsibility encourages everyone to "raise their game", forcing executives to operate at the level they should. Emerging managers, displaying the potential to develop and to make a greater business contribution, wanting the freedom and discretion to use their initiative and make their own decisions, keep a constant pressure on their superiors. The insecurity which intensive rivalry creates across the executive ranks is no doubt a negative force, encouraging political gamesmanship. But a strong pipeline of genuine talent ensures that no one individual is tempted to believe they are indispensable.

FACING UP TO UNPLEASANT REALITIES

In most instances succession management is triggered by unhappy rather than happy events. The departure of a colleague to a better-paid position in a more successful company, for example, triggers not only a vacancy to be filled but possibly envy and dissatisfaction. And the replacement process may result in disappointment and resentment from those candidates who were not successful. At the extreme, death is a circumstance that few of us want to contemplate. If you are a CEO running a successful enterprise you have personally founded, succession and the identification of a successor is a reminder that you are mortal. As one CEO told his colleague when confronted by the need to draw up a succession plan, "But I don't want to die." Sandy Weill of Citigroup made it clear, only half in jest, that he didn't need to name a successor because he never planned to leave. Confronting one's succession is a tough exercise. "It's a little like writing your will. Most CEOs don't want to think about it. They're consumed with the business and don't want to consider their own mortality."[18] There is no shortage of examples of CEOs who didn't know when it was time to move on. Harold Geneen of ITT Corp and Harry Gray of United Technologies had to be pushed out by their Boards. And it was only on his way to the operating room for a heart operation that Disney CEO Michael Eisner began writing down his successors on a sheet of paper. Manfred Ket de Vries, the organisational psychoanalyst, describes this as the "edifice complex".[19] Having devoted your career to building a legacy, it is uncomfortable to think that this legacy may be destroyed by your successor, that your former subordinates may reject your personal vision and dismantle your brilliant strategy. It is tempting to hold on to power for as long as possible.

QUICK-HIT FORCE-FIELD ANALYSIS

Thinking about your organisation, what forces are driving the succession agenda? Don't just list the "it's a good thing in principle" factors; highlight the specific drivers that are increasing its relevance for your organisation.

What forces will hold back the introduction and implementation of succession management? What will operate as a constraint?

For each theme, draw a force-field indicating the strength of each positive and negative force.

Review each in turn. What lies behind this theme; what might be the cause? What actions might need to be taken?

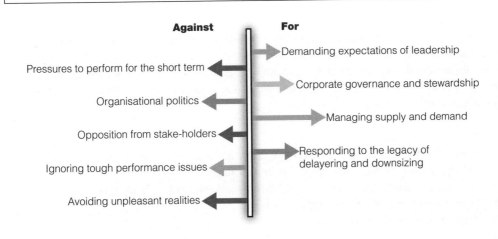

Figure 1.1 Generic force-field analysis

Tactical choices

In bleak summary, succession management asks us to think about the future (when we are preoccupied with immediate survival); to bring into the open deep-seated organisational tensions (when it is easier to keep a lid on potential conflict); to balance competing stake-holder expectations (when it is clear that no one group really wants succession); to tackle under-performing individuals (which can only rock the boat and create organisational disruption); and reminds us of our mortality! A tough nut to crack indeed!

NO POINT SO GIVE UP

What happens when an irresistible force meets an immovable object? Faced with the sheer speed of business change, a common view in the HR community is that any attempt to introduce and implement a systematic approach to succession is ultimately doomed to failure. The uncertainties of the organisational future mean that any structured attempt to plan leadership development is likely to be irrelevant at best or counter-productive at worst.

Instead we need to establish a resourcing game plan based on a mix of recruitment, interim management and greater use of external agencies such as consultants and professional advisors. In a world of business uncertainty and portfolio careers perhaps this is the only realistic approach for some organisations. The first rule of organisational change

— "whatever you do don't make things worse" — applies. Attempts to implement succession processes when the forces against outweigh the drivers for seem destined to fail. Either nothing changes and time and effort is expended fruitlessly, or even worse solutions are imposed which backfire and constrain future resourcing flexibility.

Organisationally we may still need to create that piece of paper, the formal succession plan, for the benefit of the audit and remuneration committee or some other stake-holder group. But this is largely an exercise in rhetoric. The reality is that succession, as a driver of resourcing and development, is sidelined as an issue.

KEEP DOING THE SAME BUT DO IT BETTER

"Keep doing the same but do it better" represents perhaps the most typical response we've encountered in our consulting experience. While the common problems are recognised, succession management is nonetheless still seen as a goal worth pursuing. This is the belief that incremental improvement will improve execution. There is a standard consultancy prescription for the design and introduction of succession processes, an approach that can be summarised as follows:

- Agree your business strategy
- Translate these strategic imperatives into a "blueprint" of accountabilities and a management structure of roles and responsibilities
- Assess management competency for key role holders and their reports
- Review succession coverage and exposure
- Agree and implement actions.

Apart from the sheer vagueness of this strategy, this succession recipe begs many fundamental questions. The implicit assumption in this scenario is that we know what we need to do; the problem is doing it. Our fundamental assumptions about succession are correct; it is the detail of implementation that is letting us down. And when we experience difficulties in implementation, we then move on to the "if only" response: if only the top team would give us better direction; if only we had the budget to introduce a high potential development centre; if only we would stop reorganising so often; if only we had better technology to manage our leadership database.

This approach has now dominated Human Resource thinking for the past two decades. This is the mind-set which looks for inspiration from best-in-class firms, seeking to import their resourcing and development practices. And it isn't working.

RETHINK THE FUNDAMENTALS AND DO SOMETHING DIFFERENT

Could it be that organisational and business realities require us to go beyond the incremental improvement of existing processes and systems? For many organisations succession management isn't "working". It may be that we are at the point where we need to conduct a "root and branch" review of our succession activity to rethink existing practices before we can set a more realistic agenda. Much conventional thinking in the area of succession management has evolved through a combination of word-of-mouth networking and consultancy recycling from the practices of high-profile organisations going back to the 1960s. However, life has moved on. What worked for

Shell or Procter & Gamble 30 years ago will not work for your business now. And what is working now for BP Amoco, IBM and Dow Chemical won't work for your organisation in the future.

If we are serious about succession management we need to examine the fundamentals of what we are trying to achieve and be willing to rethink how we get there. For too long we have been achieving ordinary results in succession management. Perhaps we need to think extraordinary things in order to achieve extraordinary things.[20] For example, designing yet another competency model will not advance strategic resourcing. On the other hand, questioning the fundamentals of how we think about the realities of leadership success and failure might. Updating the documentation to support a succession review forum may or may not move things forward. Thinking imaginatively about how we can recognise and reward managers for the development of talent will make a difference.

We need to rethink much of what we do when we design and implement succession processes. Many effective practices were encountered in our research, sometimes in unexpected places, and there is much we can learn from these experiences in mapping out the detailed tactics to advance succession management. But simply cranking out the familiar succession machinery faster will not provide the kind of response we need to future-proof our organisations. We need to think critically and imaginatively:

- What is it we really want succession to do; what solutions is succession activity providing to which business problems?
- What would an effective succession process look like for our organisation? How would life be different? What specifically would be happening which isn't happening now? What wouldn't happen; what would we stop doing?
- Do we need to rethink our views of leadership?[21] How do we do this? What is leadership and why do we need it?
- How do our views about organisational structures and how we configure roles and reporting relationships need to change?
- Do we understand what we mean by the concept of potential? Are we willing to accept that it may present part of the reasons for our difficulties rather than part of the solution?
- How do individuals develop to take on greater leadership responsibility? What processes make a difference?
- Who takes responsibility for advancing the succession agenda and managing the process?

The structure of this book

Part I maps out the themes of *sustainable business success, strategy and how resourcing and development practices might be positioned*. There might be certain core principles that drive "best practice", but a one-size-fits-all model of succession management is unlikely. Different businesses with different strategies, management structures and operating cultures may need to establish their own priorities and processes in advancing succession. Part I then asks you to think strategically about your organisation, the scale and scope of its business aspirations, in order to identify the beginnings of a game plan for managing succession activity. For those readers with the inclination to cut to the chase and rush onto the practical "nuts and bolts" material, I would encourage you to review this first section even if it is only briefly. Part I tackles some conceptual themes; I would remind you of Einstein's advice, "There is nothing more practical than a good theory."

There is no fixed A to Z of succession, an amalgam of standard "best practice" prescriptions which can be bolted on to work for your organisation. The founder of a new start-up, in discussion with a venture capitalist firm looking for additional investment, will have a very different take on succession from that of a CEO heading a multinational that is attempting to "localise globalisation"; this multinational in turn will have a different agenda to the head of a family firm planning their retirement and evaluating how best to secure the business's future. How you approach succession and the specific sequence of actions that need to be established will reflect the scale, direction and scope of the business ambition within your organisation. This part also addresses the *realities of leadership*. For too long our leadership models have proved inadequate in facilitating the debate about succession and progression. Or put more assertively, "Virtually everything our modern culture believes about the type of leadership required to transform our institutions is wrong. It is also dangerous."[22]

Part II of the book maps out *three "battle-grounds"* of succession. In the short term, *appointments* need to made, vacancies filled and managers and professionals redeployed within a restructuring programme. How these appointments are made is the immediate driver in succession. At another level, the *business risks* of succession exposure or the loss of key personnel need to be identified and managed. In the longer term, emerging *talent* needs to be identified and proactively developed to provide sufficient capability within the leadership pipeline. Either we rely on a Darwinian survival of the fittest to progress individuals on the basis of organisational contribution (or advance those more scheming individuals versed in managing the system to their own ends) or we may need to rethink what talent really means, its drivers and how it is developed.

The last part of the book addresses the *specifics of the implementation* of succession management: what are the processes and systems that need to be introduced to ensure succession management is not a discrete activity but rather part of the organisational fabric that shapes how things get done. We don't necessarily need more policies and procedures or to produce a "succession manual". But we do need to comprehend of the *information flow*, up, down and across the organisation, in order to develop more integrated processes for the management of succession. The current situation, typical of many organisations, of people placing data in folders and filing cabinets across different locations is not sustainable. Although buying in a new succession software package may not be the ideal solution, we do need to have a thorough awareness of management intelligence if we are serious about strategic resourcing. What role should the human resource function have in succession management? What are the responsibilities of the top team; where should its time be directed? And how do line managers and professionals contribute to "future proofing" the organisation; what is their distinctive role and how is this best maximised? Above all we need to see effective succession practice as part of an ongoing way of doing things throughout the organisation rather than as an initiative which every year senior executives need to be cajoled into supporting.

Broad-brush themes

For those readers wanting a broad overview before working through the detail, below is a description of some of the themes to be developed.

"Classic" succession planning, the exercise in organisational charting which maps out lists of nominated successors against the management structure, most of the time for most companies is largely a futile activity, misdirecting valuable resources and effort. Although a handful of key roles do need to be identified and back-up successors nominated, the formal organisational charting of nominated coverage across the corporate hierarchy is largely a pointless exercise. Even worse, it "freezes the present" rather than stimulating a discussion that shapes the future. Although *conventional charting may be a largely irrelevant and tedious chore*, thinking strategically about the organisation and the business scenarios it faces, and your people and their development may be the best investment of your time and energy in helping the organisation advance and sustain for the longer term.

Managing succession is *managing today's performance for the future*. If your organisation doesn't possess robust performance management disciplines, you will struggle to implement an effective succession strategy. Clear thinking is needed about the organisation's business model and the basis on which it competes and operates; you need to recognise that this will evolve and change over time. And the way in which we set objectives and priorities, and how we reward performance, needs to shift if we are serious about future-proofing our organisations.

Organisational success is better achieved and sustained by leaders who quietly get on with the business of running profitable enterprises rather than by high-profile charismatic individuals. "Boring is not better", but *leadership character* counts for more in the long run than charisma. Our processes and practices for assessment and career management therefore need to shift to identify and develop the right qualities for our next generation of leadership. Despite (or maybe because of) the best attempts of the competency movement we have developed and promoted, in many instances, the wrong people.

Establishing accountabilities through the use of business metrics to track executive effectiveness in succession management is important. Rigorous process mapping to clarify the sequence of resourcing and development activities is valuable to build greater discipline in execution. By and large, however, succession management is about the day-to-day interactions between individuals. Succession management *hinges on a series of interpersonal encounters* and is dependent on the management of organisational relationships. Successful implementation will lie not so much in formal policies and procedures as in the relationships between individuals and their line managers, in the interactions line managers have with their peers, and above all the interpersonal dynamics of the top team and their relationships with senior executives. Sincerity, honesty and respect may be more important drivers of sustainable succession than process maps, charts and databases.

The *concept of potential should be abandoned*. It means too many different things to different people. Typically, attempts to establish detailed criteria and indicators to provide a global evaluation of promotability or readiness of progression have consumed huge amounts of organisational time but often with little meaningful action. The drive for consistency through the formulation of competency frameworks has hindered rather than helped attempts to grapple with the realities of leadership.

Talent and succession management is a key priority for managers and professionals. External consultants and other advisors can and should make a contribution to informing your thinking about options and solutions. Ultimately, however, succession is not an organisational activity that can be hived off and outsourced. Instead it is a *mainstream responsibility of your managers* which should be a focus of their time and energies.

Above all the design and implementation of robust succession management practices that make a difference is *contingent*, requiring an understanding of the "if – then" concept. *If this* is the situation, *then* we need to do *that*; and if the situation changes, then we need to do something else. Practical succession management is not lifting policy statements, procedure manuals or the associated paraphernalia of templates, guidelines, and so on from other organisations. Practical succession is working out what works when, under which circumstances, and mastering the art of timing to know what to do at the right organisational moment. There are obvious "dos" and "don'ts"; these may speed things up or avoid unnecessary mistakes. But they won't in themselves make succession management "work" for your organisation.

In essence, succession management is not a difficult concept. Indeed, it is much simpler than the consultancy world would sometimes have us believe. However its design, implementation and execution can be difficult, with risks and hazards to be navigated. Embarking on succession with our "eyes wide open" will ensure that we formulate a robust game plan rather than launch another initiative that will dissipate within a few months.

Although we provide a series of work sheets, templates and protocols, with examples of promising and innovative practices, they do not represent a "succession solution". This book will *not tell you "what" to do, but it will indicate "how"* you might develop a succession process that works for your organisation. Above all, finding a succession solution for your organisation lies in the aspiration of your senior executives to accomplish something great, worthwhile and long lasting, with the spirit and resolve to achieve this through integrity, character and honesty.

Some gaps in this book
We don't address the employment law implications of succession management. Analysing the variations and vagaries of employment law across different countries is outside the scope of this book. More importantly, an overarching theme within this book is that sustainable processes which make a difference, which drive development, are defensible and robust. While aspects of succession data are commercially sensitive and rightly need to be confidential,[23] highly secretive processes, apart from their potential legal problems, just don't work.

Neither does this book address the highly specific issues tied up in succession within family-owned firms. The legal and financial vagaries and complexities of inheritance taxation make this a specialist area.

Notes

1. This digest draws on the excellent book by Judi Bevan, *The Rise and Fall of Marks & Spencer* (UK Profile Books Ltd, 2001).
2. "Best Practice Succession & Resourcing: Survey Results", Andrews Munro Ltd, 1999; "Strategic Resourcing Alignment Index Survey", Andrews Munro Ltd, 2002.
3. Booz Allen Hamilton survey, 2002; Drake Beam Morin survey, 2002.
4. The Burston-Marsteller and Wirthlin poll (2003) found that 54 per cent of senior executives would turn down the CEO position, a refusal rate which had doubled from the previous year.

5. Peter Drucker, *The Practice of Management*, 1955.
6. Rakesh Khurana, *In Search of the Corporate Savior*, 2002.
7. William G. Flanagan, *Dirty Rotten CEOs*, 2003.
8. Peter Drucker, "Peter's Principles", *Context*, Spring, 1998.
9. Rakesh Khurana, *The Chief Executive*, April 2003.
10. "The Combined Code of Corporate Governance" Higgs, 2002. This initiative, like many previous efforts in this area, has had a mixed response. It is tempting to agree with Alan Greenspan that "the state of corporate governance to a very large extent reflects the character of the CEO". Or put simply by Warren Buffett, "CEOs don't need independent directors, oversight committees or auditors absolutely free of conflicts of interest. They simply need to do what's right" (James O'Loughlin, *The Real Warren Buffett*, 2003).
11. Arguably much management development and business education activity is directed at providing structured substitute experiences to compensate for the lack of real-life leadership challenge.
12. John Kay makes the observation that dynastic succession in comparison with "meritocratic" succession doesn't do all that badly (although he does point out, for example, the bankruptcy of Australian newspaper group Fairfax, triggered by Warwick Fairfax, the 26 year old who succeeded his father, and the business decline of retailer Littlewoods caused in large part by family squabbles). Kay argues that dynastic succession may work because it emphasises leadership as a responsibility not as a prize, and with responsibility comes a sense of obligation as well as privilege which establishes greater legitimacy (*Financial Times*, 4 June 2002).
13. There are a number of tactical factors that explain the difficulties of implementation which we will explore later throughout the book; here the focus is on why in principle succession represents such an organisational challenge.
14. Nigel Nicholson, *Managing the Human Animal*, 2000. This provides a good business perspective for those interested in developments in the field of evolutionary psychology and the implications for organisational and leadership life.
15. Gerard Egan, *Working the Shadow Side*, 1994.
16. Politics is the competition for power and resources and the compromises reached as part of that competition. It is an inescapable factor of organisational life. While an organisation dominated by rivalry, factions and cliques will find it next to impossible to sustain succession effort, and an organisation with clear business purpose, committing effort to its customers rather than internal squabbling will find it easier, an understanding of political realities is fundamental to the successful implementation of succession management. Resourcing decisions — who gets fired, promoted, transferred and outplaced — are at the heart of corporate power plays, indicators of the balance of power within the political dynamic.
17. "Boards that have a high level of connectivity to other Boards through prominent Directors are more likely to appoint outsiders than those Boards that do not have such connections" (Rakesh Khurana, *In Search of the Corporate Savior*, 2002).
18. Dennis Carey of Spencer Stuart.
19. Manfred Kets De Vries, *Leaders, Fools and Impostors*, 1993.
20. "It is not likely that you are going to be able to achieve outstanding success by doing what everyone else does. You can't be 'normal' and expect to achieve 'abnormal' returns." J. Pfeffer, *The Human Equation*, 1998.
21. Increasingly throughout this book we will focus on leadership. This doesn't imply that succession is only targeted at the top team or senior executive population. Rather, we want to encourage the disappearance of the "management" word in order to establish leadership as relevant at every organisational level.
22. Jim Collins, "The Conference Board", 2001 Annual Essay.
23. While individuals rightly can access the data an organisation holds about them, provisions exist in the UK Data Protection Act for the confidentiality of "management forecasts" which should incorporate scenario planning around succession. "Data can be withheld if supplying it would prejudice the employer's business, but only whilst the planning/forecasting is in progress. Once the process is completed and decisions and actions have been taken any personal data are subject to disclosure." It is difficult to work out what this quite means and seems a grey area requiring test cases to establish the practical implications.

The Context for Succession Management

Succession does not occur in an organisational vacuum. Its importance and positioning should be informed by strategic priorities and business pressures. The following three chapters provide the basis for thinking clearly about succession, to see it as strategic resourcing rather than as a mechanism for generating static replacement charts. Before we can grapple with the specific tactics that need to be deployed in advancing a succession agenda, as a first step, we need to stand back and ask:

- What impact does succession management have in achieving and sustaining business success?
- Under which circumstances is succession a critical component of corporate success; when doesn't it make much difference?
- What does succession management in practice involve?
- What solutions is succession management providing to which resourcing problems?
- How do we need to rethink our priorities to implement improved processes for leadership succession?
- Why are standard leadership competency models part of the problem rather than the solution?

2 *The Business Imperative*

"Our commitment must be to continue the vitality of this company...so it will last through another 150 years. Indeed so it will last through the ages." Former CEO of Procter & Gamble

"At Berkshire Hathaway we have no view of the future that dictates what businesses or industries we will enter...we prefer to focus on the economic characteristics of businesses that we wish to own and the personal characteristics of managers with whom we wish to associate...and then hope we get lucky in finding the two in combination" Warren Buffett[1]

> Well-managed succession makes a difference to the business, but its relevance depends on the scale and scope of business aspiration and the ambitions of the executive team. For some organisations succession management may be an unnecessary distraction, raising difficult issues which ignite political tensions; for others, continuity of capable leadership from within is a critical component in the realisation of their strategy. Different strategic stances have different implications for the way in which resourcing and development policies and practices are designed and implemented.

Why is it that some start-ups succeed while others don't even get off the starting blocks? Why do some organisations go from initial success to maintain solid performance but other firms after the promise of early success fall by the wayside? And why do some organisations make the breakthrough from operating reasonably well and delivering respectable returns to performing at a far superior level than their rivals? What dynamics are at work in sustaining excellence, decade after decade? And what is the role of succession management; how does it help organisations achieve and sustain success? Does it really matter where leadership, managerial and professional talent comes from? Talent is talent, isn't it?

Although we have seen family firms, drawing on a pool of leadership from within the family circle, struggle to stay the distance (for example, Barings, Littlewoods), there are other companies with a major family influence (for example, Mars) that continue to be highly successful. And there are examples of organisations that have reinvented themselves through the injection of external talent (for example, Asda). So does succession make any difference or is it largely irrelevant in determining which organisations will succeed and prosper? And why, in the first place, are some organisations more successful than others?

Who moved my Holy Grail?

We have a deep-seated obsession with success. The alchemists' pursuit of the "philosopher's stone", the catalyst that transformed base metal into gold, and the quest for Christ's chalice with its mythical life-giving properties are archetypes of our need to find that magical ingredient which is the secret of success. An entire management industry has grown up, spanning the range from heavy-duty academic research to trivial froth, in search of the corporate equivalent of the "Holy Grail": the secret of organisational success.

IN SEARCH OF EXCELLENCE

In the 1980s, the "In Search of Excellence" concept pioneered the way to the Holy Grail. As a response to Japanese inroads into US competitiveness, the knights templar of management consultancy Peters and Waterman provided a motivational uplift to executives looking for a model of business success that would make sense of their problems and provide the reassurance that a solution was possible. Eight principles for excellence were outlined: bias for action; staying close to the customer; autonomy and entrepreneurship; productivity through people; hands on, value driven; stick to the knitting; simple form, lean staff; loose-tight properties. This prescription provided a set of big ideas shaping much of the management consultancy industry's efforts over the next decade.

The problem was the subsequent dismal failure of many of the apparently excellent companies, several within a remarkably short period of time. Richard Pascale noted that, of the 43 companies studied, less than one third could be described as excellent and nearly one half had serious performance deficiencies — this within only five years of original "excellence". Michelle Clayman tried an alternative experiment — "in search of disaster" — to identify companies that yielded the worst combination of financial characteristics used by Peters and Waterman. The bizarre outcome: the portfolio of "unexcellent" companies outperformed the Standard & Poor 500 by 12.4 per cent as compared to the portfolio of "excellent" ones.[2] Nonetheless undeterred by these findings, the "excellence movement" gained momentum, providing inspiration to the next generation of "Holy Grail" seekers.

BUILT TO LAST

Disillusioned by ad-hoc attempts to identify the Holy Grail of business success, another research group[3] outlined a more ambitious agenda: to look beyond a snapshot of currently successful organisations to identify what had sustained outstanding performance *over the long haul*. Short-term success is relatively easy to achieve. But we need to avoid generalising about those organisations who, through good luck and fortunate timing, have attained only fleeting and temporary acclaim. To determine the fundamental and enduring principles that underpin corporate performance we need to look over a longer time frame, over decades and generations, at those organisations that have delivered consistently superior business results. More importantly we need to compare this select group of "visionary" organisations with a control group matched by sector. This will pinpoint the differentiators of success.

The "Built to Last" research work mapped out the dynamics that make the difference, challenging many of the myths that have grown up around business success. Specifically the following assumptions were questioned and identified as the "myths" of business success, myths which had until that point been the foundation for many change management enterprises.

Myth 1: It takes a great idea to start a great company.
Myth 2: Visionary companies require great and charismatic visionary leaders.

Myth 3: The most successful companies exist first and foremost to maximise profits.

Myth 4: Visionary companies share a common subset of "correct" core values.

Myth 5: The only constant is change.

Myth 6: Blue-chip companies play it safe.

Myth 7: Visionary companies are great places to work, for everyone.

Myth 8: Highly successful companies make their best moves by brilliant and complex strategic planning.

Myth 9: Companies should hire outside CEOs to stimulate fundamental change.

Myth 10: The most successful companies focus primarily on beating the competition.

Myth 11: You can't have your cake and eat it too.

Myth 12: Companies become visionary primarily through "vision statements".

THE WISE GRANDFATHER

It is the year 1926 and your grandfather is planning his long-term investments in order to provide future generations of his family with financial security. His specific challenge is to identify those organisations that will deliver an outstanding return over the long term.

In 1990, as one of the grandchildren you are pleasantly surprised to hear the news that the $100 investment he made on your behalf is now worth $635 600. Intrigued by the far-sighted business acumen of your grandfather, you find that the equivalent investment made in the general market over the same time frame would have yielded $41 500. Your grandfather has out-performed the market by 15 times.

You are further astounded when you examine the collection of businesses your grandfather backed. Among a host of other positive qualities and attributes, the out-performing organisations were much more likely to have pursued a policy of progression from within and to have established robust practices for managing succession.

From the "Built to Last" research, home-grown talent and the importance of succession from within emerged as an important driver for sustaining long-term success. "The visionary companies were six times more likely to promote insiders to chief executives than the comparison companies." The question then is why; why does succession management make such a difference?

Long-term success hinges on a dynamic, a tension between two forces, what has been called the "ying and yang" of success: the impulse for innovation, exploring the new and a willingness to experiment versus the dynamic that seeks stability, control and to maintain the current order. Visionary organisations manage to balance these fundamental tensions in a way that defies their competitors. They manage to do two simultaneous and potentially conflicting things. On the one hand, they have clarity of business purpose, a clear understanding of what it is they stand for and represent. They possess a set of principles and values that run through the entire fabric of the organisation and its operating culture: they "*preserve the core*". This is not the "mission statement poster and coaster" approach to corporate culture: the sudden appearance of a new set of values on the wall, or the baseball caps, coffee cups and badges to announce the new culture. Visionary organisations live and breathe their values, values that direct and shape every decision and action. But visionary companies also keep searching for ongoing incremental improvements while embarking on major high-risk projects and ventures: they "*stimulate progress*". Preserving the core is not enough. On its own it probably amounts to a recipe for introspective complacency which is overtaken by more entrepreneurial competitors. Stimulating progress is the renewal force which keeps seeking improvement, taking on new challenges to do things better. But nor is stimulating progress a sufficient dynamic to sustain success. Organisations that stimulate progress without maintaining a sense of their fundamental values and principles are likely to rush headlong into unrealistic ventures and unsustainable expansion.

The challenge then is balancing these competing forces. The question is how? Succession management provides part of the answer. Succession management is the vehicle to deliver *continuity of capable management*. Without continuity, preserving the core is difficult. It is the critical mass of a management group that has progressed from within which understand the organisation, its purpose and values, and ensure that it maintains its focus on what fundamentally matters. Without the willingness to stimulate progress, capability doesn't develop. Capability is created through the organisational willingness to take on new and unfamiliar challenges — challenges which encourage its managers and future leaders to experiment and innovate. Management continuity without capability is the emergence of a leadership generation that lives on the past but cannot see the future. Capability without continuity is the dismissal of the past in search of the promise of the future (see Figure 2.1).

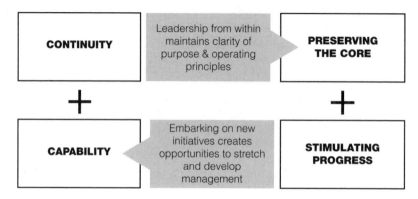

Figure 2.1   Continuity and capability

The message then seems clear and simple. Succession management is a critical activity to provide both the continuity and capability of leadership to sustain long-term organisational success. But then the bad news: "over the last 10 years just six of these visionary companies managed to out-perform the Dow Jones industrial average. The other twelve have gone from great to merely OK."[4] Of course this finding in itself doesn't disprove the findings of the "Built to Last" concept. It could be that a number of visionary organisations embarked on actions which lost sight of the ongoing drivers of their success. This is almost certainly the case, for example, with Disney, presided over by outsider Michael Eisner ("the world's most overpaid executive"), and criticised as losing touch with its customers.[5] But the difficulties of a number of these visionary organisations did make the Holy Grail more elusive.

CREATIVE DESTRUCTION

In 2001, two consultants from McKinsey published an attack on the concept of "Built to Last". "Creative destruction"[6] was a systematic examination of the difficulties of corporate longevity. Noting that, of the United States Standard & Poor 500 Index in 1957, only 74 remained on the list by 1997, and of that 74, only 12 had outperformed the index over that 40-year period, they suggested that "the corporate equivalent of El Dorado, the golden company that continually performs better than the markets, has never existed". In other words the odds are stacked hugely against long-term organisational success.

The argument ran as follows: companies that are "built to last" can't possibly sustain competitive advantage because the forces that help organisations survive – order and control – assume continuity. However, an increasing rate of business change requires the complete opposite: discontinuity. "Creative destruction" is the name of the new game: the willingness to keep tearing up the corporate rulebook. The dynamics for organisational longevity lie in constantly eliminating marginally performing business units, encouraging innovation from the periphery, and always looking for novel configurations.

And significantly, succession management doesn't actually feature in this new way of doing business.[7] In this scenario, capability may be important; indeed it is critically important. But the kind of continuity provided by leadership from within represents a potential drag on the kind of fast-moving radical innovation that is required. "Creative destruction", as the formula for business success, received a blow when one of its flagship case study companies, Enron, an outstanding exemplar of this new-look organisation, an organisation prepared to reinvent the rules to transform itself from conventional energy generation to trading in weather forecasts, ended in spectacular bankruptcy. Maybe some rules are there not to be broken. At this point the search for the Holy Grail was proving to be a futile exercise.

Good to great

Drilling down from an initial corporate database of 1435 companies, another research enterprise[8] went on to ask: not what sustains long-term success — perhaps that is next to impossible to answer — but a question of more pressing relevance to most organisations. What is it that takes an organisation operating at a "satisfactory" level to go on to perform at an outstanding level? What dynamics are at work to take organisations from good to great? This research enterprise focused on 11 firms that had met the demanding criteria of greatness: achieving returns at least three times the market value, sustained for 15 years or more. What triggered the "leap to greatness"? What differentiated these "great" companies from their peers who, despite their best efforts at corporate transformation, failed to make the transition? (See Figure 2.2.)

The results must have made depressing reading for the change management industry, the experts in translating the "big idea" into a programme of organisational renewal. Going from good to great does not seem to involve the kind of "change jamboree", that mix of structured and facilitated programmes, motivational events, elaborate project management methodology and new initiatives, which are the essential armoury of the management consultancy profession. Instead it requires lots of hard work, an ongoing attention to the detail of getting lots of things right, a refusal to be deflected by setbacks and a ruthlessness to stop doing the things that are hindering progress. Introducing a new initiative is exciting; calling a halt to established practices and processes is more hazardous as it is more likely to challenge vested interests and create political opposition. The good to great transition is not about change management gimmickry; rather it is a relentless and ongoing drive expending disciplined effort. There is no one defining moment that triggers the momentum of success. Instead there is a series of well-taken decisions, each moving the organisation in the right direction based on a frank and honest appraisal of the issues and a clear-headed strategic model to drive the business forward.

A distinctive leadership style at the top
- A rare combination of personal humility and resolute determination
- Emphasis on continuity from within and succession planning

A culture of discipline
- A consistency about what matters and a ruthlessness to stop doing what doesn't
- Encouraging personal responsibility, not building in bureaucracy to compensate for incompetence and a lack of self discipline

Getting the right people "on the bus"
- The rigour with which people decisions are made – putting the right people in place and removing the wrong people

A simple business model
- Creating that insight which makes sense of complexity and uncertainty
- Knowing: what we can and can't be the best at; what drives our financial engine; what we get passionate about

Confronting the "brutal facts"
- Accepting that good is not great, and that current success is no guarantee of future success
- Creating a climate in which the truth is heard and tough issues are confronted

Applying carefully selected technologies
- Seeing technology as the tool (not the end point) to accelerate momentum
- Building in technology as part of the business model, not pioneering for its own sake

Continual momentum
- There is no one breakthrough moment
- Greatness is a cumulative process, resulting from a series of decisions and actions, not one-off change programmes

Figure 2.2   The dynamics of "good to great" organisations

Going from good to great is also about a shift in leadership outlook and priority: a "distinctive leadership style at the top". It wasn't simply that good to great companies put much more emphasis on succession from within. They did, overwhelmingly so. Organisations who travelled the trajectory to achieve greatness were *six times less likely* to have appointed a CEO from outside than the comparison firms who had failed to make the transition. Across the time lines of the research survey, only 4.7 per cent of outsiders were appointed to the post of CEO in good to great firms in contrast to 30.7 per cent for the comparison firms (see Figure 2.3). Indeed the evidence indicates that in over three quarters of the comparison companies, "executives set their successors up for failure or chose weak successors, or both". This is succession as organisational sabotage.

Going from good to great involves a distinctive leadership style and approach. Reviewing the business press coverage, researchers found that much less was written about the leaders of good to great companies than for the comparison companies; those organisations who matched by sector had failed to make the breakthrough. This is extraordinary. The leaders of those organisations who had delivered and sustained superior returns were less well publicised than their comparisons. Either this is a chance finding or an indicator of something fundamental about the nature of leadership.

Further investigation revealed that the group of good to great leaders shared a similar mind-set: personal humility and an intense will to see their organisations succeed. "They are somewhat self-effacing individuals who deflect adulation yet who have an almost stoic resolve to do absolutely whatever it takes to make the company great, channelling their ego needs away from themselves and into the larger goal of building a great company."[9] Humility is not a word in common currency in business leadership. But it was a theme

	No. of Companies	Total No. of CEOs	Total No. of Outsiders	% of Outsiders
Good to Great Companies	11	42	2	4.7%
Direct Comparison Companies	11	65	20	30.7%
Unsustained Comparison Companies	6	25	6	24%

Figure 2.3   Insiders and outsiders in "good to great" companies

marking out this exceptional group of individuals who had achieved something quite remarkable for their organisations and shareholders. Conversely, in the comparison group, "ego", that is, striving for personal status, public plaudits and peer approval, was a running theme. This, to jump ahead, has important implications for the way in which we identify the kinds of leaders we need for the future. Many talent management programmes seem almost intentionally designed to nominate ambitious and self-seeking individuals, keener to move on to the next level to further their personal aims, than those individuals who want to get on with the job of achieving something worthwhile for their teams and the organisation, who are quietly getting on with the business of achieving excellence right now in their current role. We may need to change where and how we look for the kind of talent required for genuine leadership.

Achieving and maintaining success is extraordinarily difficult. In a ferociously competitive business world, getting started is tough enough. When technological developments keep changing the rules of the game, outperforming your competitors even for five years will be extraordinarily difficult, unless you have the good fortune to operate in a monopoly industry, protected by a favourable regulatory environment. Sustaining consistently superior performance over decades borders on the impossible.

The secret of long-term organisational success may be that there is no Holy Grail. Attempts to map out a definitive list of "success factors" are fundamentally flawed. Instead there is a moving target.[10] Identifying a definitive listing of factors which drive corporate success and longevity is likely to be an impossible goal. So does this mean there are no enduring and timeless principles that underpin success? Not necessarily. Although the specific dynamics will shift and change for different organisations in different sectors and at different points in their evolution, there may be overarching themes, themes "hard-wired" into the nature of competitive advantage. These themes, "strategic story lines",[11] are timeless, but the themes need to be reinvented and renewed to keep them relevant. Succession management, the processes to ensure continuity of capable leadership to manage the organisational tensions of competing and conflicting dynamics, may be one of these story lines.

AN ACADEMIC FOOTNOTE

Business case studies based on small sample studies or retrospective methodologies may not be the best way to determine the impact of succession activity on organisational outcomes.[12] What does a more dispassionate view from academic research suggest? Are effective succession practices associated with sustained and superior corporate performance? Reviewing the available research it is initially tempting to agree with screenplay writer William Goldman in his analysis of Hollywood and its attempts to predict the next movie blockbuster: "No one knows shit."[13] The sheer number, complexity and interaction of organisational and environmental variables makes it extraordinarily difficult to conceive the kind of controlled experiment that would provide a definitive answer, never mind conduct it.

One of the more illuminating studies[14] found moderate correlations between different aspects of succession practice and corporate performance across 200 firms. Although by no means conclusive this research found that high-performing firms had a different approach to succession than low-performing firms. Significantly, as regards formalisation of succession procedures, there was no differentiation across the two sets of organisations. So what do high-performing firms do that is different from that of the low-performing firms?

Firstly, high-performing firms simply spend more time on succession activity. Notably one of the best indicators was the time spent by the CEO and top team. On average, it was found that the average time spent by the CEO on succession issues was 11 per cent of his or her total work time. In high-performing firms this was much higher. High-performing firms reinforce succession practices and outcomes. They are, for example, more likely to reward their executives for attention to employee development. Higher-performing firms display greater commitment and "earnestness" with regard to talent review processes. As well as running talent review exercises more frequently, the process is more likely to be owned by line management rather than sponsored and driven by human resources.

"Succession roulette"

Walk into a casino, head for the roulette table and observe the game. The croupier stands by the roulette wheel, a wheel numbered from 0–30, alternating black and red. Surrounding the table, displaying the betting options, are the players, the gamblers. They place their bets on the table. Some put down only a few chips; others a large stack. Some bet on one number only; others spread their bets, odds or evens. The croupier spins the wheel, throws in the ball and waits. The wheel stops. The bets are reviewed and paid out. Some gamblers who have lost walk away from the table; no more gambling action for them that night. The winners check their chips; a few walk away, but most stay to play again.

Since our consultancy involvement over the last few years with a gaming organisation we have found gambling, and specifically roulette, a powerful metaphor for succession management.

THERE ARE NO CERTAINTIES

In "succession roulette", there are no guarantees of winning. Appointments are made and managers are promoted but there are no certainties. We are placing our bets on the future. We're gambling that we've made a good call and have selected the right person for the job. We like to think we've done all we can to maximise our probabilities, but it is still a bet. Our call depends on the business scenarios that open up over time. Only as the strategic game unfolds do the winners and losers become clear.

PLAYING WITH LIMITED CHIPS

Even the wealthiest, highest-rolling gamblers have a limit on their stake. All of us have to play "succession roulette" on a budget. The budget can be spent on the "chips" of external recruitment, betting on managers from outside the organisation and/or spent on the "chips" of the development and progression of internal candidates. But there is a limit to this budget. In "succession roulette" we cannot place our bets on all employees and cover every possible resourcing eventuality. We need to find the optimal balance of internal and external "chips" and make choices to back some individuals rather than others.

CHOOSING A GAMBLING STRATEGY

Roulette players have several gambling options. Placing all their chips on number 17 is a bold bet with a potentially big pay-out but a low probability of winning. Spreading bets, a modest number of chips on, say, odds or evens, has a higher probability of winning but a smaller pay-out. The challenge in "succession roulette" is to use our finite budget wisely. Backing a well-regarded and talented senior executive from outside on premium remuneration or providing proactive and intensive development to groom a handful of internal candidates may be lucky and beat the succession wheel and win the big strategic prize. Or, if the wrong choices have been made, to lose it. Alternatively, spreading the resourcing and development budget across a broad range of individuals at different organisation levels covers the strategic bases, but will dilute effort — less risky but a smaller pay-off.

Of course, like most analogies, "succession roulette" breaks down. We can walk away from the roulette table. We can't, however, walk away from the realities of succession management. The replacement for a key role will be made, eventually. It may happen after a period of delay, creating organisational uncertainty and stalling strategic implementation. It may result in the appointment of a senior executive whose actions go on to terminally weaken the organisation. But succession will happen and we can't avoid playing the game. The challenge is to play the game in a way that maximises the odds of success.[15]

PLAYING SUCCESSION ROULETTE: AN ORGANISATIONAL PERSPECTIVE

MOTIVATION

How keen are we to play this game? How serious are we as an organisation about strategic resourcing?

STAKE

How much organisationally are we willing to bet? What investment needs to be made? How much time will we commit to this activity? What resources need to be deployed to play this game properly?

RISK	GAMING AWARENESS
What level of risk are we willing to accept? Will we continue to bet on the "usual suspects", the predictable internal options or the obvious short-list from the executive search firm? Or will we look for unusual sources of talent and be imaginative about who we will back and invest in for the future?	How do we need to play this game to maximise the probabilities of success? How shrewd are we in the way we identify, develop and deploy our talent?

The strategy succession connection

It may be that how you play "succession roulette", the kind of stake that needs to be placed and the tactics you deploy will depend on your organisation's fundamental strategic outlook. There is no one game with one approach to succession. Instead different strategies will require different tactical responses to resourcing and development.

FOUR ORGANISATIONAL CARICATURES

Consider these four fictional organisations within the IT sector:

1   Three precocious students at MIT set up FST in the early 1990s. Possessing outstanding talents, the trio blazed a trail in software for logistics management when a major food retailer spotted the potential of their early prototypes. The mid-1990s saw a period of rapid expansion for FST and its distinctive culture attracted the attention of the financial press. "Free-wheeling, flexible and fun" was how Jerry Fischer described the organisation. By 1997, FST had disappeared from the software landscape. "It was never our intention to become part of the whole corporate thing," said Pat Tyrrell. "We wanted to make some money, but we also wanted to have fun doing things our way."

2   From nowhere PSG became a credible player in the competitive accountancy software market. The robustness and dependability of its products combined with the responsiveness of its customer support established a solid reputation for PSG. From its initial series of highly profitable niche applications, PSG expanded rapidly to become an obvious choice for small to medium-sized companies. Through a combination of shrewd commercial judgement and product reliability, PSG claimed a 30 per cent share of the small to medium-sized business market. However, things began to unravel by 2001. By 2002 PSG had been acquired by a smaller rival. One investor commented, "Two things contributed to PSG's downfall: a belief in its innovation which didn't recognise it was being out-paced by smaller rivals, and an arrogance that its customers would always remain loyal to PSG."

3   WAS specialised in software applications for human resources, most notably in databases for management audits and succession planning. The popularity of its first suite of products provided a platform for aggressive growth throughout the 1980s and early 1990s. The business formula was clear: sell the basic product, then maximise revenues through "customisation, consultancy and contracts". Perceiving the emergence of the Internet, WAS recognised that the rules of the game were changing and knew it had to

rethink its proposition. But while internal debates prolonged the review of its options, WAS was outflanked by more pioneering competitors quicker to exploit the potential of on-line data capture integrated around highly flexible databases.

4   BBF was formed in the mid-1990s as a break-away of one of the established market research firms. Initially it had no particular product offering; instead it had some preliminary business ideas about what might be possible and an empathy with client dissatisfaction over the high cost and slow turnaround of typical market research surveys. Bringing together a high-powered software development team with its own market research capability, BBF is set to launch its first product. "Although the risks are high — no one knows if the market is ready for this kind of radical innovation — the potential gains for BBF are phenomenal," commented one industry commentator. "If it takes off they will revolutionise this sector and blow the socks off the competition. If it doesn't they're going to look rather foolish."

These four organisations are caricatures, each representing one of four over-arching strategic positions an organisation can adopt at any point in time (see Figure 2.4).

FST symbolises the *Focus on the Short Term* posture. Here business energy is directed towards the immediate: either to tackle those pressing problems that threaten survival or to exploit obvious commercial opportunities quickly before making a rapid exit. As a response to adverse business conditions, this can be a valid manoeuvre. It is not one, however, which can be sustained over the long term. In this scenario succession management is likely to be largely irrelevant. Instead the resourcing emphasis will be on bringing in people as and when they are required and allowing a "survival of the fittest" to determine progression.

PSG is an example of *Playing the Same Game*. Here the assumption is that the rules of

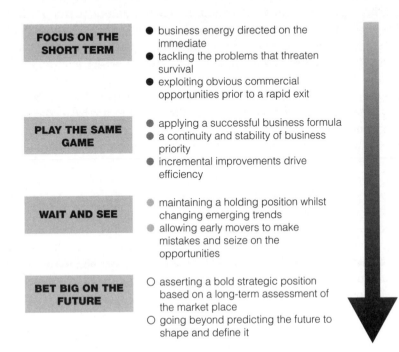

Figure 2.4   Strategic stances

business engagement that determined previous success will hold good in the future. Corporate strategy is the ongoing application of the same formula of business success. The upside is continuity and stability of approach. Stake-holders — shareholders, customers and employees — understand the organisation and where it is coming from and see it as a safe and dependable investment. The downside is vulnerability to that competitor who decides to play according to a different set of rules. In this scenario, Playing the Same Game is in difficulty. Nonetheless, as a business position in a relatively stable environment it works for many organisations for much of the time. For these organisations the aim of succession management is to generate an ongoing supply of leadership talent, following a well-worked resourcing model. Here, succession activity is likely to be driven by a tried-and-tested formula, which ensures that the same management "breed" is identified, developed and groomed for leadership responsibility.

WAS is indicative of the strategic posture of *Wait and See*. During times of business uncertainty, when the economic, political and social landscape is shifting and the competitive rules of engagement are unclear, Wait and See holds back from staking out a particular business battle-ground or committing itself to a specific investment in technology, product development or operating system. Instead Wait and See maintains a holding position, looking to gauge when a trend or pattern emerges. At best this is a sensible tactic allowing early movers to make "beginner mistakes" and then seize on emerging opportunities. At worst it is strategic procrastination, at risk of being overtaken by bolder and more ambitious rivals. For Wait and See, succession management represents an acute dilemma. On the one hand it cannot direct longer-term resourcing and development effort in any specific business direction. On the other hand, if it doesn't establish a succession agenda to build its future leadership capability then it is at risk of lacking the leadership to compete when it decides to show its hand and declare its business intentions.

BBF is *Bet Big on the Future*, an assertive and risk-taking strategic position, which takes a longer-term assessment of how the marketplace may evolve and the opportunities that may present themselves. It then commits itself to pursuing a particular course of action. The mind-set is not simply one of predicting the future, but of acting quickly and boldly to define and create the future before competitors get there first and set the rules of the game. For Bet Big on the Future it can be argued that succession management is at the heart of successful implementation. In the game of "succession roulette" the stake is bigger and more chips need to be put down if it is to win. Bet Big on the Future is either a remarkably risky gamble or the astute deployment of the available "chips" based on the shrewd development of emerging talent.

These four stances and the competitive interplay between them represents the chessboard on which business strategies evolve, shift and are redefined (see Figure 2.5). "Strategy involves judgements about when to commit and be willing to bet, when to delay making a commitment, when to kill something, when to hedge and ensure a bet, when to hustle, and when to try to change the rules of the game."[16] An attempt to Bet Big on the Future during tough economic times may be successful but may also be countered by an expedient rival who is Focusing on the Short Term. As a consequence the organisation retreats from its initial ambition to Play the Same Game. Here it faces a new set of competitor pressures and a different "strategic squeeze". Like the Red Queen in *Alice in Wonderland*, "it takes all the running you can do to keep in the same place. If you want to get somewhere else you must run at least twice as fast."

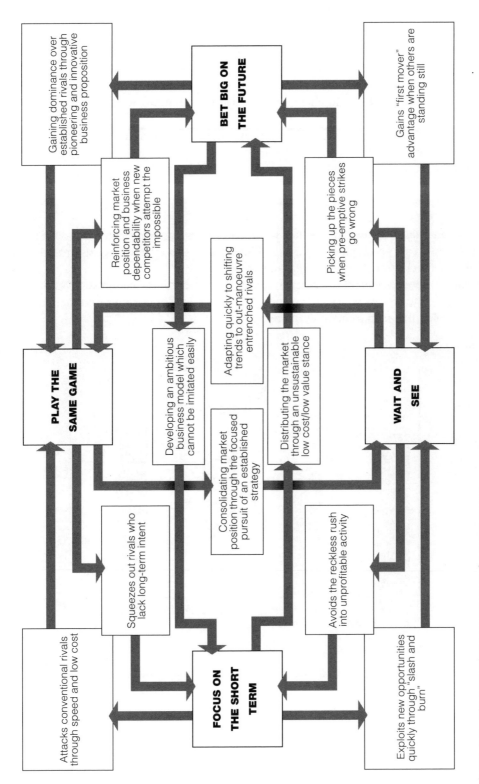

Figure 2.5   The strategic game: moves and counter moves

THE STRATEGIC RESOURCING ALIGNMENT INDEX[17]

In 2002 we conducted a research programme across our database of UK organisations. We wanted to identify which of these four strategic stances are more or less prominent? Which patterns of resourcing and development activity were evident across these organisations? And was there a relationship between different strategic outlooks and how organisations manage resourcing and development activity? Do organisations with different strategies approach succession management in different ways?

Figure 2.6 shows the spread of different strategic stances across the organisations within the survey sample. The most common themes were: Play the Same Game and Wait and See, with Bet Big on the Future the least frequent stance.

From the 20 survey statements of resourcing and development practices, we identified two themes:

- *Corporate Impact*: the extent to which talent and succession management is driven by the centre to create an organisational-wide blueprint and to establish consistent processes across different functions and departments
- *Proactive Development*: the degree to which the organisation commits investment to accelerate the process of leadership and professional development beyond that provided by ongoing line-management coaching.

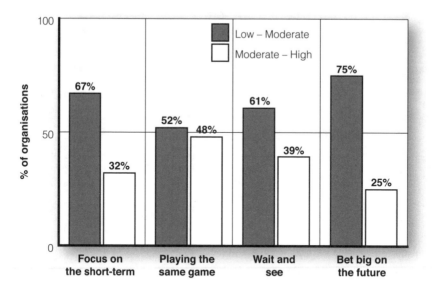

Figure 2.6   Strategic resourcing alignment index: four strategic positions

STRATEGIC RESOURCING ALIGNMENT IN YOUR ORGANISATION

Rate your organisation in each of the following areas, rating each of the activities on a 1–5 scale, where 1=absent, 2=largely ineffective, 3=moderately effective, 4=effective; 5=very effective

1. The impact of the top team in the regular review of high potential managers.
2. The application of a robust business planning process which clarifies overall resourcing requirements against strategic priorities.
3. The application of a clear set of guidelines from the centre to determine resourcing and development policy and share best practice.
4. The implementation of a performance management process to reinforce business priorities and operating values.
5. The utilisation of a corporate-wide framework, specifying the values and capabilities required for career progression at different organisational levels.
6. The planning, coordinating and monitoring of expenditure for resourcing and development throughout the organisation.
7. The influence of a "review forum" of senior management to coordinate career development activity within and across business units.
8. The implementation of consistent assessment methods for selection — internal and external.
9. The utilisation of smart information technology to capture, retrieve and analyse data about individuals and roles.
10. The coordination of resourcing activities to link talent management, succession planning and the appointments process.

For the next ten activities, provide a 1–5 rating, where 1=none, 2=minimal, 3=moderate, 4=much and 5=considerable.

11. The level of financial investment made in the development of your management and professional groups.
12. The extent to which your organisation provides additional development (to complement ongoing self-development and line-management coaching).
13. The targeting and coordination of development to those individuals seen as critical to the business.
14. The extent to which all employees at every level have a set of goals for improving personal effectiveness.
15. The degree to which senior managers are actively engaged in the mentoring and coaching of key managers.
16. The recognition and reward of line managers for their effectiveness in developing staff.
17. Your organisation's innovation in implementing progressive approaches to the development of its people.
18. Your organisation's willingness to "take risks" and invest in the development of "non obvious" individuals.
19. The extent to which any potential external providers of development activity are evaluated carefully before commencing any assignments.
20. The evaluation of the impact of your organisation's development efforts and initiatives.

Total up your score for statements 1–10. The total score is your organisation's *Corporate Impact* index. Total up your score for statements 11–20; this is your *Proactive Development* index. Scores less than 23 indicate a low score; 24–37 a moderate score; 38 and above, a high score.

Do different strategic stances have a different set of resourcing and development priorities (see Figure 2.7)? Is there any alignment between organisations and their strategic outlook and how they embark on succession? Yes and no seems to be the answer from the UK organisations we surveyed in 2002.

For those organisations Focusing on the Short Term, succession management could be expected to be a relatively low priority and this was confirmed in the findings. They reported much less activity generally. The centre makes less impact in driving priorities or establishing consistent processes. There was also much less evidence of Proactive Development. Put simply, for organisations where the strategy was Focus on the Short Term, they did exactly that, looking only at today's resourcing demands rather than investing and planning for the future.

For organisations Playing the Same Game we predicted that there would be less Proactive Development but that the centre would exert greater influence over succession activity, that Corporate Impact would be higher. The succession priority for these organisations is to ensure processes and systems are in place and adhered to throughout the organisation in order to identify and progress that breed of management that has been successful in the past. The results confirmed this approach: greater influence from the centre but less investment in additional development.

For Wait and See organisations we anticipated a different approach to succession. Here, since there is no clear business emphasis but more of a holding position, it makes little sense for the Centre to determine priorities and practices. Rather the reverse: different business units should be encouraged to experiment and innovate and establish local processes that reflect their specific requirements. Corporate Impact should therefore be lower. However, there should be more Proactive Development. Although leadership and professional development should not be constrained by an overall corporate template, there should be a greater willingness to encourage talented individuals to drive their own development and a commitment to invest in development. The findings broadly supported this analysis: Wait and See is associated with lower Corporate Impact and higher Proactive Development.

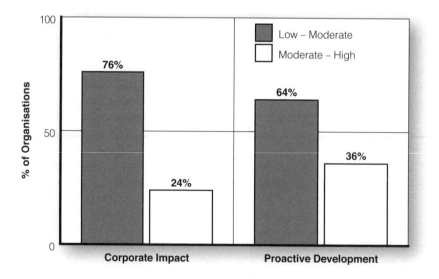

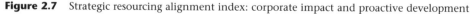

Figure 2.7   Strategic resourcing alignment index: corporate impact and proactive development

Intriguingly it was those organisations Betting Big on the Future that proved more problematic. A bold and assertive strategic stance should suggest higher Proactive Development and Corporate Impact. While some organisations in the sample exhibited this profile, overall there was little alignment. Further investigation within the overall survey database highlighted two categories of organisations:

- Organisations where the business strategy was genuinely one of Bet Big on the Future but which had failed to think through the implications for succession and resourcing. Here a gulf was opening between business intention and practical implementation, a gulf which in succession terms meant a future lack of leadership capability to support their strategic aspirations.
- Organisations where the resourcing and succession infrastructure was running ahead of business requirements. In some instances the human resources function had hijacked the agenda, implementing initiatives to support a Bet Big on the Future game plan when the organisation, on greater analysis of its competitive position, was pursuing a much less ambitious course of action. This is human resources jeopardy — implementing a solution to a problem that doesn't exist. In other instances a "succession infrastructure", a set of activities and processes, had built up to support past strategic ambitions but the organisation had changed course to focus on new priorities. The momentum of previous resourcing and development activity was rolling on, regardless of current organisational requirements.

Succession management doesn't take place in a vacuum. It is played out in the context of a highly competitive business world in which organisations keep shifting, adapting and evolving their strategies. Organisational success, the "Holy Grail", stems from this willingness to accept the nature of this strategic change, recognising the opportunities to Bet Big on the Future, when it makes commercial sense to Wait and See or Play the Same Game. There will also be times of business pragmatism, when organisations Focus on the Short Term. This is the nature of competition, that business success is never a one-off victory but an ongoing series of battles, of advance and retreat, of attack and defence. But this campaign can only be sustained if your organisation is serious about the long term and has a commitment to succession management. For some organisations, some of the time, succession should be driven from the centre. For other companies at different moments this will be a mistake, with a high likelihood of distracting executive time and energy from their own distinctive resourcing pressures. For others, a calculated investment in professional and leadership development will provide the momentum to advance the business agenda. For others this investment may well be an expensive and irrelevant exercise.

The point is to align succession management priorities and practices within the overall strategic outlook of your organisation. Work through the framework of Figure 2.8 to establish your organisation's current stance and how well aligned your approach to succession management is in which to support this set of business priorities.

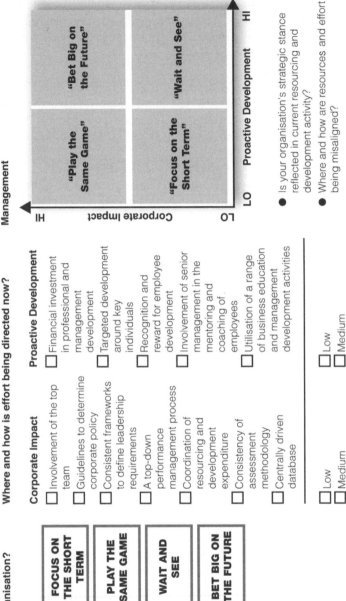

Which of these four positions is most and least descriptive for your organisation?

Review:

- Its fundamental outlook, ambition, purpose and willingness to accept risk
- The business challenges it is actively facing and those it is avoiding
- The competitive scenario it is operating in
- Those customer groups it sees as priorities
- The focus of the top team; where it is and isn't directing its time
- Its dominant cultural mind-set and operating values

FOCUS ON THE SHORT TERM

PLAY THE SAME GAME

WAIT AND SEE

BET BIG ON THE FUTURE

Current resourcing and development activity. Where and how is effort being directed now?

Corporate Impact

- ☐ Involvement of the top team
- ☐ Guidelines to determine corporate policy
- ☐ Consistent frameworks to define leadership requirements
- ☐ A top-down performance management process
- ☐ Coordination of resourcing and development expenditure
- ☐ Consistency of assessment methodology
- ☐ Centrally driven database

☐ Low
☐ Medium
☐ High

Proactive Development

- ☐ Financial investment in professional and management development
- ☐ Targeted development around key individuals
- ☐ Recognition and reward for employee development
- ☐ Involvement of senior management in the mentoring and coaching of employees
- ☐ Utilisation of a range of business education and management development activities

☐ Low
☐ Medium
☐ High

Alignment of Strategy and Succession Management

- Is your organisation's strategic stance reflected in current resourcing and development activity?
- Where and how are resources and effort being misaligned?

Figure 2.8   Strategic stances and resourcing and development priorities

An initial stock take

At what point in the cycle of "business excellence" is your organisation?

- Struggling to survive?
- Operating effectively but lacking the aspiration to go from "good to great"?
- Successful and with the commitment to achieve "greatness"?
- Highly successful but showing signs of arrogance and complacency?
- Highly successful and with a passion to sustain excellence?

What are the implications for how succession is managed?

- When playing "succession roulette" are you at the game, or not even near the table? Do you need to increase your stake? By how much?
- Do you need to change your betting tactics? If so, do you need to bet more or less on external recruitment; on internal development?
- How clear are you about your specific bets? Are you gambling on a few individuals to stay in the game, or are you keeping your options open?

What is the emphasis of your organisation's strategic stance and business outlook?

- Focus on the Short Term: the need to survive on a day-to-day basis?
- Playing the Same Game: the ongoing application of a successful business formula which has worked in the past?
- Wait and See: tracking emerging trends to maintain a holding position before making a strategic commitment?
- Bet Big on the Future: the confidence to embark on an ambitious agenda to create the future?

How well aligned are your resourcing and development priorities to reflect this stance?

- How much consensus is there within the organisation about the focus of succession and the best approach to resourcing and development? Within the human resources community? Between business executives and the human resources function?
- What impact is the centre currently making? What impact does it need to make in the future? Less? More?
- How much investment is being made in the development of emerging talent? Should this investment be less or greater given your business outlook?

Notes

1. During his 37-year tenure as chairman and chief executive of Berkshire Hathaway, Warren Buffett has increased the company's market value at a compound growth rate of over 25% per year. Personally the second wealthiest individual in the USA, his investors have also benefited. A $10 000 stake in the company in 1965 would have grown to over $40 million today (compared to $144 000 if invested in the S & P 500).
2. These findings are summarised in R. Eccles and N. Nohria, *Beyond the Hype*, 1994.
3. J. Collins and J. Porras, *Built to Last*, 1993.

4. G. Hamel and L. Valikangas, "The Quest for Resilience", *Harvard Business Review*, September 2003.
5. Peter Drucker, "Peter's Principles", *Context*, Spring 1998.
6. R. Foster and S. Kaplan, *Creative Destruction*, 2001.
7. Importantly there is no reference anywhere to succession management in the case study organisations quoted in *Creative Destruction*.
8. J. Collins, *Good to Great*, 2001.
9. Jim Collins, "The Conference Board", Annual Essay, 2001.
10. Imagine, for example, a scenario in which every enterprise embarked on the attempt to introduce and implement the principles of "good to great". No doubt many organisations would find this too demanding a challenge. But nonetheless a substantial number might go down this route. At this point the rules of competitive advantage would shift and the dynamics of business success would change. Success is achieved by doing something different and better from your competitors. If competitors copy this approach a new set of differentiating success factors would emerge. This is the moving target.
11. "There exist incontrovertible truths that apply and can be expected to hold in the long-term." James O'Loughlin, *The Real Warren Buffett*, 2003. These include the laws of business economics, value creation, organisational dynamics and human nature.
12. A general observation. Research in the area of organisational success has been dominated by studies identifying the practices of currently successful organisations. Here any association between specific practices and organisational success is interpreted as cause and effect. But correlation does not imply causation. The fundamental empirical test is prediction. From our knowledge of cause and effect can we predict future outcomes? This is the bottom-line test of our knowledge. (It is also of course the goal of stock-market investors.) But I know of no study in which a Holy Grail researcher has analysed, say, 100 organisations, made predictions based on their business theory of which would and wouldn't be successful, sealed their predictions in a safe, and opened it ten years later to report the accuracy of their predictions.
13. William Goldman, *Adventures in the Screen Trade*, Abacus, 1983.
14. S. Friedman, "Succession Systems in Large Corporations: Characteristics and Correlates of Performance", *Human Resource Management*, vol. 25 (1986).
15. "Succession Roulette", *Business Types Facilitators' Manual*, Andrews Munro Ltd, 1998.
16. R. Eccles and N. Nohria, *Beyond the Hype*, 1994.
17. "The Strategic Resourcing Alignment Index Survey", Andrews Munro Ltd, 2002.

3 The Battle-grounds for Succession

"If the trumpet give an uncertain sound who shall prepare himself to the battle?" 1 Corinthians 14:40

"In preparing for battle I have always found that plans are useless but planning is indispensable." Dwight D. Eisenhower

> Succession management is a solution to a business problem. What problem is it attempting to solve? Succession can be tightly defined as the specific plan to determine who takes on the "baton" of corporate leadership. For organisations, thinking strategically about the long-term future, and the capability needed to realise that future, this is a limited definition. Succession management needs to operate across a number of battle-grounds, short and long term, focused and wide-ranging. A coherent and consistent game plan relies on coordinating activity and aligning processes across three different arenas: managing the appointments process to improve current leadership and professional capability; tracking those business risks that are emerging as "resourcing pressure points", and identifying and developing talent proactively to maintain a strong leadership pipeline for the future.

A NEW CEO OF A PROFESSIONAL SERVICES FIRM IS MEETING WITH THE HR DIRECTOR

New CEO: "What's the story then on succession management? Where are we at?"

HR Director: "The Organisation and Management Review worked through the senior executive population as they do every year. We've just finished presenting the succession plan to the Board."

New CEO: "OK. What's the view from the business? What practical difference has this made?"

HR Director: "I'm not sure I know what you mean."

New CEO: "At the same time as the succession plan is being finalised I see that Bill was appointed as a regional director. There is no way that guy should have been put into that role."

HR Director: "I know what you mean. But there were a few other factors at work…"

New CEO: "I'm also a bit worried that we haven't drilled into the detail of Business Systems. It's all very well looking at the senior people. They're doing a great job right now. I'm more concerned about the problem we've got if Hilary and Gemma leave. My impression is that we've got a big resourcing hole in that division. What analysis has been done there?"

HR Director: "The problem is that the OMR looks only at levels 7 and 8. Business Systems haven't been too keen on cascading the process further down. But you're right, we have big problems ahead in that division."

New CEO: "I see that Marketing are launching a high potential programme. What's that all about? It looks a pretty expensive initiative to me."

> HR Director: "Marketing think they need a more proactive approach to career development. They ran a survey and a lot of their people are very unhappy about progression."
> New CEO: "This is ridiculous. We both know that Marketing are going to have a painful time in the next six months when we restructure; this programme is going to send out completely the wrong message... All of this is making me think our overall succession strategy is a bit half baked. There is no sense of overall business priorities and not much joined-up thinking. Can we get together next week to go through this properly?"

Perhaps the greatest challenge in planning a programme of succession management is the lack of clear definition. Succession management seems to mean many different things to different people. When an organisation approaches us to say it wants to "do" succession, the resulting assignment can go down a variety of avenues with different outcomes. At one extreme, succession is tightly defined as the "charting of successors" for a handful of top management roles. Here we have been involved with projects that have required us to draw the succession plan on a piece of paper, indicating succession coverage and exposure within the senior management structure. These projects have sometimes been no more than an exercise in impression management to persuade a stake-holder group, a regulatory agency or Board committee that succession is an important priority for the organisation, and that the leadership bases are covered.

At the other end of the spectrum, succession management is a sprawling set of loosely connected activities, covering business planning, workforce planning, resourcing, performance management, assessment and career management; this makes it difficult to pin down and prioritise the key issues. Indeed for some organisations a kind of "succession forest" has grown up as different business areas have embarked on a series of programmes while the corporate centre has launched its own initiatives. In this scenario, much organisational effort is expended, but in this "forest" it can be difficult to navigate a path to guide organisational activity around a clear purpose. Before progress can be made, a certain amount of "ground clearing", that is, the removal of the tangle of irrelevant, overlapping and confusing activities, is required.

THE "IS–IS NOT" OF SUCCESSION

One exercise we run with managers as an introduction to the practicalities of succession management is a variation of the Kepner Tregoe methodology: the "is–is not" technique. Faced with a problem, ask: "Where is the problem; where isn't there a problem? When is it a problem; when isn't it a problem? Who is the problem; who isn't the problem?" And so on. The discipline of answering both "is" and "is not" is a simple but powerful way of outlining the scale and scope of the problem to be addressed. "Is" is usually easy to answer, but "is not" requires a more incisive analysis. If organisationally there is no clear consensus about succession, what

it is and isn't attempting to accomplish, it is difficult to see how progress can be made.

Working with your management group, erect a flip chart with two columns headed "Is" and "Is Not". Give the group a few minutes of reflection to prepare their thoughts. Then ask the group for their observations. What do they think succession is? What do they think succession isn't? Depending on the group and the time designated for the session, either encourage comments as issues are noted or summarise the group's output quickly. Then work through each of the observations systematically. If the group's output is too general, prompt them by asking: "What does succession mean for us as an organisation? What doesn't it? What will it require us to do; to stop doing?"

If the group is motivated to advance the discussion and think through the implications, present the question in a different way: What would our organisation need to do to ensure that succession management *won't* get "off the ground" at all? Or if we did manage to introduce succession, what would we need to do to ensure it *didn't* make a practical difference? The aim here is to invert the argument and help reframe the issues from another perspective and stimulate a debate about the realities of managing succession.

Succession as a set of solutions

Figure 3.1 summarises the range of possible succession solutions and associated organisational commitment.

REPLACEMENT CHARTING

For many organisations replacement charting is the be-all-and-end-all of succession management activity. Within the organisational structure, key roles are identified and successors are nominated as potential replacements. Certain individuals are designated as contingency back-ups, who are equipped to provide immediate cover in the event of the sudden departure of the current incumbent, hence the disturbing reference to "drop dead" charts. Jerry Junkins, CEO of Texas Instruments, said, "I'm as lean and healthy as a horse", noting that a succession plan was in place to coincide with his planned retirement in two years. A few months later he died of a heart attack, and Texas Instruments was left without an immediate successor.

Replacement charting
● Nomination of back-up successors

Grooming successors
● Proactive programme to equip individuals for specific roles

Managing "Pools and Flows"
● Resourcing for clusters of position from pools of talent

Catalysing organisational change
● Shifting resourcing priorities and practice to drive cultural transformation

Strategic resourcing around business scenarios
● Asking "what if" questions about the future

Increasing Organisational Commitment

Figure 3.1   Succession solutions and commitment

Short- to medium-term successors are those individuals who, over time and with appropriate development, represent potential candidates to progress into the role. Replacement charting for a highly select number of roles, those pinpointed as critical to the organisation's future, may be a basic discipline of succession management. Embarking, however, on an annual exercise to assemble an organisational chart across every business unit and covering all roles is a highly wasteful activity. It may be there was a time when this served some useful purpose. But in a period of ongoing business change when structures repeatedly shift with some roles disappearing and new ones emerging, then the standard replacement chart for organisations now seems to be part of the problem rather than providing a meaningful resourcing solution.

GROOMING NOMINATED SUCCESSORS

If replacement charting is the summary of coverage and exposure for the "big roles", then "grooming" represents another succession response. Here it isn't simply a case of who is on the "slate"; it is how we intend to develop these nominated individuals to prepare them to assume greater leadership responsibility. Given our view of emerging successors, what needs to be done to equip specific individuals for more senior roles? Nominated successors either simply sit tight waiting for their moment of destiny when the target role becomes vacant, or a development plan is established to ensure they are prepared and ready to take on their new responsibilities. At best this "succession solution" gives the nominated successors clarity about their future and time to plan their development. At worst the identification of "crown princes" creates animosity from those colleagues who perceive their personal ambitions have been thwarted. "Grooming" also assumes that the projected role doesn't change between the point of nomination and the succession event itself, a questionable assumption.

MANAGING "POOLS AND FLOWS"

Instead of preparing an organisational master plan indicating who is in the running for which job, some organisations have mapped out a looser approach to succession, thinking in terms of clusters of roles and pools of available talent. Since organisational structures and the configuration of roles are continually shifting, succession management should be directed at proactively directing the flow of talent to create a grouping of candidates for categories of position. For example, one of the UK's banks overhauled its succession strategy to move away from classic charting against current structures and roles to a more flexible framework. This identified five groupings of role within the middle/senior management and professional population (see Figure 3.2):

- *Leading the strategic future*: formulating a long-term vision and direction and strategic positioning in the marketplace.
- *Managing customer operations*: maximising resources and focusing priorities to ensure high standards of quality and efficiency in the delivery of products/services to customers.
- *Facilitating organisational innovation*: providing the ideas and policies to support organisational renewal and build long-term capability.
- *Providing professional advice*: providing best-practice professional expertise to inform business decision-making and to maintain and improve the "organisational infrastructure".
- *Others*: miscellaneous roles with a mix of different or unusual requirements.

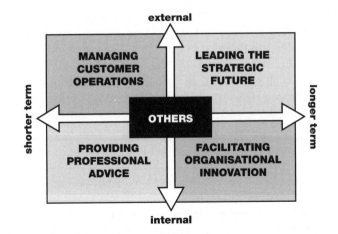

Figure 3.2 "Pools and flows" succession

The management population, based on an assessment of their business experience, management competency, technical know-how and career aspirations, was also coded against these five groupings. The succession debate became less about agreeing progression for individuals against specific roles and more about mapping out the strength of each talent pool at senior executive levels and the flow from middle ranks.

This is a more contingent approach, accepting that nominating and grooming successors for roles, which in all likelihood will not exist in future, does not make much sense. The aim then is to look at the pools of emerging talent within the "pipeline" to identify who is capable of progressing not to a specific position but to take on a range of responsibilities.

CATALYSING ORGANISATIONAL CHANGE

The development and deployment of talent is a key lever in changing organisational culture. If we are serious about creating business change, then we need to rethink our policies and practices in who we promote and progress as professionals and leaders. Motorola, for example, in the late 1980s, concerned about its lack of workforce diversity, redesigned its succession processes to make the development of women and minorities a priority. Managers, when reviewing the pool of available talent for progression, were asked to submit not just one list of high-potential individuals, but names under four categories: white men, women, minorities and technical staff. The aim here was to create a more socially diverse workforce more representative of the society in which Motorola operated.

This is succession management as "social engineering", rethinking the criteria for progression, the mechanisms for career development and the appointments process to catalyse a shift in the make-up of the workforce and its business leadership. This "succession solution" becomes an important lever in creating greater organisational diversity.

STRATEGIC RESOURCING AROUND BUSINESS SCENARIOS

A more ambitious "solution" is one in which succession management is closely integrated with the strategic and business planning process. Rather than take the current structure and executive/professional population as the starting-point for succession activity, the trigger to succession planning is a debate about the long-term strategic options for the organisation. This approach begins with "what if" scenarios: "what if" we moved into this market, "what if" we decided to develop this product range, "what if" we changed our fundamental service proposition? If we did, what would be the implications for our future leaders and professionals? What skill sets would be needed? What technical know-how would be required? What leadership styles would be appropriate when operating within a different business and organisational agenda? Does this capability exist at the moment? If not, can we go on to develop this capability internally? Who within the organisation represents a potential source of this capability? What would we need to do to develop this talent? How long will this take? Or will we need to go outside to buy-in this capability?

Clearly this is not a succession response for those organisations where the stance is Focus on the Short Term or Play the Same Game. There, succession management is either absent or operating to supply the same leadership mix as it has supplied in the past. This set of succession priorities is for organisations where the stance is Wait and See, or more typically, Bet Big on the Future. This is succession management, not simply as a mechanism to implement strategy, but as a trigger to initiate a dialogue about business possibilities. This is succession driven by the top team as a key priority to move the organisation forward.

This listing of succession solutions is not definitive, nor does it imply "either–or". Organisations should and do pursue a number of different priorities. Microsoft, for example, if it is serious about maintaining its dominance long after the departure of Bill Gates and Steve Ballmer, should be approving possible successors and putting in place plans to prepare them for future roles. It also ought to highlight the categories of roles that will be critical to the organisation's future and looking at the pool of available personnel and evaluating the breadth and depth of its capability. In addition it should be generating long-term scenarios of the kind of organisation it will be in five to ten years' time and thinking imaginatively about the talent it has and how this can be developed over that time frame.

Different succession solutions require different levels of organisational commitment, an investment in time and a willingness to integrate different strands of activity with implications for wider stake-holder involvement. Replacement charting for a handful of top executive positions is a manageable activity, an exercise in succession management requiring a focused but mature dialogue at Board level. At the other end of the spectrum, strategic resourcing around business scenarios needs to bring together a variety of executive and professional groups, requires a substantial time commitment and a preparedness to rethink and redefine current structures and personnel policies and practices.

Succession battle-grounds

An alternative way of thinking about succession management is to break it down into three connected strands of activity across different time horizons: the *appointments process*, *business risk assessment* and *talent management* (see Figure 3.3).

In the short term the appointments process needs to ensure the optimal selection decision is made to get the right person in place. This will be informed in the medium term by a business risk assessment: the identification of critical roles, the review of coverage and exposure, and agreeing those key players to be retained and progressed. Anticipation of resourcing pressures, risks and hazards will enable proactive planning to highlight those individuals requiring organisational attention and investment, or target where external

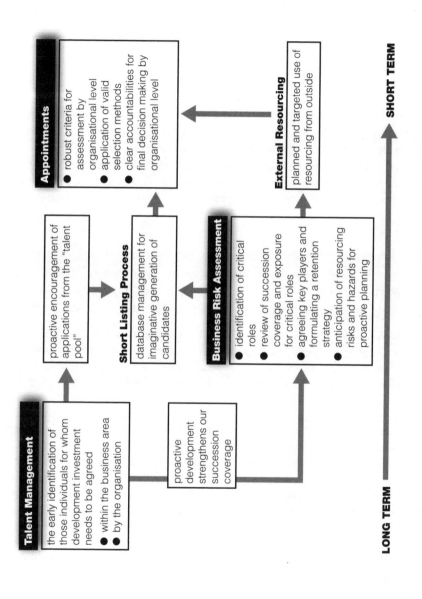

Talent Management

the early identification of those individuals for whom development investment needs to be agreed

● within the business area
● by the organisation

proactive development strengthens our succession coverage

proactive encouragement of applications from the "talent pool"

Short Listing Process

database management for imaginative generation of candidates

Appointments

● robust criteria for assessment by organisational level
● application of valid selection methods
● clear accountabilities for final decision making by organisational level

Business Risk Assessment

● identification of critical roles
● review of succession coverage and exposure for critical roles
● agreeing key players and formulating a retention strategy
● anticipation of resourcing risks and hazards for proactive planning

External Resourcing

planned and targeted use of resourcing from outside

SHORT TERM

LONG TERM

Figure 3.3   Three battle-grounds of succession

recruitment may be needed. Business risks of succession exposure will be minimised by strengthening the pipeline of leadership and professional capability through the insightful identification of emerging talent and proactivity in its development.

Succession management, like a military campaign, has to fight across different fronts. At the front line, the battle is at its most intense. Making good selection decisions at all levels is important, but especially so at senior levels. Here selection decisions are strategic decisions; choosing the battle-ground that will be waged with competitors.[1] But fighting on the front line requires ongoing logistical back-up and the flow of supplies from base camp. Battles are won not at the front line; they are won as a result of months and years of preparation and effort. Each of these three battle-grounds — the appointments process, business risk assessment and talent management — needs to be waged simultaneously. Clearly there are a number of supporting components: recruitment and induction practices; the performance management process; systems for recognition and reward; training and development activity. All these elements need to be aligned to ensure the organisation has the infrastructure in place to compete effectively across all three areas.

Above all we need to make the connections across these three battle-grounds and to map out the specific processes that underpin these activities and create an information flow which informs review and decision-making processes at different organisational points and times.

SUCCESSION DISCONNECTS

DISCONNECT 1: THE "SUCCESSION BLACK HOLE"

Business units conscientiously work through the corporate succession template provided by the centre, filling in documentation to review management structures, highlight succession coverage and exposure, and identify resourcing pressure points. The paper work is returned to head office, the "succession black hole", and life goes on. Individual managers leave or are promoted, new roles are created, some roles disappear, and resourcing realities — who gets which job — carry on regardless of the formal paper work. This disconnect, *the gap between the appointments process and business risk assessment*, initially creates management annoyance and irritation at wasted time, leading to the compliant ticking of boxes when the same paper work is demanded the following year, and finally, that most dangerous of all responses, cynicism.

DISCONNECT 2: HIGH POTENTIAL PROGRAMMES IN A VACUUM

Identifying gaps in the leadership pipeline — the lack of enough credible and capable candidates — the organisation embarks on some kind of fast-track programme. The graduate entrant intake is, for example, expanded, induction and training is bolstered, and job rotation programmes are established. Over the next two years the organisation finds itself facing the cost of high turnover of this high-potential group, while still experiencing resourcing problems further up the organisational hierarchy. Here, efforts to accelerate the development of emerging talent is disconnected from the workforce planning and resourcing cycle. *Talent management is disconnected from the outcomes of business risk assessment.*

The strategy–talent debate

Conventional human resource thinking over the last two decades or so has operated on the belief that we cannot establish a meaningful set of priorities for talent management and succession planning until we have clarified an organisational vision: a statement of strategic intent and business direction, organisational philosophy and culture. *Strategy drives talent.* The argument here is that different strategies have different implications for the number and kind of people we need to move the organisation forward. Unless our strategic aims are clearly articulated it is difficult to design a framework for meaningful resourcing and development activity.

Significantly, two widely divergent perspectives, coming from very different backgrounds, have recently challenged this assumption, with the view that *talent drives strategy*. Succession management, rather than waiting for the strategic steer, needs to focus on people, to identify capability and allow it to set the direction of the organisation. One view could be loosely described as "give talent freedom";[2] the other as "get the right people on the bus".[3] Both views recognise that strategic purpose does not pop out of a business "black box" simply as an outcome of the number-crunching of market research and competitor intelligence data. Instead strategic decisions are made by individuals reflecting their own interests, preferences and biases.[4]

In "give talent freedom" the organisational challenge is to give talented individuals the freedom and discretion to pursue business ideas, to venture out and explore new strategic possibilities. And out of this process, strategy evolves and develops. Indeed it is the generation of new business ideas that is the fundamental criterion in the assessment of talent and potential. Rather than looking at progression within established structures, namely, who moves up a level to fill which job, talent is the dynamic that helps the organisation to keep reinventing itself, to keep shifting roles and reporting relationships to respond to new business challenges.

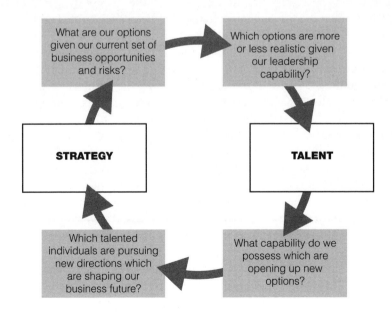

Figure 3.4   The strategy–talent debate

"Get the right people on the bus" expresses the view that it is more important to assemble a strong team of people, to "get them on the organisational bus" before deciding where the "bus" should go. Success stems not from a one-off strategically brilliant concept. Rather, successful strategies arise out of a close-knit group operating around mutual respect and trust, and successful implementation relies on collective ownership. Here the focus is not on strategy but on recruiting and developing a strong team of people. It is this team which then sets the strategic agenda.

The "talent drives strategy" philosophy works best in the early days of start-up when no definitive strategic position exists, and insightful analysis and creative thinking is required to agree and finalise a business position. It also works in a strategic vacuum when the organisation is unsure of its future. In both scenarios talented individuals come to the fore to shape the business future. But at worst the "talent drives strategy" position has the potential for "strategic chaos" in which competing egos and political agendas clash to battle for the future of the business.[5] This perspective also assumes that there is a group of super-talented individuals with the objectivity and flexibility to master any business and strategy. But as the "sage of Omaha", Warren Buffett, has commented, "When a management with a reputation for brilliance tackles a business with a reputation for bad economics it is the reputation of the business that remains intact."[6] In other words there are good businesses to be in and there are bad businesses, and there are no right people who can "drive the bus" in a bad business. In business there are no "Martini managers" with the talent to succeed "any time, any place, anywhere". The organisation that bets its future on the super-talented leader for all strategic seasons will lose to market realities.

The sensible view of course is that the strategy–talent debate is an iterative process, an ongoing series of discussions in which the organisation is constantly cross-referencing its strategic requirements with the available talent pool, talent that can be easily accessed from within or brought in from outside. It is also listening to the proposals and ideas of its emerging talent to highlight new strategic possibilities and to refocus its business direction.

For organisations operating in those sectors where the rules of the game are known and established and where the fundamental strategy has been well defined and articulated, the challenge is to build the talent base and manage the succession process to realise that strategy. Here, "strategy drives talent". The strategic template determines the skill sets, the business and technical know-how and the operating approach which drives succession priorities and practices. The risk of this approach is that the business environment changes and the current strategic game plan becomes obsolete. The current management and professional resources lack the flexibility to shift gear in order to respond to new challenges.

For other organisations "talent drives strategy". Here, the resourcing emphasis is on building a collection of talented individuals around a sense of overall purpose, a business concept and a set of beliefs about how they should operate. There is no definitive strategic master plan; rather a set of overall aspirations and a loose set of ideas about what needs to be done to succeed. Strategy flows from the efforts of these individuals, and the strategy keeps evolving as the talent base keeps shifting. The risk is allowing the mind-set of the "talented" to determine a strategy that flies in the face of market economics. Highly capable individuals with high levels of self-esteem resulting from past success have a positive energy to make things happen. They may also have an overweening arrogance to overcome business realities. This is the "masters-of-the-universe" syndrome, the belief that if we are smart enough we can dominate our competitors, and a pattern that is a common dynamic in business decline.

Strategy, in essence, is the interplay of customers, competitors and capability. A robust and sustainable strategy deploys capability shrewdly to out-manoeuvre competitors in order to identify profitable customers. The "strategy drives talent" philosophy focuses on market economics to capture the business space of current and emerging customers where competitors are slow to move. It then asks whether we have the capability to exploit this opportunity? "Talent drives strategy" asks: what could we achieve if we allowed our most talented individuals to rethink our business space? What possibilities would open up if we allowed our most talented people to redefine the basis on which we compete?

This debate is the core dilemma of succession management. This is succession management as an ongoing dialogue which examines strategic options based on a cool and dispassionate view of business fundamentals, conducting reviews of the leadership and professional capabilities that are accessible to implement these options. Succession management is also a process where sufficient imagination and flexibility is needed to be receptive to the fresh thinking of talented individuals and to provide opportunities to test out new ideas.

Next steps

How is succession currently perceived within your organisation? What set of solutions is it providing to which problems? Is succession:

- replacement charting and "names on the door" listings to reassure external constituents of business continuity in the face of the loss of key personnel?
- the proactive grooming of nominated successors to prepare them for future roles?
- the management of pools and flows of talent to provide future leadership and professional capability to respond to shifts in organisational structure?
- operating as a lever to help the organisation reinvent itself through a shift in the make-up of the workforce and management population and to create greater diversity?
- a strategic planning tool to inform future business manoeuvres and to inform the debate about the organisation's future?

Why? Is this a reflection of:

- the history and baggage of previous attempts to implement succession management?
- the business ambitions and outlook of the organisation?
- the priorities of the top team and their own personal operating priorities?
- the status and reputation of the human resources function?

Is the "succession solution" working? Is it achieving what it is intended to do?

- What are the positive outcomes?
- What problems is your succession solution failing to address?
- What are the negative consequences or side-effects of your succession solution?

What are the emerging battle-grounds of succession management? (See Figure 3.5.)

A QUICK-HIT ANALYSIS OF RESOURCING PROBLEMS	Where are the priorities for strategic resourcing?

Appointments
● spectacular high-profile failures in recent critical appointments
● increasing costs or falling revenues associated with:
  ○ reliance on expensive external resourcing
  ○ lost opportunity through excessive delays
● short-listing of low-calibre internal candidates
● high levels of turnover within critical roles
● difficulty in re-deploying people during reorganisations
 	
Managing Business Risks
● pending retirements but limited succession coverage
● succession exposure within critical roles is creating unease from external stake-holder groups
● reorganisation plans to configure roles and reporting relationships are constrained by an insufficient number of capable successors
● dissatisfaction with current role incumbents but limited choice of replacement candidates
● high dependence on few individuals to provide coverage across a broad range of critical roles
● high cost and difficulty and/or low retention in external resourcing
 	
Identifying and Developing Talent
● difficulties in filling vacancies at middle-senior levels from within
● the loss of highly regarded younger managers/professionals
● a strategic shift which requires a different managerial skill set and operating style to the current leadership
● a low level of management turnover at middle-senior levels which is blocking the progression of emerging talent
	Drivers
	Which actions will have a direct impact in moving forward?
	
	Blockers
	What factors will hold back progress and need to be overcome?
	
	Measures
	What performance measures need to be used to track activity and evaluate success?

Figure 3.5   Identifying priorities

* *The appointments process*: the need to put in place better processes to improve selection.
* *Assessing business risks*: concerns about succession exposure and the potential loss of key personnel.
* *Talent management*: a concern about the breadth and depth of professional and leadership talent within the pipeline.

How is the strategy–talent debate being played out in your organisation?

* A clear strategy in which the requirements for leadership and professional capability are well defined and articulated? How is this being reflected in your approach to succession? What are the risks of this approach?
* A vague strategy which involves "second guessing" about future organisational priorities and the consequences for resourcing and development?

- Imaginative in responding to the aspirations of talented executives and engaging them actively in the debate about the organisation's future?
- An ongoing iteration between the top team, the strategic planning function and human resources?

Notes

1. Leadership is a strategic weapon. "The term 'head-to-head' competition is literal. Global competition is not just product vs. product, company vs. company, or trading bloc vs. trading bloc. It is mind-set vs. mind-set, managerial frame vs. managerial frame." G. Hamel and C.K. Prahalad, *Harvard Business Review*, March 1993.
2. This is the dominant emphasis in *The War for Talent* (Ed Michaels, Helen Handfield-Jones and Beth Axelrod, 2001); the belief that talent should be given freedom and discretion to express itself.
3. Jim Collins's research in *Good to Great* suggests that good strategies come from good teams, not vice versa.
4. This now seems intuitively obvious, but until relatively recently was a neglected theme in classic strategic planning. "Management, after all, is people, and businesses are made successful by people, not by plans", Kenichi Ohmae, *The Mind of the Strategist*, McGraw-Hill, 1991. Tucked into a footnote in *Competitive Strategy* (2004), Michael Porter makes the observation that "the current strategy being followed by a business must reflect assumptions management is making about its industry. Understanding and addressing these assumptions can be crucial...a great deal of convincing data and support must be mustered to change these assumptions and this is where much if not most attention needs to be focused. The sheer logic of the strategic choice is not enough; it will not be convincing if it ignores management's assumptions." John Kay remarks that "when human nature conflicts with business strategy, human nature will usually win." *Financial Times*, 17 December 2003.
5. Enron was an obvious example of the risks of the "give talent freedom" approach. Appropriately, one book, detailing the Enron story, is titled *Smartest Guys in the Room*, B. McLean and P. Elkind, 2003.
6. "Many managements were apparently overexposed in impressionable childhood years to the story in which the imprisoned handsome prince is released from a toad's body by a kiss from a beautiful princess. Consequently, they are certain that their managerial kiss will do wonders for the profitability of company T(arget)...we've observed many kisses but very few miracles." Quoted in James O'Loughlin, *The Real Warren Buffett*, 2003.

4 *Rethinking Leadership Progression*

"If Martians descended to earth and demanded that we take them to our leaders, we would have to think twice about where to take them." James Bolt, *The Leader of the Future*, 1996

"No single set of competencies can be meaningfully applied across all leaders." Morgan McCall

There is a proliferation of leadership perspectives, largely dominated by the competency movement which, rather than helping, may be constraining efforts in succession management. Managing the succession pipeline at all levels within the organisation requires a clear insight into leadership success and failure and an understanding of the causes and consequences of leadership. An overarching model, the Four C framework, is mapped out to indicate how leadership frameworks need to broaden out to incorporate Credibility, Career management and Character as well as Capability, in order to provide a more insightful analysis of leadership and open up a mature debate about progression and succession.

If we are serious about succession as a driver of long-term organisational effectiveness we need to shift our criteria or certainly emphasise some aspects of leadership previously neglected.

THE FUTURE OF LEADERSHIP

At a conference on "The Future of Leadership", bringing together a combination of leading-edge researchers and pioneering practitioners, a breakout session is taking place. The moderator is a successful CEO.

CEO: "Could someone provide an overview of what we really do know about leadership; not speculation but, from the research, what have we discovered?"
Participant 1: "Well, we've found that it depends...it depends..."
CEO: "On what?"
Participant 2: "There are a number of variables, but to summarise a complex body of research it looks like effective leadership is a complex interaction of task, situation and individual."
Participant 3: "And don't forget 'followership'; that's important to the leadership equation."
CEO: "So where has this research taken us? What are the practical implications for running a business enterprise?"
Participant 2: "Mmmm."
CEO: "Can I check something; have any of you led anything other than a leadership research programme?"

Why the world doesn't need another book on leadership

One of our clients commented that she thought there were more books on leadership than there were genuine leaders in the world. I agreed with her. We have become very good at talking about leadership. We can run conferences on the subject. We are increasingly sophisticated in our research and conceptualisations of leadership. We can even produce a new book on leadership almost every day of the week. But where are the real leaders? There are now over 7000 books on leadership, thankfully not all still in print. At a conservative estimate there are over a quarter of a million articles on leadership. A search on the Amazon website yields 13 000 references. A scan of the listings highlights a confusing and contradictory set of themes. There is action-centred leadership, authentic leadership, brainSmart leadership, charismatic leadership, collaborative leadership, digital leadership, dynamic leadership, enabling leadership, ethical leadership, frontier leadership, global leadership, high-involvement leadership, high-velocity leadership, inclusive leadership, leadership for the millennium, managerial leadership, military-style leadership, political leadership, portable leadership, primal leadership, principled leadership, quiet leadership, results-based leadership, servant leadership, spiritual leadership, strategic leadership, total quality leadership, toxic leadership, transformational leadership, values-based leadership, visionary leadership. No doubt researchers are out there to ensure that we soon have the full A–Z of leadership models.

Leadership should have "soul"; leadership is an "art"; there are secrets of leadership. But it is also a challenge, a paradox and a quest. Leadership is like being on a "trapeze"; it is also largely common sense but there are no easy answers. For the numerate we have four obsessions, five essentials, eight revolutionary rules, nine keys, ten instincts, 20 secrets and 21 indispensable qualities. For the literary-minded, we can follow in the leadership footsteps of historical figures such as Attila the Hun and Moses, learn the leadership secrets of soldiers and politicians such as General Patton, Abraham Lincoln, Winston Churchill and Rudolph Giuliani. Winnie the Pooh also has leadership insights!

Faced with this alarming and bewildering array of leadership vocabulary, where do we start? The standard response going back over the last two decades continues to be the design of a leadership competency framework.

The incompetency of competency

Hailed in the 1980s as the "big idea" for Human Resources, the competency movement promised much.[1] Designing and implementing a competency programme would, it was claimed:

- ensure that employee time and effort was aligned around business goals
- integrate different streams of activity, from recruitment and induction to training and performance management and management development and succession planning
- provide a common language in which individuals could be evaluated to create greater consistency and objectivity in decision-making
- clarify leadership requirements to set an agenda for forward-looking succession management.

The underpinning assumption seemed to be that if we looked at what effective managers and leaders did, we could map out a set of competency dimensions. Knowing what these competencies are, we could then identify ways to improve how competency is acquired. If our managers and leaders learned these competencies they would be more effective. As with any big idea the consultancy sector saw its opportunity and, in the words of one critic, "a gravy train moved out of the station and picked up speed".[2] The typical assignment runs as follows:

- an opening pitch by Gravy Train Consulting to explain why your organisation needs its own distinctive competency framework
- desk-top research to review "best-in-class" firms and their leadership models
- in-depth organisational research requiring extensive interviews and focus groups utilising repertory grid, critical incidents and associated profiling methodology
- extensive consultation with different stake-holders
- production of a series of iterative draft versions
- final presentation to senior management
- publication of extensive support documentation.

The result of this exercise is the design of a competency framework, typically a listing of somewhere between 10 and 15 competency dimensions (see Figure 4.1).

The last 20 years have seen a remarkable amount of this kind of effort. Indeed there has probably been more collective effort at mapping out leadership competency in the past two decades than throughout the entirety of human history. Several critics[3] have questioned the fundamental assumptions on which this movement has been built. After the intensity of this activity the nagging question is: why do so many of these research programmes from varied sectors and industries with different strategies, structures and cultures end up with a listing of dimensions which pretty much look the same as each other?[4] Even more troublesome is that so many of these competency-profiling activities result in much documentation but break down when applied to real-life situations. Competency frameworks only have any purpose in so far as they refocus our recruitment and selection practices, direct the design of training activity, inform how we manage career progression and shape succession reviews. But so often they don't do this. Why is the end-point of many competency-profiling activities an unopened manual which sits on management shelves? And why do these exercises take so long to complete that by the time they have been conducted the business has moved on and the original research is out of date? And why, after this massive effort in competency assessment and development, *do we have a "leadership crisis"?*

The first point that needs to be made is that competencies do not exist! Or at least they do not exist in the sense that trees, chairs and teacups exist. Competencies are abstractions, conceptualisations to help us make sense of the complexity of professional, management and leadership life. There are thousands of management activities and behaviours. Competency frameworks are an attempt to group and organise these activities and behaviours into a manageable format.[5] The issue then becomes: is competency the best way to think about the realities of management and leadership? From a succession perspective, does a listing of competency dimensions illuminate the factors that underpin who emerges as a leader, who is effective as a leader, who despite initial success subsequently fails, and who sustains success over the long term? What does seem highly unlikely is that the

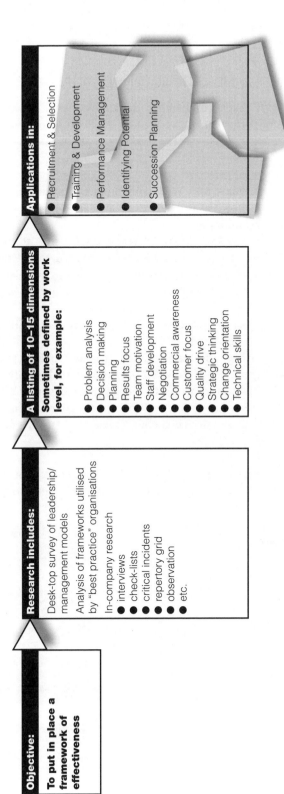

Objective:

To put in place a framework of effectiveness

Research includes:

Desk-top survey of leadership/management models

Analysis of frameworks utilised by "best practice" organisations

In-company research
● interviews
● check-lists
● critical incidents
● repertory grid
● observation
● etc.

A listing of 10–15 dimensions

Sometimes defined by work level, for example:

● Problem analysis
● Decision making
● Planning
● Results focus
● Team motivation
● Staff development
● Negotiation
● Commercial awareness
● Customer focus
● Quality drive
● Strategic thinking
● Change orientation
● Technical skills

Applications in:

● Recruitment & Selection
● Training & Development
● Performance Management
● Identifying Potential
● Succession Planning

Figure 4.1 Typical competency model

complexities and uncertainties of leadership can be boiled down into a listing of 10–15 competency dimensions.[6]

CONFUSING THE CAUSES AND CONSEQUENCES OF PERFORMANCE

The principal problem with many competency models is that they misunderstand the causes and consequences of performance (see Figure 4.2). Performance can be described as occurring at four levels:

- *Outcomes* are the outputs of effective performance, the end point and fundamental rationale for the existence of any role. Well-defined outcomes, tangible outputs of sales, service, productivity, efficiency and the like, make a clear connection between the role and the purpose of the organisation.
- *Tasks* are those activities which, when executed effectively, produce the desired outcomes. At this level the activities and functions required to deliver outcomes are defined to clarify where time and effort needs to be directed to maximise results.
- *Behaviours* are those patterns of talent and skill which, when deployed appropriately, ensure that time and effort is well directed around these tasks. Some behavioural styles are likely to be counter-productive; others will be more likely to optimise impact in those activities, which will drive overall results.
- *Attributes* are the underlying and fundamental personal qualities and traits that maximise behavioural impact. These represent the fundamental qualities and traits,[7] the personal assets an individual can draw on to maximise effectiveness and performance. They draw on those deep-seated cognitive and emotional patterns, dominant values and motivations which, translated into behaviour, drive task effectiveness and achieve outcomes.

These four levels provide the basis for mapping the "cause and effect" of performance (see Figure 4.3). Outcomes and Tasks clarify more about the "what" of performance; what is to

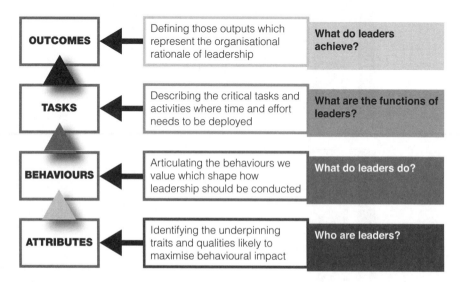

Figure 4.2   Levels of performance: cause and consequence

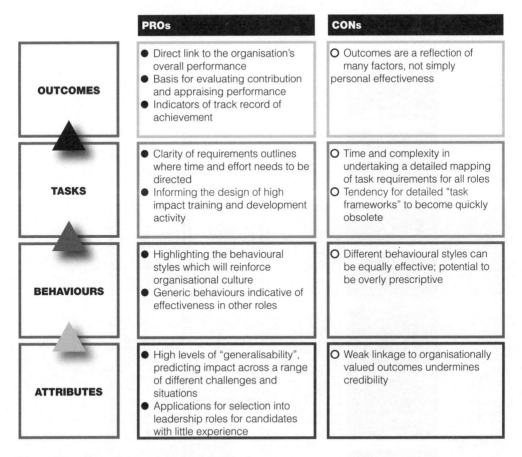

	PROs	CONs
OUTCOMES	● Direct link to the organisation's overall performance ● Basis for evaluating contribution and appraising performance ● Indicators of track record of achievement	○ Outcomes are a reflection of many factors, not simply personal effectiveness
TASKS	● Clarity of requirements outlines where time and effort needs to be directed ● Informing the design of high impact training and development activity	○ Time and complexity in undertaking a detailed mapping of task requirements for all roles ○ Tendency for detailed "task frameworks" to become quickly obsolete
BEHAVIOURS	● Highlighting the behavioural styles which will reinforce organisational culture ● Generic behaviours indicative of effectiveness in other roles	○ Different behavioural styles can be equally effective; potential to be overly prescriptive
ATTRIBUTES	● High levels of "generalisability", predicting impact across a range of different challenges and situations ● Applications for selection into leadership roles for candidates with little experience	○ Weak linkage to organisationally valued outcomes undermines credibility

Figure 4.3   Pros and cons of performance levels

be achieved. Behaviours and Attributes identify more of the "how" of performance. Condensing outcomes, tasks, behaviours and attributes into a competency listing of 10–15 dimensions jumbles causes and consequences, making it difficult to distinguish those individuals who are currently effective from those who might be effective in the future.

Figure 4.4 outlines an adapted example from one of our clients who had previously utilised the standard competency framework but found it was constraining efforts to integrate human resource activity across different organisational applications. Attributes are an expression of those qualities that set the agenda for recruitment and selection. These apply to employees at every level and are fundamental assessment criteria. Behaviours are the themes the organisation wanted to establish as its way of doing things, and again are applicable to all, and are reinforced in the performance management process as well as in training and development activity. Tasks are specific to different roles at different levels and, for key roles, summarise the functions and activities where time and effort need to be directed. Outcomes are overall groupings but translated into specific targets for each individual.

This format allows business managers to "work from top down" in managing performance. What do we need to do to achieve the outcomes we value?

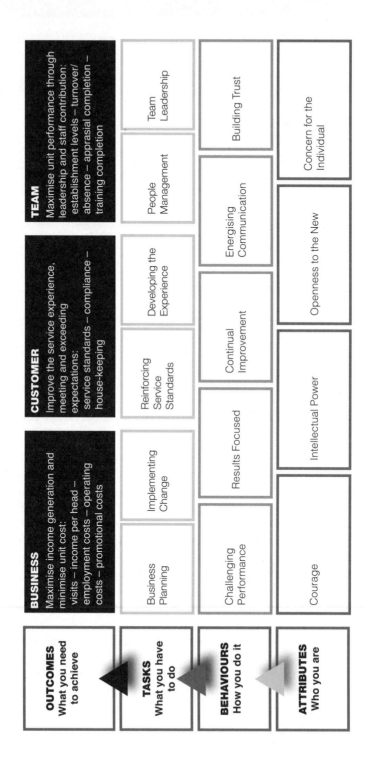

Figure 4.4 Example framework

- Direct effort more productively? (Where?)
- Deploy key behaviours more consistently? (Which?)
- Recruit the right attributes in the first place? (What?)

And for the Human Resources function this approach helps them "work upwards" to connect their initiatives explicitly to business outcomes. Why are we focused on improving our selection and induction systems? Because it will:

- make it easier to train our employees in the behaviours we value as a business
- focus organisational effort on the tasks critical to us as an organisation
- maximise the results we need to achieve.

EXCELLENT MANAGERS DO NOT THINK COMPETENCY

In 1999, Marcus Buckingham and Curt Coffman of Gallup[8] broke competency ranks to provide the most insightful critique of conventional competency profiling. Their view, "competencies if you do use them be careful. Competencies are part skills, part knowledge and part talent. They lump together some characteristics that can be taught with others that cannot. Consequently competencies can wind up confusing everybody…If you are going to use competencies make it clear which are skills and knowledge and, therefore, can be taught; and which are talents and therefore cannot."

This wasn't just sniping from the theoretical sidelines. From their analysis of high-performing individuals, identified from their database of 80 000 managers, they noted that those managers associated with superior performance had a view of the world that was very much at odds with conventional competency mind-set. Rather than attempt to describe "the how" of the role, excellent managers focus on the end-point: the outcomes that need to be achieved. They then allow individual employees to direct their talents (or attributes) to achieve these defined goals. Neither do excellent managers look for across-the-board threshold competency. Instead they focus on identifying the specific strengths that individuals display and look for ways of deploying and developing these strengths further.

Excellent managers do not work through a competency check-list with the expectation that team members will show competency across all themes. They make clear their expectations of what needs to be achieved. They then allow individuals to deploy their talents to maximise their contribution, and also commit high-quality time to nurture and coach these talents. They don't spend time on what the individual isn't so good at; they focus on those underlying attributes and traits that represent strengths.

PRACTICAL PROBLEMS OF COMPETENCY

Wrapping up attributes, behaviours, tasks and outcomes into a package of competency dimensions might seem an economical way of summarising leadership and management requirements, but by bundling cause and consequence there is a risk of confusing who is currently effective (displaying the achievement of outcomes) from who might be effective in the future (evidence of those attributes predictive of outcomes). In addition, they lack the precision needed for real-life applications. Competency profiling and the publication of competency manuals may be the end-point for consultancies. In themselves, however, nothing changes. Competency frameworks are only useful in so far as they focus and direct activity around specific applications. Does your framework, for example,

- pinpoint the attributes and experiences to shift your recruitment blueprint from bland generalisations to zero in on the specific criteria that will differentiate between applicants?
- provide sufficient detail to design practical induction and training events?
- identify the specific factors of experience, capability and motivation, which will facilitate a discussion about who will advance and who won't, and why?
- establish a robust framework to differentiate different levels of contribution to provide an equitable basis for reviewing and recognising performance?
- map out a detailed brief to guide a coach about the focus of a coaching assignment for one of your senior executives?

If the answer to any of these questions is no, that more work is required, then the chances are that Gravy Train Consulting has developed a generic model, which looks plausible but is so bland it is also relevant to any other organisation. Gravy Train Consulting is exploiting the fact that there are generic practices and processes applicable to most professionals and managers most of the time. But if it is no more than a mapping of the basic building-blocks of effectiveness, relevant to any organisation, then why conduct the research in the first place? And importantly, many generic competency models fail to map out the specific technical and professional expertise that is critical to the organisation's future.

Competency profiling also neglects leadership realities, failing to address the specific reasons for leadership failure. Is incompetency the absence of competency? We don't need psychoanalytical training to observe that the underlying causes of many flawed and incompetent managers and leaders are more complex than that described by a set of 10–15 dimensions. Competency frameworks don't quite seem to hit the mark in accounting for what has been called the *"sad, mad and bad"*.[9] The *"sad"* are those sorry individuals who, overwhelmed by organisational events, find solace in drink, drugs or inappropriate relationships and spiral into depression. The *"bad"* are the lying, bullying, jealous and venal individuals who exploit others for their own selfish ends. The *"mad"* are those individuals who become disconnected from the realities around them and operate in a world of their own dreams, fantasies and self-delusion or, even worse, descend into "functional psychoticism".

If the objective of classic competency frameworks was to provide a diagnostic tool to explain why some managers are more or less effective than others and to predict who will be more successful in future, they have failed. At what point does the typical competency model identify the arrogance, laziness, cowardice, spitefulness, humourlessness and other ugly traits that underpin incompetency? There is an irony that employees in their description of flawed and incompetent leadership readily access the vocabulary of character, a frank and direct language that tends to be absent in most leadership competency frameworks. For example, was the negative evaluation of a senior executive's competency in planning an indication of a lack of project management expertise? No, reviewing the open-ended comments in his 360° feedback, he was, to put it bluntly, selfish, dumping work on colleagues at 5.30 pm with the expectation of a turnaround for 9.00 am the next morning. The issue here wasn't his competency in planning; it was one of a fundamental pattern of self-centredness. This diagnosis sets up a very different type of development and coaching assignment.

The language of competency was invented to provide a consistent and objective vocabulary to talk about leadership. But a set of words seems to have been created that constrain from us talking frankly and directly about the causes of leadership success and failure.[10] Despite these criticisms we are not advocating the wholesale abandonment of competency frameworks. But we are suggesting that the way in which they are designed and implemented needs considerable rethinking. Specifically in the context of succession management and the identification of future leadership, we need to be much more insightful about the causes, consequences and complexities of leadership success and failure.

Alternatives to competency (charisma and EQ)

CHARISMATIC LEADERSHIP

Competency on its own hasn't "worked". Despite at least two decades of intense investment in competency we have a leadership and succession problem. Henry Wendt, former CEO of SmithKline Beecham, remarked "We're in the most severe shortage of CEO talent in corporate history. Most of the people I see are not leaders; they are managers who know how to work the system and have worked it well."

If we have a leadership crisis it isn't because we lack competency models or haven't invested effort in assessing and developing competency. Perhaps we've been missing that essential ingredient which represents the essential of leadership: charisma. Competency has the connotation of mediocrity, ordinariness, of being good enough but not exceptional. Charisma could be the pizzazz to make the leadership difference. Faced with intense business challenge and complexity, we need leaders who are more than competent. We need leaders with charisma, leaders who can inspire others to make them believe in a mission and to engage them in a purpose.

For Jim Clark, the Silicon Valley entrepreneur, "charisma is almost the definition of leadership". Charisma is viewed as that bundle of qualities incorporating:

- aura and personal magnetism to command attention
- an up-front communication style which distils complex ideas into simple messages
- an empathic charm; the ability to step into others' shoes and engage others easily
- an enjoyment of risk, to do the things that haven't been done before
- a willingness to "think outside of the box" in challenging conventional wisdom, to rebel and to defy the status quo.

These traits and qualities may be valuable assets. However, after a period of initial enthusiasm and an excitement about a shift in the leadership agenda, a certain nervousness is emerging. Charismatic leadership, like an exciting night out, is fun at the time but is leaving organisations with a dreadful hangover. Charismatic leadership has its risks.

"Sizzle or steak"

Interpersonal engagement and compelling communication are persuasive and influential. They help leaders get things done. We all want to feel special, to be valued and feel involved in a larger enterprise, and charismatic leaders excel in this area. But after the firm handshake, the gesture of encouragement, the barnstorming conference speech, what is there of substance? Leadership must be more than interpersonal appeal and the feel-good factor of the moment. It must make a long-lasting positive difference. The problem is that charismatic leaders seem better at arousing energy and motivation to exhort everyone to work harder rather than address the systemic issues that are constraining work effectiveness in the first place.

Personal heroics

Ted Turner, the media mogul, commented that "a full moon blocks all the stars around it". Charismatic leaders seem to come with a psychological baggage of self-aggrandisement and a need for personal acclaim, more likely to create a business enterprise around themselves and their own ambitions than build an organisation with the resilience to outlast their personal legacy. Lee Iacocca, the "saviour" of Chrysler and one of the first of the celebrity CEOs, observed, "Running Chrysler has been a bigger job than running the country. I could handle the national economy in six months." After Chrysler's initial turnaround, stock fell 31 per cent behind the general market during the second half of Iacocca's tenure. The German automotive giant, Daimler, subsequently acquired Chrysler. Al Dunlap, aka "Chainsaw Al" and "Rambo in Pinstripes", another celebrity CEO of the mid-1990s, commented, "Corporate America, what a bunch of boring guys...I have zero problems with being called an egomaniac." Recruited to Sunbeam on the back of rescuing Scott Paper (on his arrival in 1996, shares rose by 50 per cent) he was then fired. It transpired that Dunlap had been dismissed earlier in his career due to his involvement in an accounting fraud that had culminated in one firm's bankruptcy. Peter Drucker has observed that, "90% of the trouble we're having with the CEO's job is rooted in our superstition of the one-man chief."[11] Charismatic leaders reinforce this superstition.

Why do we need charismatic leadership? Charismatic leadership appeals to organisational weakness. When vulnerable the organisation looks to the charismatic leader who can transform its fortunes. The organisation is in denial; it isn't confronting the "brutal facts". It wants a positive view of the future and an individual with a big-hitting track record who can help it believe it can achieve that future. The problem is that the organisation often gets those individuals who, after the first burst of enthusiasm, go on to weaken the organisation further.

WHY DO WE NEED LEADERSHIP?

Arguably an imaginative organisational design, progressive personnel policies and practices and self-managed teamwork dispense with the need for leadership. So why do we still need leadership (see Figure 4.5)? Firstly, *uncertainty and challenge* are ongoing facts of competitive life. Leadership is needed to make sense of uncertainty and decide the best way to respond to challenge. For the foreseeable future, hierarchy, in one sort or another, will continue to be the dominant organisational pattern, and leadership is needed to manage that hierarchy of authority and accountability. In the face of ambiguity, decisions need to be made about what to do.

Secondly, *trust*, that critical but fragile dynamic of organisational life, will always need leadership. Organisations are social groupings, a collection of individuals who need to work together to get things done. Working together requires more than procedures and rule-books. It involves honesty, respect and care; it requires trust. Leadership is needed to maintain the "trust momentum".[12]

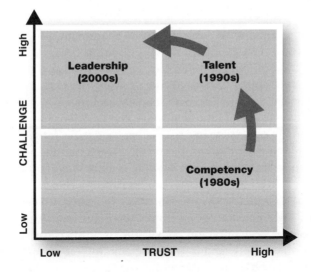

Figure 4.5   The leadership rationale: challenge and trust

This is leadership at its most fundamental: the response to *challenge and uncertainty* and the building of *trust* to engage others in that response. Anything else is either tyranny or straightforward management, coordinating others' activity to do what we've always done. Or put another way, "the leader will determine the corporate dream, and will define the corporate character".[13]

Using this framework we can chart the leadership story of the last two or three decades. Back in the economic good times of the 1980s, for many organisations the issues were simple and straightforward. After the turmoil of the 1970s and the political changes that ensued, for many organisations the business rules were well defined and employee mood was positive. In these relatively good times it is perhaps not surprising that the "competency movement" took off. Competency was enough. As we moved into the 1990s, the business landscape shifted and familiar landmarks began to disappear. Competition intensified and, as the high-tech revolution unfolded, organisations were faced with greater uncertainty. The rules were changing and many organisations didn't know how to respond. For many, "Wait and See" was the dominant strategic stance. For others who were more bold and pioneering it was the opportunity to "Bet Big". Challenge was greater and competency didn't seem to be enough to respond to these business complexities. Rather, what was demanded was exceptional talent: outstanding skills to tackle the tough issues. Employee trust at this point was still relatively high, but showing signs of wobbling. Performance ruthlessness was becoming a dominant feature of organisational life. It was not enough to meet your objectives if 90 per cent of your peers had met their targets. You were in danger of falling into the dangerous territory of the bottom 10 per cent and about to undergo the "rank and yank" experience. Employee trust began to plummet. The outstandingly talented individuals who had been recruited into senior executive positions began to look exposed. They simply were not up to task of establishing a leadership agenda which employees could believe or engage in.

In the early days of the twenty-first century we are at a time of high challenge and low trust, when neither leadership competency nor talent seem enough. We are at that point when competency and talent need not charisma but something more substantial.

LEADERSHIP AS EMOTIONAL INTELLIGENCE (EQ)

If the longer-term organisational consequences of charismatic leadership were beginning to make people nervous, then another leadership solution emerged in the 1990s: emotional intelligence.[14] The EQ movement seemed to position itself as a reaction to the apparent failure of intellectual ability as a predictor of work success.[15] Here the view was that leadership assessment and development had focused largely on intellectual skills and neglected a key theme: the ability to manage the emotional stuff. Specifically, effective leadership requires the capacity to understand yourself, to be in touch with your feelings, to understand others and their feelings, to connect, reach out and relate to others. The key message seemed to be that relationship building is more important than technical skills.

Reviewing this field a couple of years ago, as part of a client assignment, turned out to be a breath-taking experience for me. The sheer intensity of views from advocates and opponents of EQ highlighted a certain irony. Advocates were evangelical in their claims, displaying a passionate certainty and conviction that this perspective on leadership was exploring unknown territory and a turning-point in leadership research and practice. Opponents were equally fervent. Critics dismissed EQ as:

- lacking a clear and precise definition ("the sum total of all positive qualities that could be imagined")
- essentially a repackaging of established personality theory and research (marketing old wine in new bottles)
- making extravagant and unsupported claims (the contention that EQ is twice as important as IQ plus technical skills for outstanding performance seemed to trigger particular anger from opponents).

At times the criticism verged on the hysterical but nonetheless carried a certain weight as serious academics were drawn into the debate.[16] What most balanced and sensible observers can agree on is that the EQ movement might not be saying anything intrinsically new, but it is saying old things in a fresh and interesting way. It highlights an important leadership theme, a theme that had probably not received sufficient attention. To caricature, if IQ simplifies that component which helps leaders make sense of the complexity and uncertainty facing an organisation, then EQ is attempting to map out the self-management skills and interpersonal impact that builds trust and engages the workforce.

Making sense of leadership: the four Cs

Is there a way of making sense of the range of varied frameworks and models? Our approach has been to work backwards from the questions which the top team, directly or indirectly, ask of their organisation's emerging leadership. Boards do not systematically work through the formal competency documentation which Gravy Train Consulting has compiled. Neither are they engaging fully with the "touchy feely" language of EQ. Our view is a pragmatic one but one that is striking a chord and engaging senior executives more actively in the discussion of leadership talent, progression and succession. Figure 4.6 summarises a Board's perspective of leadership. Our framework asks four questions:

	Credibility	Capability	Career Management	Character
Leadership Criteria	Background, credentials and connections to establish leadership legitimacy and authority	Mastery of the functions and tasks of leadership and the skills to respond to new challenges	The management of the "rules of the game" to advance a leadership agenda in overcoming political dynamics	The ethics and principles to provide leadership meaning and stewardship and fulfil the full range of the obligations of the leadership role
Resourcing Emphasis	Greater use of external recruitment and head-hunters to buy in prestigious leaders from outside A focus on established credentials and an employment history with blue chip firms	An encouragement of promotion from within through a recognition of personal competency Objectivity and consistency in career progression Moderate use of external recruitment to "buy in" specific expertise	Appointments made on the basis of corporate loyalty and support Highly politicised resourcing decisions as a trade-off to preserve the political dynamic	Prolonged and demanding selection and induction processes to evaluate the fundamental leadership qualities Looking to promote from within based on a shared understanding of values
Attitude to Development	Relatively minor emphasis placed on internally driven development initiatives Moderate use of business education with "big badge" names Encouragement of networking and making connections with players across the industry and political arena	Greater investment and a higher usage of internal skills development Fostering personal growth and development	Overall moderate application Extensive use of networking and mentoring and relationship building The importance of formal and public events to lobby support and build commitment	Substantial use of real life experience and the assignment of tough challenges to drive development Top management involvement in coaching emerging leaders in business strategy and organisational values
Risks	A danger of drawing from a narrow pool of talent of like-minded individuals with similar backgrounds Assuming leadership effectiveness through association with high-performing firms and allowing those who "look and sound the part" to take on leadership responsibility	Developing a leadership population which is naïve and fails to grapple with the complexities of organisational reality An arrogant belief in own problem solving talent which may be dismissive of other organisational talent	The advancement of self seeking games players into leadership positions Organisational politics and deal making drives out genuine talent	Creating a narrow definition of leadership talent which encourages dogmatism rather than diversity

Figure 4.6   Leadership: a Board perspective

- Is this individual *credible*?
- Is this individual *capable*?
- Is this individual proactive in *career management*?
- Does this individual display *character*?

CREDIBILITY

The first question senior executives might ask is: is this individual credible and believable? If their name is mentioned, does it pass the first test of leadership, the "laughter test"? Has this individual, for example, worked for successful blue-chip organisations at senior levels and demonstrated a consistent track record? Do they have a breadth of business experience to reassure others of their right to operate as a leader? Do they project that kind of self-belief and social confidence which others will respect?

Credibility is the first hurdle of leadership. Credibility provides authority, legitimacy and a reassurance that the individual can operate effectively within leadership roles. Skills and competency, no matter how exceptional, will not be enough. Without credibility an individual will find it next to impossible to succeed in a leadership position. At best credibility is shaped by a consistent track record of achievement, through relevant experience, and through the regard and respect of peers. Here, credibility is the meritocratic outcome of effectiveness. But credibility is also fickle and can be deceptive. Credibility is driven by many factors, some of which have little to do with real leadership talent. A career resumé, the listing of impressive job titles within big name companies, looks good but may be more a reflection of good luck and smart career management than of any personal talent on the individual's part. Self-belief, social confidence and positive communication at cocktail parties may be nothing more than that — social impact over cocktails — and say little about leadership effectiveness in the real world. The big problem is that credibility hinges on stereotypes and prejudice, on judgements based on factors that have relatively little to do with effectiveness (physical appearance, accent, dress sense) but affect our overall assessment of the individual. Human nature is such that we do judge a book by its cover (or our expectation of what the cover should look like) rather than taking the time to read the book.

In our experience Boards are particularly swayed by credibility in their evaluation of leadership. They want to know who has this person worked for, what positions they have held, and who they know. But too much emphasis on credibility immediately constrains the choice of suitable leadership candidates. Reputation can go a long way in establishing leadership status. However, a robust evaluation of future leadership effectiveness requires more than credibility. The intrinsic problem with credibility is that it is essentially a superficial analysis of leadership. It answers the question: does this individual look and sound the part to meet our current expectations? But effectiveness is less about past reputation and more about the qualities, skills and expertise to tackle the challenges of the future.

CAPABILITY

The capability component of leadership represents the range of skills and talents that enable individuals to take on the problems and challenges facing the organisation. This is the area in which the competency movement has directed most attention. If we can define the specific capabilities, talents and competencies, key to the organisation's competitive future, we will have constructed a leadership road-map to guide who we recruit, how we focus our training and development efforts, and how we manage the succession process. In a completely fair and rational business world, well-designed capability frameworks would provide the definitive blueprint for leadership succession. But few, if any, organisations are complete meritocracies, and no business operates in a just world.

In the late 1980s,[17] an intriguing study was devised to address the question: does effectiveness equal success? In the world of competency, competent managers would be effective, their effectiveness would be recognised, and as such they would be more successful than their less effective peers. But is this the case?

Four hundred and fifty-seven mainstream managers were evaluated against two measures. Management *effectiveness* was determined by business unit performance and by employee satisfaction and commitment. In summary, effective managers were making a better business contribution and levels of employee motivation and loyalty were higher. *Success* was measured by an index of speed of progression. Who for their age had "out-performed" their peer group to attain a higher organisational salary and level? The result of this research? Of the 60 most *successful* managers, only 15 were highly *effective*. Effectiveness, therefore, does not equate to success and successful managers may not be the most effective managers. Competency is not the only factor in determining progression; we need to broaden our perspective on leadership.

CAREER MANAGEMENT

Leadership operates in the real world, in the organisational "shadow side", a world in which organisations do not operate with perfect rationality. The most talented candidates do not necessarily get the job and the "cream does not always rise to the top". At its most basic, leadership success is not win-win for everyone. It is a competitive game in which one person's advancement threatens the position of their peers, and the progress of peers constrains the individual's options. Talented individuals who do not understand the realities of corporate life or how to advance their own personal agenda will find it difficult to compete with peers also keen to achieve their goals. To progress to a leadership role it is not enough to be competent; an individual must compete more successfully than his or her peers. This is career management, the third strand of leadership effectiveness.

Career management isn't simply highlighting that aspect of leadership which recognises and skilfully plays the political game. Career management is also the shrewd deployment of self-management skills, of directing time and energy around the "art of the possible", of balancing competing life and work priorities to advance personal aspirations. If capability maps out the functions, tasks and skills needed by the organisation, this theme outlines the personal ambitions and the career tactics and manoeuvres which are required for the individual to advance and compete in the leadership arena.

Top management, in their review of succession coverage, are not naïve. They do not simply look at credibility or capability. They also look at the individual's understanding of the rules of the game, ability to manoeuvre effectively through the political system and self-management skills to cope with a gruelling work schedule.

"IS TALENT ENOUGH?: A SURVEY OF CAREER TACTICS"[18]

In 2002 we undertook an exercise to examine the impact of career tactics in determining speed of progression (see Figure 4.7). Using a self-assessment questionnaire we analysed which of 90 tactical themes were most likely to be deployed by those individuals who, for their age, had achieved a higher salary and organisational level than their age peers. The first and most significant finding was that the individuals who were more "successful" were more likely to report the greater deployment of career tactics. Specifically the successful individuals were more likely to:

- play to their personal strengths to concentrate on priorities and direct effort around making the maximum contribution rather than taking on everything the organisation might throw at them
- use controlled delegation to ensure they kept on top of work activity, deploying the efforts of others well but still ensuring they received the credit for their achievements
- work out who they should and shouldn't work with and gravitate towards successful projects and activities rather than accept the impossible and thankless assignments
- project confidence to build quick credibility at high-profile organisational moments
- utilise feedback to gain a better insight into others' perceptions of their personal impact.

Importantly, the use of career tactics was correlated with work satisfaction. The stereotype of the highly career-focused but unhappy individual was not confirmed. Rather the opposite: individuals deploying more use of tactics were more satisfied in their careers.

CHARACTER

The fourth component required for leadership is character. Character is about the fundamental inner qualities, principles and ethics which shape a full understanding of the role of leadership and what is required to operate effectively. Historically, character has been the dominant theme of leadership but somewhere along the way we forgot its importance. Given recent corporate scandals and the failings of a number of business leaders we are now paying the price. At first sight character seems an old-fashioned concept, a return to an era that we thought we'd grown out of in a period of scientific management. But it is now showing signs of a re-emergence.

Jim Collins highlighted the leadership requirements associated with the good to great transition ("There are really three dimensions of what the right person must have: competence, chemistry and character."). Martin Seligman, the respected academic psychologist, observed, "the time has come to resurrect character as a central concept to the scientific study of human behaviour."[19] And Norman Schwarzkopf, the US general who oversaw the 1991 Gulf War, stated "95 per cent of all leadership failures in the last century have been failures of character". Daniel Goleman, proponent of EQ, acknowledges that the vocabulary of emotional intelligence is an attempt to grapple with the theme of character: "there is an old fashioned word for the skills that Emotional Intelligence represents —

Building a Reputation	Managing Complex Relationships	Optimising Personal Energy	Recognising Organisational Realities	Strategic Self Management	Maximising Learning Potential
Projecting Confidence	Managing Upwards	Establishing Life Disciplines	Working within Corporate Politics	Playing to Strengths	Curiosity to Discover More
Creating a Distinctive Image	Building Broad Based Commitment	Focus on Priorities	Mastering the Art of Timing	Flexible Goal Setting	Responding to Feedback
Gravitating towards Success	Forging Alliances	Controlled Delegation	Sensitivity to Key Players	Managing Ego Emotions	Using New Challenges to Speed Development

Figure 4.7   Career tactics framework

character."[20] There is nothing new here. Peter Drucker, 50 years ago, said, "It is character through which leadership is exercised, it is character that sets the example... It is not something one can fool people about." He was right: character is the fundamental component of leadership. He was also wrong. In recent times we have allowed ourselves to be fooled by leaders without character.

So what is meant by character? The Board and senior executives freely use the "character" word in their debate about succession candidates and emerging talent. What are they attempting to describe? In our research to explore the concept of character, we found three recurring themes. Firstly, character is about *integrity*: moral and ethical purpose. It is a leadership outlook based on the fundamental principles of honesty, truth and honour. Leadership without this element is leadership without a moral compass. Secondly, character comprises *resilience*: the robust toughness that keeps going in the face of adversity to recover from disappointments and setbacks. It is the mental and emotional strength to persist and persevere in order to overcome challenges and the flexibility to adapt and shift to changing circumstances. The third component is *distinctiveness*, about standing out as different, as unique and special. It is difficult to think of character as boring or dull. Character seems to have a certain "stamp", a way of marking individuals out and differentiating them from others. Figure 4.8 maps out a framework we have utilised in our leadership assessment and development assignments.[21]

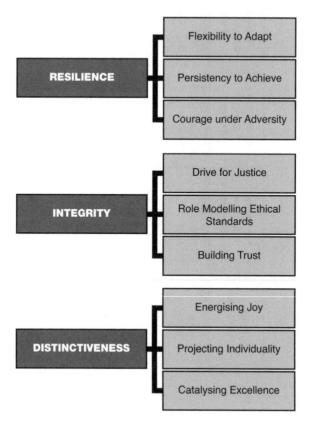

Figure 4.8   Leadership character profile

Character hinges on the interaction of these three themes. Integrity on its own will be well intentioned and honourable in its commitment to the long term. It establishes a long-term purpose around authentic principles and ethics, but in itself it won't stand out and stay the distance. Resilience has a certain relentless purpose but without integrity and distinctiveness simply becomes ruthless determination without a fundamental purpose or creative flair. And distinctiveness might stand out as different but it needs integrity and resilience to sustain its promise and build something lasting for the long term. *Leadership character is the point at which these three themes come together in balance.*

THE FIRST ONE HUNDRED DAYS OF A NEW CEO

High-*credibility* leaders want to establish themselves and assert their legitimacy quickly. They look to make an authoritative impact to signal that they mean business and are now in charge. The first hundred days is about high-profile presentations, extensive meetings across the organisation, and establishing contact with as many different people as possible. Decisions are taken rapidly to assert control, and announcements are made to raise their profile. To reinforce credibility these CEOs remove those senior executives with the potential to undermine their authority. Any challenge and disagreement that might threaten their position will be highlighted and dismissed.

High-*capability* leaders want to understand the real challenges facing the organisation, to go beneath the superficial issues to identify the fundamental problems. They spend the first hundred days out and about throughout the business, taking time to understand the detail of the operation, asking questions to identify the specifics and reviewing management information to determine what is really going on. These leaders identify those senior executives who are part of the problem and those who will become part of the solution, and refocus the management team around their view of the priorities.

High-*career management* leaders immediately eliminate the second layer of management, replacing half of those they have fired with managers from the third level. The other half, former colleagues, are recruited from outside. The aim here is to ensure high levels of commitment to them personally from the management ranks and to consolidate their leadership position. This provides the backdrop of support to ensure their initiatives can be implemented.

High-*character* leaders spend the early days getting to know each of their direct reports and their team members. They want to establish: what kind of management team is in place? Is this a group of individuals with the ethical principles, integrity and business purpose that we can move forward with? High-character leaders spend considerable time at the front line, listening to the views of employees and taking time to understand the culture of the business. They keep a low profile, listening rather than talking, thinking rather than launching initiatives.

This of course is a caricature. All leaders are a mix of all four themes and most leaders will adapt their approach and set a different agenda in response to different situations. But each leader has a dominant motivation and an operating approach that will surface to shape their organisational priorities.

The four themes — credibility, capability, career management and character — provide the fundamental building-blocks of leadership. However, they are not stand-alone components. There is an inter-play between them. Credibility on its own is largely leadership reputation: the superficialities of looking and sounding the part. Credibility with career management describes that leader who has been in the right place at the right time and knows how to play the game to advance his or her own interests. Arguably, it is this breed of leaders that has dominated the succession agenda over recent years.

High levels of capability can drive credibility, but a superficial factor of credibility (for example, dress sense) can also weaken perceptions of capability. Career management through polished interpersonal skills and positive impression management can be "disguised" to look like capability, or it can maximise the impact of capability through shrewd self-management and political influence.

Character without credibility is irrelevant, but credibility without character is dangerous. Capability and character identify that leader who takes on the complex challenges facing the organisation, refusing to take the short-term easy way out but committed to building something worthwhile which will stand the test of time. This may describe the leaders highlighted by Collins in his analysis of good to great leadership. Warren Buffett endorses these individuals: "when you have able managers of high character running businesses about which they are passionate, you can have a dozen or more reporting to you and still have time for an afternoon nap."[22] However, without credibility and career management, there is a danger that these individuals will be under-rated and over-looked by their organisations. While their more ruthless and self-seeking colleagues "play the game", these leaders are more concerned to do what is right for the organisation rather than advance their own personal agenda. Here they are outmanoeuvred by peers more skilful at impression management and political influence.

Perhaps for organisations the riskiest leadership choice is high credibility, high capability, high career management and low character. These individuals look and sound the part. Their reputation and past accomplishments combined with their interpersonal charm build status and respect within their peer group. Their exceptional talents provide them with the opportunity to take on greater and greater responsibility. Their skills and charm conceal the absence of character. And it is the absence of character, which provides them with the freedom of manoeuvre to achieve results quickly in the short term, which their more principled peers would find difficult. It is this type of leadership which mostly in the long run wreaks the greatest havoc on organisations.

LEADERSHIP REALITIES

In exploring this area we conducted a survey programme[23] to identify how people saw the current realities of leadership. Drawing on our experiences of organisational life and the leaders they have worked with and observed in action, we asked which themes are more or less important in determining who gets on and who doesn't? Who progresses, and who makes most and least impact? The focus of the survey wasn't *who should* make it as leaders, but *who in reality does?* What are the key drivers: credibility, capability, career management or character? We then asked the survey sample: what for you as an individual are the key priorities; which leadership themes are more or less prominent in your own leadership approach and outlook? A forced choice response format was utilised to indicate relative priorities. We analysed the results across the four themes. Figure 4.9 summarises the results of survey perceptions of *leadership realities*. Figure 4.10 highlights the findings from respondents' evaluation of their own *personal leadership priorities*.

If the competency movement has achieved its aims then capability should have won by a mile. It didn't. Career management emerged as the most relevant component in driving leadership progression and success. The survey respondents saw the combination of skilful self-management and political influence as the most determinant of leadership progression. Capability did emerge as a relevant theme but it was less important. And character and credibility were seen as much less relevant in determining leadership realities. Leadership was seen as

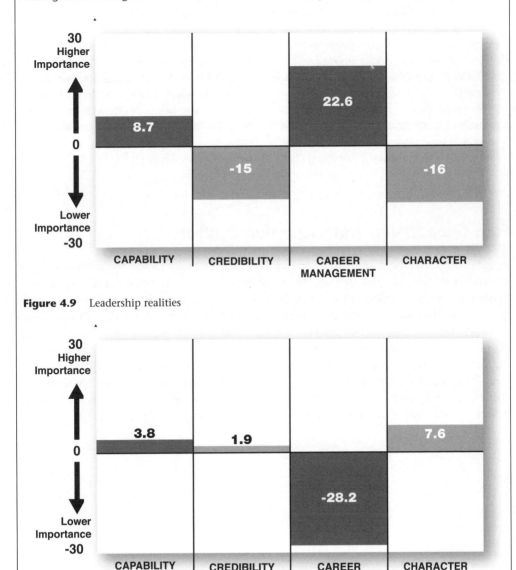

Figure 4.9   Leadership realities

Figure 4.10   Personal leadership priorities

less about consistency of track record and experience or about long-term purpose around authentic values and more about those reasonably talented individuals who know how to get on and advance their own interests. Is this respondent cynicism or a realistic evaluation of the realities of succession they have encountered?

What about the survey respondents' own leadership outlook and approach? The contrast is remarkable. The message seemed to be: "organisations are advancing those career-minded individuals who know how to play the game. But I don't. I'm more focused on doing the right thing through my talents and competency."

No doubt there is a self-serving bias in this survey, a tendency to emphasise some aspects of leadership in our peers and play down others in ourselves. Nonetheless the analysis indicates yet another dilemma in succession management. Most of us, most of the time would rather be part of an enterprise engaged in building something positive for the future, to be part of a meritocracy in which leadership is governed by capability and character. But we operate in the real world in which we compete with others, some of whom are less concerned with the substance of long-term and meaningful success and more preoccupied with personal advancement through impression management and political gamesmanship. It is in this world that potential leaders have to operate; talented individuals wanting to do the "right thing" are in head-to-head conflict with those who have mastered the rules of the game and know how to play the system to their own personal advantage.

Four C leadership and succession conflicts

At executive levels there needs to be a vigorous and mature discussion about the realities of leadership within the organisation. Here the debate about succession, the disputes and disagreements surrounding which individuals are ready to advance and progress and make a bigger contribution, is essentially a battle of competing theories. Succession decisions, like all other decisions, are a trade off between the ideal and the realism of different options. Figure 4.11 provides a summary of a number of "succession conflicts", conflicts arising out of the Board's own outlook and response to different types of emerging leadership. Some of these conflicts are potentially disastrous for the long-term health of the organisation. Others, like any conflict, possess a tension which can be worked through in an informed debate to focus not on leadership rhetoric but on leadership succession realities.

	BOARD'S LEADERSHIP OUTLOOK			
EMERGING LEADERSHIP	**Credibility**	**Capability**	**Character**	**Career Management**
Credibility	succession as the straightforward selection of those individuals with the reputation, track record and experience reflecting the Board's own background	the Board is less impressed by track record and reputation and questions their relevance in facing the future challenges of the organisation	a Board which is more concerned about the long-term future puts less faith on established reputations from the past	a Board is divided in its views, with some members impressed by track record and others feeling threatened by the emergence of those with a big-hitting reputation
Capability	in this scenario the established leadership utilises its authority and status to resist the innovative challenge which emerging talent may provide	succession as the meritocratic process in which the organisation renews its leadership through the progression of talented and gifted individuals	a commitment to build greatness to sustain for the long run which looks to nurture and educate emerging talent	here the Board feels challenged by the emergence of highly talented individuals and seeks to protect its own position by resisting their progression
Character	here the Board may be defensive in protecting its record against a new generation of leadership keen to take a more principled and ethical stance	here a talented Board keen to see quick results resists the agenda of those emerging leaders who want to take a longer-term view of the business	nurturing a generation of leadership around shared values and ethical purpose to maintain an organisational legacy	a politicised succession process discouraging those individuals who take a stand and work towards a longer-term organisational purpose
Career Management	a messy scenario in which the shrewd challenge of ambitious individuals adept at political management results in short-term compromises and expedient decision-making	a focus on business achievement and contribution which seeks to discourage political gamesmanship and self-advancing impression management	a drive towards the longer-term based on ethical business purpose which is quick to identify and remove from the succession process those individuals motivated by short-term expediency	succession as the result of a series of compromises and political trade-offs to preserve the power and status of specific individuals and encourages self-seeking personnel

Figure 4.11 Succession conflicts

Next steps

How much consensus is there about leadership requirements across the different stake-holder groups?

- What are the expectations of *outside stake-holders* (institutional investors, media, general public); what is the external view of current leadership and the strength of future capability from within the organisation?
- How does the *Board* view the current CEO, top team and internal talent? Which components of leadership do they value in particular?
- What leadership agenda is the *top team* discussing? What factors are influencing their perception of the current leadership talent pool? Which individuals are seen as having the "right leadership stuff"; which individuals are being overlooked?
- How do *professionals and executives* see the rules of the game of progression? Which leadership practices and behaviours do they see recognised and rewarded?
- Throughout the *human resources* community is there recognition of leadership realities or a naïvety about what is required to progress? How similar or different is the HR perception of leadership to that of mainstream business leadership? Is the HR function pushing through a model of leadership that is out of synch with career realities?

What, if any, framework is in place to help articulate your organisation's leadership requirements? Is this framework "working"?

- Is it being actively used by the top team or senior executives to guide the review of talent and shape resourcing recommendations? Or are real-life decisions being made against a different set of criteria?
- Is it effective in making meaningful differentiations across the target population to highlight different types of individual and business contribution? Or is your framework simply a variation of "good guys" and "bad guys"?
- Is it pinpointing the specific factors which explain why some individuals are ready to advance and clarify development priorities; is it indicating why some individuals are stuck and identifying the reasons?
- Is your framework integrating a range of different people applications, connecting role profiling, and performance management with personal development planning with succession? Or does your framework sit as a separate initiative?

If no framework is in place, what needs to be done to establish a template to guide succession and resourcing decisions and support the identification and development of talent? (See Chapter 7.)

What do you need to do to refocus your leadership model?

- Politically are you stuck with a "Gravy Train Consulting" model you have to live with for another year?
- Evolve the current approach to provide a more insightful analysis of leadership?
- "Rip up" the existing framework and establish a more robust approach?

What do you want your framework to do? Is it:

- a language only for discussion about emerging talent at succession reviews at senior levels?
- a way of directing attention onto our expectations of leadership at every level and shaping new priorities throughout the organisation?
- a unifying model to integrate recruitment, induction, training and development, performance management and succession priorities?

How specifically is the Board's view of leadership being played out against the pipeline of leadership talent which is being identified and developed?

- What is the dominant leadership "theory" at the top: a balanced evaluation or skewed towards particular elements of leadership? Which of the Four Cs is more or less important to the Board? Which leadership approaches are valued; which are being dismissed?
- How do they view the leadership population that is emerging? Which individuals are being encouraged and supported; which individuals are ignored and neglected?
- What tensions are there? How will this be played out? What are the implications for the range of leadership talent that is being identified and developed?

Notes

1. R. Boyatzis, *The Competent Manager: A Model for Effective Performance*, 1982.
2. I can't remember the name of the delegate who made this observation but it summarises well the disillusionment with the "competency consultants". A big factor behind the bland conformity of competency has undoubtedly been consultancy cynicism of "cut and paste" models from a recycled library of competency statements under the pretence of original research.
3. See, for example, R. Jacobs, "Getting the Measure of Management Competence", *Personnel Management* 6 (1989), pp. 32–37. Adrian Furnham, *The Incompetent Manager*, 2003, has suggested that "we dispense with the concept of competency because of its associations and ambiguities".
4. The reality is that most competency models look the same because they tap into generic managerial processes and practices, now well established and publicised. (Dulewicz has highlighted 12 dimensions that provide a "periodic table of competency"; V. Dulewicz, "Assessment Centres as the Route to Competence", *Personnel Management* 11 (1989), pp. 56–59.)
5. One of our clients, working alongside a "Gravy Train" consultancy, had developed a competency list of 32 dimensions. Challenged to design an assessment centre around these dimensions, I pointed out this might prove troublesome, and perhaps we should find a way of grouping the competency dimensions into a more manageable number. The consultant was reluctant to accept this compromise. "But in the research we conducted we found these 32 competencies." Well, he didn't find them in the sense that he walked into a forest and picked up 32 logs. He found them in his head as his own way of making sense of the data he had collated from his fieldwork. But his way of thinking about competency was unworkable.
6. Peter Vaill in *Managing as a Performing Art*, 1989, asks the question: "Why do most lists of competencies omit what may be the most strategic competency of all, capacity to shelve one's competence in favour of an openness to the new?"
7. There was a period, 1970s to mid-1980s, when attributes were seen as pretty much irrelevant. The message seemed to be that anyone with appropriate experience, training and development could be a leader. The last decade has seen the return of fundamental cognitive, motivational and interpersonal traits as an important component of leadership effectiveness.
8. M. Buckingham and C. Coffman, *First Break All the Rules; What the World's Greatest Managers Do Differently*, 1999.

9. Adrian Furnham's *The Incompetent Manager: The Causes, Consequences and Cures of Management Failure*, 2003, is a good overview of different perspectives indicating why conventional competency listings might be simplistic.
10. "Competency speak" stifles the debate around the realities of work-a-day life, realities well portrayed in the worlds of Scott Adams's Dilbert and Ricky Gervais's David Brent of *The Office*.
11. Peter Drucker, *The Practice of Management*, 1995.
12. And at an economic level trust is an important business asset. "In economies where trust is lacking the cost of transactions is so high that it seriously damages economic activity." Brian Pearce, Director, Centre for Sustainable Investment, January 2003.
13. Barry J. Gibbons, *Dream Merchants and How Boys*, 2002.
14. Daniel Goleman, *Emotional Intelligence*, 1998.
15. Not too bad a failure though. The consistent finding in peer-reviewed journals over the past few decades has been that cognitive aptitude is the single best predictor of work effectiveness, across different roles, organisations and sectors, accounting for at least 30 per cent of the variance in work effectiveness, and more in roles of high complexity and ambiguity (that is, leadership positions). See, for example, M. Cook, *Personnel Selection and Productivity*, 1998. EQ needs to establish a similarly impressive track record of consistent empirical research reported in serious academic literature.
16. For an interesting perspective on EQ, visit the website http://eqi.org/busi.htm. This includes a review of the EQ phenomenon by Robert Sternberg, which first appeared in *Personnel Psychology*, Autumn 1999.
17. F. Luthans, R. Hodgetts and S. Rosenkrantz, *Real Managers*, 1988.
18. "Is Talent Enough: A Survey of Career Tactics", Andrews Munro Ltd, 2002.
19. M. Seligman, *Authentic Happiness*, 2002.
20. Why then, it might be argued, invent the new vocabulary of EQ rather than utilise the rich language of character?
21. See www.azureconsulting.com for details of supporting tools for self-assessment, 360° feedback and interviewing.
22. James O'Loughlin, *The Real Warren Buffett*, 2003.
23. Leadership Dynamics Profile survey, Azure Consulting International, 2003.

Formulating a Succession Game-plan

This section moves on to the more practical aspects of succession management, addressing in turn each of the three battle-grounds: the appointments process, business risk assessment and the identification and development of talent.

How should the current appointments process work to support succession? What safeguards need to be put in place to manage the succession for key positions, the CEO, top executive roles and other business critical roles? What assessment criteria and processes should be utilised to improve the calibre of the organisation's professional and leadership capability? How should the selection decision-making process operate?

What mechanisms need to be established to ensure the organisation is identifying its resourcing pressure points and spotting emerging business vulnerabilities? What alternatives to classic succession charting will provide a shrewd insight into future resourcing opportunities and risks?

What systems for the identification and development of emerging talent will strengthen the pipeline of leadership capability and create "organisational resilience"? What processes will manage talent proactively, ensure key individuals are retained and nurtured, and any blockages to the pipeline are addressed? Which development methods should be deployed to accelerate the progression of promising professionals and executives?

5 Managing the Appointments Process: Who Gets Which Job?

"Yesterday I died. That is unquestionably bad news for me. But it is not bad news for our business." Warren Buffett's letter in a sealed envelope to be opened on his death naming his successor

"What surprised us was the evidence of amateurishness with which so many key appointments were still made." "Taking Charge: What Makes CEO Succession Work", Judge Institute of Management Studies

"The interview is the most flawed process in business." Larry Bossidy, former CEO of Allied Signal

The appointments process is the bottom line of an effective succession planning process. It provides the strategic opportunity to raise the corporate game, move the organisation in a new business direction, or, if badly managed, weaken the organisation. And the problem is compounded by the tendency for bad leaders to hire even worse leaders.

An effective selection decision doesn't simply appoint from within or recruit from outside. It begins with a clear understanding of role requirements and looks imaginatively at the range of resourcing options. The risks and hazards of a typical selection process need to be avoided to improve the speed and quality of key appointments. Good selection isn't overly impressed with the credibility of career resumés; it examines rigorously the capability and character of candidates.

THE SEARCH COMMITTEE

The search committee has conducted its first stage in short-listing candidates for the CEO role.

Chair: "Well, what do we think so far? Bill looks pretty impressive. He did a sterling job in turning around Third Tree."

Member 1: "Maybe. But can we afford him? Maybe he's too good for us."

Member 2: "But if we want to move into the premier league we have to recruit a premier league player."

Member 3: "Third Tree is a very different business to ours. And I'm not sure we're ready for a rerun of the Third Tree experience."

Member 1: "There are a couple of candidates we haven't looked at properly. And what about the internal candidates? We haven't even considered them."

> *Chair:* "OK, we'll come on to them. But I want to talk about Theo. The search firm reckon he might be our best bet. Look at this guy's track record. He's worked with some good firms and with some pretty special people."

Challenges and dilemmas

The appointment decision is a critical moment of truth in the management of succession, cutting through the rhetoric of how in principle succession should be managed, to clarify what happens in practice. It represents a summary of the organisational *past*. The appointments process, where outstanding candidates are short-listed and a quick selection decision is made, is an indication of an established legacy of robust succession within organisations. Difficulty in drawing up a short-list of credible candidates reflects previous failings in resourcing and development activity. The appointments decision is also a statement for the *future*. Making the right decision, playing "succession roulette" well to place the right bet, provides an opportunity to raise the organisational game through the selection of superior leaders and managers. Alternatively, it is at this time that badly managed succession and a weak appointment damages the organisation, sometimes irreversibly. The appointments process can also be a key lever in driving organisational change to select those individuals who, rather than maintaining the status quo, will shift it in new directions and shape the future. It is the impact of selection decisions, not only at senior levels but throughout the organisation, that explains why robust succession practices are a key factor in driving organisational performance. Succession management to improve selection decision-making is "success management".[1]

The resourcing strategy that looks outside the organisation to appoint individuals to fill key roles is a valid tactic. But when deployed frequently as a substitute for a lack of home-grown talent, rather than as a proactive game plan to target key capabilities from the external market, it is a risky approach. It assumes that suitable candidates are available easily, can be brought in cost-effectively, will "get up to speed" quickly, will make a positive impact and will reinforce and bolster the culture of the organisation through a commitment to its ethics and values. In a resourcing world in which these assumptions are valid then succession management as an organisational activity loses its relevance. But external resourcing is not like a trip to the supermarket where, armed with a shopping list, we load the trolley, pay at the check-out, and return home to restock our kitchen shelves. Suitable candidates are not necessarily easily found. They can be a hugely expensive option. They may struggle to come to terms with their new role. They may damage the culture and reputation of the organisation. Those organisations that repeatedly look outside for their leaders are in danger of undermining that fragile dynamic, which balances change and challenge with continuity and stability.[2]

Competing on this "battle-ground" of succession includes:

- anticipating vacancies to *get "ahead of the game"* by exploring all resourcing options and agreeing and planning responses before a selection decision is required
- linking plans for reorganisation and redeployment to an effective appointments process and connecting succession planning with the drawing up of *informed and imaginative short-lists*
- developing an *internal search mechanism* to review the available talent pool and identify

those candidates whose long-term development may be best met through an imaginative appointments decision

- agreeing *clear and consistent criteria* to guide decision-making and implementing a robust assessment methodology to evaluate candidates
- building *relationships with trusted external partners*, headhunters, interim agencies and so on, to keep up-to-date with marketplace developments and resourcing options.

While a well-managed appointments process provides perhaps the most powerful mechanism with which to implement robust succession and trigger organisational change, it is not without its dilemmas.

- How, for example, should line management discretion with regard to hiring decisions be maintained while using specific appointments to build long-term corporate capability? Line managers rightly want to make their own selection decisions; after all they will be accountable for the outcomes of these appointments. But the organisation may want to utilise a specific appointment to provide an up-and-coming professional with the development experience they need to build leadership effectiveness.
- How should the need for an immediate contribution within the role be balanced with the option of selecting the candidate who represents a better bet for the longer term but will take longer to get up to speed? Who gets the job? The best-matched candidate due to retire in 12 months' time or the high-potential candidate who will gain from this experience and provide leadership for the longer term?
- How should you restructure and refocus roles to play to the distinctive strengths of an exceptional candidate while avoiding the organisational chaos from reshuffling responsibilities and reporting lines each time you make an appointment?

Working backwards: success factors

Perhaps the best piece of consultancy advice I ever received was to "work backwards": to start at the end not at the beginning. Most projects and assignments are a process that goes from A (the current situation which, in one way or another, is unsatisfactory) to Z (the end-point which represents the ideal or at least a significant improvement on the present). A is clear and tangible, and the steps to reach B and C can be plotted out in detail. But Z is a long way off and more difficult to visualise. Typically Z represents a hazy sense that organisational life in one way or another will be better. But without clarity of Z and specifically what makes Z distinctively different from A, projects will either lose their way or end up at a different destination. The starting-point then is to map out the specific factors that will define success and provide the criteria against which progress can be evaluated (see Figure 5.1). As with all metrics the trick is to keep things simple, focusing only on those measures that highlight significant trends and provide a reliable gauge to pinpoint emerging problems.[3]

The first category is measures of *efficiency*. The longer an appointment takes to fill, the greater the business disruption and the potential for lost opportunity. One IT client estimated that its difficulty in making a senior sales appointment, a role that took more than nine months to fill, cost the organisation £750 000. Delays in appointments also create uncertainty. The organisation stalls as employees are reluctant to embark on any new

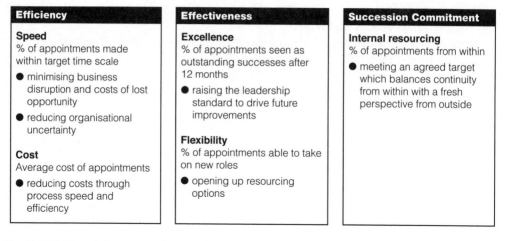

Efficiency	Effectiveness	Succession Commitment
Speed % of appointments made within target time scale ● minimising business disruption and costs of lost opportunity ● reducing organisational uncertainty **Cost** Average cost of appointments ● reducing costs through process speed and efficiency	**Excellence** % of appointments seen as outstanding successes after 12 months ● raising the leadership standard to drive future improvements **Flexibility** % of appointments able to take on new roles ● opening up resourcing options	**Internal resourcing** % of appointments from within ● meeting an agreed target which balances continuity from within with a fresh perspective from outside

Figure 5.1   Appointments metrics

initiatives that may be dismantled on the appointment of a new manager. In one professional services partnership, a firm in which the executive team was elected from the partner population, the organisation essentially went into maintenance mode for a period of three months. Only once the phase of politicking and lobbying of votes was over and the new executive team announced could business life then resume. In a police force, plans and proposals for organisational improvement were shelved for several months until the name of the new Chief Constable was known and the individual's particular operating approach and priorities could then be evaluated. *Speed* then is a key measure. How long on average is it currently taking to make appointments? What target should be set to indicate improvements in managing the appointments process? Which aspects of the process are constraining speed of response: agreeing a role specification, advertising, short-listing, assessment and selection interviewing, agreeing a remuneration package, negotiating contracts? Where could improvements be made to speed up the process?

Improvements in succession management and the appointments process should also reduce the *cost of appointments*. How much on average is it costing to make appointments? For internal appointments you need to factor in the costs of professional and management time spent on the selection process as well as the opportunity costs associated with delays in filling the role. For external appointments you also need to build in the costs of advertising, search and selection. These costs should be evaluated for the average appointment as well as broken down by level and business area.

Efficiency improvements represent tangible organisational gains in utilising succession to expedite and streamline the appointments process. Measures of *effectiveness* should address the business impact of appointments. Succession management should be the mechanism that widens resourcing options, improves the calibre of short-listed candidates and raises the capability of those appointed. Again, what is the base line of A, the current situation? How is this established: through intuitive judgement from the top team or through the more objective evaluation of formal appraisal? Effectiveness can be gauged in different ways and the specific metrics agreed will depend on your organisation and its resourcing requirements. One measure is the *"excellence ratio"*: the percentage of appointments viewed as "outstanding successes" after, say, 12 months in role. This is a key index to track if the aim is to crank up the appointments process to raise the calibre of the leadership population. What is the business impact of an outstanding performer *vis-à-vis* one operating at an average level? The greater the financial difference, the greater the opportunity to use succession to drive business progress. A variation of this is the *"flexibility ratio"*: the degree to which those appointed have the breadth and depth of experience, capability and motivation to take on new responsibilities and challenges. What percentage, for example, of senior executives are specialists, individuals recruited for specific roles requiring highly technical input as opposed to those who could operate across a range of mainstream business roles?

The flexibility ratio is at the heart of resourcing priorities and how succession is managed. Is the appointments process designed to find and select the best candidate for a specific role, or is it less about matching a candidate to one role and more about selecting that overall capability which can make a wider organisational contribution in the future? One scientific-based government agency, reliant on leading-edge technical innovation, recognised there was little flexibility. Technical excellence came through organising work activity around highly specialist roles, allowing individuals to concentrate and focus on the acquisition of increasingly advanced knowledge and expertise. This process was manageable in a protected world of government funding, but problematic when the organisation was forced into the commercial world and needed to build partnerships across the private sector in order to pay its way. Here the lack of professional and management flexibility constrained its strategic options.

The final overall theme against which the appointments process should be judged is *succession commitment*: the balance of internal versus eternal candidates. A target of 100 per cent appointments from within is both unrealistic and undesirable. However, if succession management is seen as a priority a target needs to be set that reflects projections about future resourcing philosophy and priority. There is a "tipping point",[4] the moment when the number of external hires undermines organisational purpose and jeopardises the core, the organisation's fundamental purpose and ethos. There is also the point when insufficient talent is being brought in from outside and the core is in danger of falling into complacency. This "tipping point" ratio will vary from organisation to organisation, reflecting different histories, cultures and strategies. A new start-up that is expanding quickly must rely on high levels of external recruitment, but I suspect for established mainstream organisations the "tipping point" on average is around 70:30, 70 per cent of appointments through internal progression, and 30 per cent through external recruitment.

SUCCESSION IN THE NEW NEW ECONOMY

Centricorp, a well-established manufacturing firm, faced with the unexpected death of its CEO, looked for a successor outside the company. A headhunter was engaged and eventually a veteran with extensive experience, L. Enton Drake, was identified. As the employment contracts were being finalised unfortunately someone managed to misspell L. Enton Drake as Lenny Drake. This mistake was then compounded by another problem when a secretarial temp sent the contract to the wrong address, the address of a Lenny Drake.

Lenny, a salesman of bathware planning a career move, saw the contract as a sign from God and signed the contract. When Lenny arrived at Centricorp to take up his new role of CEO it quickly became clear that a terrible mistake had been made, but a mistake that was going to be hard to rectify. Either Centricorp could dismiss

Lenny, but be forced to pay a huge penalty under his employment contract and face a crisis of confidence from institutional investors, or retain him but keep him under close control. It decided on the latter option.

Lenny's first action as CEO was to fire the "stuffed shirts", replacing them with his family and friends. His next move, the initiative "Big Like a Fox", to establish a global presence, included the decision to corner the blender market in the African Upper Volta and ship out vast quantities of margarita mix... In the wake of Lenny Drake's departure, Centricorp spent the last year divesting itself of the 5978 acquisitions made during his tenure and fending off numerous lawsuits. Experts predict that Centricorp will not return to profitability until late in the decade, if at all.[5]

Triggers to appointments

There are two sets of triggers to appointments: vacancies that can be anticipated and those that can't. Anticipated vacancies arise out of planned departures, predicted by the age profile of the management and executive population and the organisation's retirement policies (who do we know will be leaving when?) or through advance notice being given of the role-holder's intentions to pursue their career aims elsewhere. Dealing with the predictable should be, but isn't always, straightforward.

A more rigorous test of succession resilience is coping with the unanticipated. How quickly can the organisation respond to the sudden departure of the role-holder through an unexpected promotion or progression to another role, their decision to leave and move to another organisation, or illness or premature death? Increasingly the need to manage appointments is now sparked by external factors requiring a refocus of the management structure and the need to reconfigure roles, responsibilities and reporting lines to redirect executive time and effort. In the business ruthlessness of the twenty-first century it is also a response to under-performance and the dismissal or demotion of the current role-holder. Robust succession management should be prepared for the unexpected and unplanned. For critical roles, short-term contingency arrangements should be in place to make a rapid response, with a game plan to indicate options and recommendations. The next chapter will address in more detail the processes needed to review structures and roles, identify key resourcing pressure points and assess any business risks and vulnerabilities. However, faced with the pressing reality or the pending expectation of an unfilled role, what are the resourcing options? (See Figure 5.2.)

- *Straightforward replacement into the existing role.* This resourcing tactic has the benefit of an established expectation of what success within the role looks like, how it should be judged and clear criteria for evaluating candidates. Here the successor profile matches that of the previous incumbent. This apparent "benefit" also has the downside that often replacement options are constrained by perceptions of the previous role-holder and their way of doing things; "we need someone like them". The short-listing process becomes an exercise in locating a similar type of individual, which can be hazardous. Role requirements change and the leadership skill set and outlook that worked in the past may not be relevant in the future.
- *A realignment of the role to shift the emphasis.* This is likely to be the most common

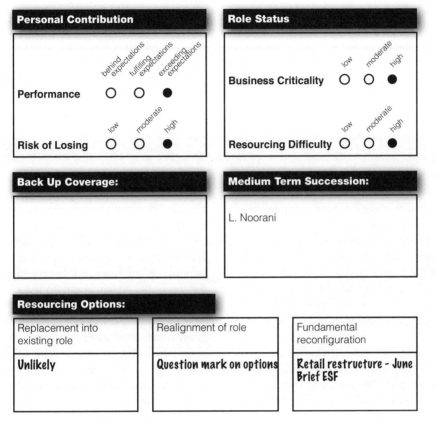

Figure 5.2   Succession role profile

experience. The vacancy creates the opportunity to review the objectives and priorities of the role. Where have time and effort been previously directed, with what outcome? How should role requirements be refocused to ensure the next role-holder is maximising the full range of opportunities of the role? Which management and leadership tasks have been neglected and need greater attention? Where is there overlap with other roles which can now be reduced?

- *A fundamental reconfiguration of the role* alongside the surrounding matrix of roles and reporting relationships to completely change the criteria for role success. Here the need to make a new appointment triggers a recognition that all has not been well and that a more radical change is required within the organisational structure. In light of emerging opportunities and risks, a shift is needed across the management structure before a role specification can be agreed. This exercise may throw up a number of resourcing options beyond conventional succession or external recruitment: the utilisation of interim management, greater involvement of professional advisers and consultants or the decision to completely outsource this organisational activity. The downsides are obvious.

Each appointment triggers a wave of organisational change, requiring shifts in others' roles and their remuneration. This is manageable in a small, fast-moving and flexible firm, but more problematic in a large enterprise, particularly those where the "bind weed" of job evaluation — the tangle of points, levels and grades — is a major constraint to resourcing flexibility.

The key challenge in reviewing resourcing options is to keep a forward-looking perspective. It is easy and tempting to opt for more of the same, to find that candidate who can mirror the successes (or avoid the failings) of the previous incumbent. But "success management" rather than succession management doesn't focus simply on current organisational structures and roles; it asks: does this appointment open up possibilities to improve how we operate and the kinds of individuals who will drive the business forward?

THE INSIDER–OUTSIDER DEBATE

Under which circumstances is an external appointment better than an internal one? *The common cliché has been that internal succession is evolution and external recruitment is revolution.* So when, for example, Compaq announced in 2000 that insider Michael Capellas would become CEO, its stock price fell; whereas at Hewlett Packard, shares shot up on the news that outsider Carly Fiorana would be the next CEO.

The thinking here is that it is only external candidates, the "new brooms", who can tackle the prevailing mind-set and cultural expectations to make that major shift in strategy to refocus and realign the organisation. Internal candidates, those individuals who have progressed through the management ranks, are seen as too closely associated with the organisation's current strategy and business performance to operate as credible agents for business renewal. At best, through their network of relationships and closeness to the organisation's decision-making, they maintain continuity of purpose and minimise disruption. They are the safe pair of hands to keep the current business model working. But if the agenda is major transformation, driven by investor perceptions of corporate under-performance, internal candidates are "lame ducks", part of the problem and carrying old baggage. By contrast, the outsider "has a clear mandate...he is not beholden to anyone. There are so many constraints on the internally promoted individual...you turn to an outsider and then you can watch the blood spray. You don't see many examples of internal candidates getting to the top of the system and then laying waste to the existing culture."[6]

How meaningful is this internal–external distinction? In the supermarket wars being played out in the UK, Terry Leahy, CEO of Tesco, who progressed through the ranks, seems far-removed from the conventional insider in the way he has led the charge to take Tesco to the number one slot. Another insider, founder Ken Morrison of Morrisons, is heading the pack to acquire Safeways, run by an "outsider". But it was outsiders Archie Norman and Allan Leighton who masterminded the turnaround of the ailing Asda, now part of the mighty Wal-Mart group. And for Sainsburys, the other big player in food retailing, it is not clear whether Peter Davis is an insider or outsider. A former marketing executive at Sainsburys, Davis left to head up insurance firm Prudential, to return as Sainsburys' CEO.

It is misleading to contrast the complete insider, the individual who joined the organisation and worked their way steadily through the management ranks, who will maintain the status quo, with the complete outsider, the executive brought in from another organisation to shake things up. The days of family dynasties are disappearing. And in the complex dynamics of business acquisitions, partnerships and membership of the "executive club", the complete outsider is also a stereotype. Instead of simply looking at the origins of the successor, that is, whether they are an internal appointment or a recruit from outside, it may be more informative to ask:

- Is the successor part of the "established order", part of the power dynamic not simply within the organisation but within the broader stake-holder community? Was James Murdoch an external appointment for BSkyB, or as son of Rupert Murdoch (owner of 35 per cent of BSkyB), an insider? Neither, but given his family connections he certainly was part of the prevailing power structure. Alternatively, it could be argued that insider Jack Welch was outside General Electric's political establishment. Brought in from the plastics division, at that time outside of mainstream business activity, he wasn't constrained by the current political dynamic and could ignite transformation with an insider's knowledge. It was, after all, Jack Welch, the "insider" who sold 200 of GE's

businesses, closed 73 facilities and reduced head count by 100 000. Quite some blood!

- What is the *dominant mind-set* of the successor and how similar or different is this to the organisation's strategic imperatives? Is the appointment in essence about continuity, about more of the same, or is it a driver of change, about moving to something quite different? An insider may seek to preserve the past; alternatively they may utilise their insights into the organisation and what is and isn't working to generate a very different set of business priorities to the current strategy. Will an outsider embark on radical transformation, or will the external recruit, unfamiliar with the specific complexities of the industry's dynamics and the organisation's culture, find themselves falling back on maintaining the status quo?

Succession should be less concerned with the source of the successor or preoccupied with the insider or outsider debate.[7] Instead it should identify more fundamental dynamics, the extent to which the successor should or shouldn't be part of the current "establishment", inside or outside the existing political structure, and the degree to which the successor should have a similar or different business approach.

CEO selection mechanisms

The Higgs code of corporate governance in the UK spells out the theory: a key responsibility of the Board is planning and managing CEO succession. What happens in practice?

THE CURRENT CEO PASSES ON THE "BATON"

The Board might have formal responsibility for ensuring well-managed succession, but distanced from the detail of organisational life it allows the CEO to take control of the succession agenda. This is hazardous and a factor that has led to the downfall of many businesses. No matter how rational and objective the CEO wants to be there is a real risk that they nominate a successor in their own image. The criteria they establish for reviewing candidate options and selecting the individual best equipped to succeed them reflects their own set of experiences, skills, outlook and leadership style. After all, if these factors have defined their self-identify and accounted for their success, why should this be different for others? But life moves on, business demands change and leadership requirements shift. At a darker, subconscious level, some CEOs, extraordinary as this may sound, nominate a weak candidate, a candidate who is unlikely to provide the business leadership to exceed their own achievements.[8] If not full-blown organisational sabotage, then CEOs certainly have the power to undermine their successor. Roberto Goizueta, chairman and president of Coca-Cola, certainly didn't make it easy for his successor, Douglas Ivester. In media briefings, Goizueta complained of Ivester's lack of impetus and having the "nerve of a night prowler". Perhaps these open criticisms of his successor reflected Goizueta's own ambivalence about retiring. Responding to a shareholder's comment that "you should be like the Pope and never retire", Goizueta began to display the "hallmarks of a King Lear, unwilling to step away from his throne, out of the spotlight, and on to a life of much diminished purpose and power".[9] Ivester himself, despite Coca-Cola's reasonable performance at the time, was fired after less than two years in the role.

Ben Cohen and Jerry Greenfield, the two maverick entrepreneurs behind premium ice-cream firm Ben & Jerry's, faced with meeting the challenge of Häagen-Dazs in the 1990s, looked at succession and accepted the need for a new CEO. The first selection process, the publicity stunt of the essay contest, "Yo, I wanna be your CEO", was eventually backed up with the help of an executive search firm, leading to the appointment of outsider Robert Holland. He left after less than two years in the role following disagreements with the founders. Here their ideological commitment and motivation to balance a broad social and environmental agenda with shareholder interests made conventional succession troublesome. "Executive recruiters said that finding a CEO who can succeed at Ben & Jerry's could be a daunting task."[10]

At AT & T the Board allowed the incumbent CEO Robert Allen to control the outside search for his successor. Allen then himself refused to exit gracefully himself. The Board agreed to Allen's nomination, John Walter, although he was their second choice, a choice which when made public was described by the business media as "puzzling". Indeed AT & T's market value fell by $4 billion on the news of Walter's appointment. Nine months later, lacking credibility with his executive team, Walter resigned or was dismissed depending on which version of events is to be believed. His replacement, C. Michael Armstrong, an external candidate from IBM, was seen as the CEO who should have been originally appointed. Armstrong has since had his own difficulties.

It is an absurd exaggeration to suggest that the incumbent CEO, in "passing on the baton", wants to bring the organisation down, although Stanley Gault of Rubbermaid appeared to have come close to this. Describing himself as a "sincere tyrant" his "successors found themselves struggling not only with a management void, but also with strategic voids that would eventually bring the company to its knees".[11] Subconsciously, however, some CEOs may not want to see the organisation go on to exceed their own personal achievements. Whatever the complexities of CEO psychology, it is a major risk to allow the CEO, overtly or covertly, to control the Board agenda with their nominated successor.

THE "SUCCESSION TOURNAMENT"

In a "succession tournament", succession is set up as an overt contest among internal executives to identify the most suitable candidate. In this scenario no one individual is announced by the CEO as the "heir apparent". Instead the likely successors are given the opportunity to demonstrate their commitment and motivation to succeed to the "throne" through virtue of their accomplishments. This isn't quite "last one standing wins", but it is based on a commitment to meritocracy, that ability and achievement should determine who will be the next CEO. This tactic has the benefit of clarifying the "rules of the succession game" and using business results as the "acid test". But, as Richard Greenbury at Marks & Spencer discovered, the tournament can require more than skill and competency. It can also arouse political gamesmanship which distract executive attention from the business of managing the organisation.

Nonetheless it is a stratagem that continues to be utilised. Gordon Cairns of Australian brewing giant Nathan Lion, impressed with Jack Welch's experience of the tournament at General Electric to determine his own successor, replicated this manoeuvre. Cairns, who had transformed an ordinary organisation into a growth company, nearing his retirement, concluded that his successor should be an internal appointment. Cairns identified three candidates who would be given the opportunity to gain greater exposure to the Board and establish their leadership credentials. The expectation was that the losers of the tournament would leave. The game plan also ensured that successors for each of the nominated candidates were being identified and groomed. Welch's advice to Cairns was direct. Keep your mind open as long as possible before selecting the succession candidate. Choose the candidate with the most potential for the future rather than the one with the best performance record.[12]

Nathan Lion's application of Jack Welch's strategy in turn owed much to Jack Welch's own predecessor, Reg Jones. It was Jones who utilised the now famous "airplane interview test". Jones would turn up unannounced with the leading succession candidates and ask, "You and I are flying in one of the company's planes and the plane crashes. Both of us die. Who should be the next chairperson of the General Electric Company?" Jones conducted this session with all the candidates and then three months later went through it all over again. Jones also interviewed the non-contenders, those senior people who had an insight into the succession candidates, to evaluate their views. He then re-ran the exercise with the succession candidates in the final set of interviews, asking, "We're flying in the plane and the plane crashes. I'm done but you live. Now who should be the chairperson of General Electric?" From these discussions three candidates were agreed and the tournament continued.[13]

EARLY CHOICE OR DELAYED DECISION? PROS AND CONS

Is it better to declare your hand and announce the successor in advance? Or should the succession decision go right "to the wire", the nominated successor becoming known only at the time it becomes "necessary"? The "early choice" tactic has the benefit of providing time and space to ensure that the nominated successor is equipped for the role. It reassures external constituents that organisational continuity is planned and that business disruption will be minimised. It clarifies the leadership agenda to allow other potential successors to make their career choices and exit the business rather than stay on to fight those battles that can only undermine the organisation.

Conversely, "early choice" has the potential to ignite interpersonal conflict and to force the premature departure of key executives who see their career options constrained and want to advance their careers with other organisations. "Early choice" also commits the organisation to a particular strategic course of direction based on the nominated successor's business background, track record and operating outlook. If there is much uncertainty, "Wait and See" might be the only and realistic option for the organisation, while "early choice" may lock in the organisation, restricting its freedom for manoeuvre. This seemed to be the scenario which CEO John Roth created for Nortel. Keen to retire, he appointed Clarence Chandran, his chief operating officer, as his successor. Chandran was within 45 days of taking over as CEO but then was forced to quit on health grounds. As the telecom industry edged into a massive downturn, headhunters found it difficult to find a new CEO, with few external candidates willing to lead an organisation when the days of reckoning were so obviously looming.[14]

While "early choice" makes a positive statement to the investment community about the organisation and its confidence in the future, it also runs the risk of becoming derailed by fast-moving events and marketplace trends. This has been the recent experience of Standard Life, Europe's largest mutual life insurance firm. Awarded the coveted Triple A rating by Moodys, Standard Life went from strength to strength throughout the 1990s. In 2001 it maintained its long-standing commitment to internal succession with the appointment of Iain Lumsden as CEO. But Lumsden's public and emphatic commitment to mutuality became unsustainable by 2003 as the Financial Services Authority (under its own pressure, following the debacle of Equitable Life, another mutual life insurance firm) began to question the scale of Standard Life's liabilities, sparking damaging speculation about its financial position. As Standard Life embarked on a fundamental strategic review, including the option to demutualise, Lumsden, the defender of mutuality, stepped down in early 2004, making way for Sandy Crombie, another insider with 37 years in the business, who had lost out to Lumsden in the previous succession competition. Analysts anticipate a round of external recruitment at top executive levels before Standard Life regains its credibility.[15]

Both early choice and delayed decision have their relative merits. It may be that early choice is the best bet when there is an outstandingly capable individual, head and shoulders above his or her peer group, and whose exceptional leadership is openly acknowledged. Here early choice sends out a strong signal to external constituents that the organisation is in control of its destiny. Delayed decision may be more sensible in the scenario where there are a number of well-established competent and credible players within the senior team, when the market dynamic is shifting and when freedom of manoeuvre is paramount.

THE BOARD SEARCH COMMITTEE IDENTIFIES A SUCCESSOR

Reliance on one individual, the CEO, to pass on the baton, has huge risks, whether it is through the nomination of a favoured individual or the testing of several candidates, tournament style. The consequences of the CEO succession decision, getting it right or wrong, can be so immense that the expectation now is that succession is the responsibility of the Board. So how does the Board process work? The answer is most of the time quite badly.[16] A combination of inadequate analysis, insufficient time, vested interests and the peculiarities of the interpersonal and political dynamics of the process conspire to make it remarkably easy to select the wrong top executive.

How should a good appointments decision be made, and how is it made in practice?

The selection decision-making process

A good decision-making process requires:

- a clear summary of the problem, a concise analysis of what is at the heart of the issue
- the involvement of those with the greatest insight into the nature of the problem and those most affected by the impact of the final decision
- a creative generation of the full range of options to highlight potential solutions
- detailed and comprehensive information about the options to allow risks and benefits to be examined and weighed up
- an implementation plan to make the decision work.

So how does the appointments process operate in practice?

A CLEAR SUMMARY OF THE PROBLEM

A vacancy to be filled represents a problem. How do we select the best candidate to operate effectively within this role? This of course immediately begs the question: what are the requirements of the role and what do we mean by the best candidate? How should the role be defined to generate clear criteria against which we can evaluate potential candidates? Framing the issues in the wrong way will produce faulty decisions, and it is here in the selection process that things can begin to go wrong. Even the most superficial scanning of the appointments section of the press illustrates how very different roles with different requirements can all sound pretty much the same, essentially a wish list of vague sentiments and positive-sounding attributes. Key words are "strategic vision", "boundless energy and enthusiasm", "inspirational change agent" and "strong commercial acumen". Like the particulars produced by estate agents to sell a house and attract potential buyers, most role specifications, especially when spun into job advertisements, are a mix of the vague, flattering and downright misleading.

In our discussions with external search firms we asked about the most common factors of client dissatisfaction, one of which is the excessive time taken to make external appointments. Their response: "clients aren't specific enough in their requirements, and when they are, they then keep changing the brief." We also asked organisations of their experiences of working with executive search firms. Their complaint: a lack of business and organisational insight which fails to pinpoint the differentiators needed to finalise a robust specification. As one report concluded,[17] establishing a role specification is "spontaneous ignition", deciding the criteria *during* rather than prior to the search for candidates. This is an elegant way of saying that often the search committee makes it up as it goes along. Areas for improvement include:

- Map out role requirements based on a clear view of the future. What are the key challenges facing the organisation and what are the implications for the problems the role-holder will face? How will these change over time? What is the likely shelf life of the role and role-holder? Is the focus of the role: trouble-shooting over the next 12 months or implementing cultural change over a three-year period? Is the dominant challenge restoring corporate reputation with different stake-holder groups or revitalising the customer service proposition? Distance yourself from the current role-holder and the challenges they faced in the past or the distinctive style they created for themselves. What is the new agenda, the new problems that need to be tackled? If this was a new role, what would be the key factors?

- Be rigorous in forming the role specification and in identifying the criteria against which candidate options will be evaluated. Go beyond a wish list of vague sentiments to zero in on those key factors where excellence is genuinely required to move the business forward. If you need to recruit a super-star, displaying excellence across the board, ask why? Look at those individuals surrounding the role — peers and reports — to identify how their experience and skill sets might modify the criteria. Succession does not take place in a vacuum; what are the current strengths within the surrounding relationships; where are the gaps? If the criteria resemble those which could apply to any top executive role it isn't a specification, and without a clear specification it will be impossible to short-list candidates objectively.

- Keep working through the role specification to keep tightening it up, not against the full array of competencies, but to pinpoint the non-negotiables of outcomes and critical attributes. After the first draft check it through with well-informed internal stake-holders. Then review it with a trusted external search firm. How realistic is the specification based on their evaluation of the market and the supply and demand of different leadership and professional skill sets? What trade-offs need to be made across the ideal mix of experience, skills, expertise and personal qualities to develop a realistic role profile?

- Don't allow short-term pressures, the need for specific expertise right now, to distort the criteria. Don't generate a narrow role specification based on today's problems; today's problems will continue to be tomorrow's problems.

ROLE TRADE-OFF

The appointments process depends on a clear specification of role requirements. This involves an acute insight into both the context and content of the role. The content of the role describes the specific leadership tasks and activities which will have most leverage in driving success. But no role exists in isolation. It is bound up in a context, in a complex web of other roles, role-holders and reporting relationships within a set of cultural expectations.

The role trade-off methodology starts from the premise that each role has a budget: the total compensation package. Specifying everything within a role profile is likely to be either highly expensive (nothing comes for free) or result in bland candidates who excel at nothing in particular but meet the minimum threshold of acceptability. The challenge is how to allocate the available "budget" across the range of possible requirements to identify what is more or less critical — namely, where money needs to be spent — and to pinpoint the criteria that will guide short-listing and selection.

Using the Four C model of leadership, (see Figure 5.3), how much of the budget would you allocate to credibility, capability, character and career management? None of these elements is free. Let's assume the total compensation package is £500 000. How will this money be spent?

How much does *credibility* cost? A consistent employment history with an established track record of business achievement with blue-chip firms will cost, say, £100 000. Breadth and depth of experience, operating across different sectors and having real-life exposure to a range of challenges will cost another £80 000. If you want a "big-hitting

Credibility

Role:

CREDIBILITY	Minimum spend	Maximum spend
will be higher when:		

- driven by "stake-holder" concern for a player with an established reputation with a "blue chip" track record
- need for breadth and depth of relevant experience
- a high profile within the industry through an extensive network of contacts

ESTABLISHED TRACK RECORD

	LOW	MODERATE	HIGH
an employment history indicating achievement of outstanding accomplishments with known and reputable organisations	☐	☐	☐

Which sectors/industries are relevant?

EXPERIENCE BASE

	LOW	MODERATE	HIGH
a breadth and depth of business experience in responding to a range of different challenges	☐	☐	☐

Which experiential factors are specifically important?

NETWORK RELATIONSHIPS

	LOW	MODERATE	HIGH
an established reputation with peers within the industry and a wide circle of professional contacts	☐	☐	☐

Capability

Role:

CAPABILITY will be higher when:	Minimum spend	Maximum spend

- driven by the complexity and uncertainty of the challenges facing the organisation
- a need for exceptional talents to tackle problems
- operating in a fast-moving environment with changing skill requirements

Management competency in:

PROBLEM SOLVING

	LOW	MODERATE	HIGH
analytical and decision-making skills to exercise sound judgement; originality of thinking to generate ideas	☐	☐	☐

INTERPERSONAL IMPACT

	LOW	MODERATE	HIGH
deploying a variety of interpersonal skills to influence, motivate and energise others	☐	☐	☐

TASK MANAGEMENT

	LOW	MODERATE	HIGH
planning, coordination and monitoring skills to maximise resources against objectives	☐	☐	☐

TECHNICAL PROFESSIONAL EXPERTISE

	LOW	MODERATE	HIGH
the possession and application of high levels of "know-how"	☐	☐	☐

Does the role require mastery, advanced proficiency or could the role be undertaken by a relative novice?

Career Management

Role:

CAREER MANAGEMENT	Minimum spend	Maximum spend
will be higher when:		

- driven by the need for proactive self-management
- operating in a political environment where there is a need to manage the "art of the possible"
- a requirement for ambition to want to advance to higher levels

SELF-MANAGEMENT

	LOW	MODERATE	HIGH
high levels of personal organisation and time management to prioritise and direct efforts without ongoing supervision	☐	☐	☐

TACTICAL AWARENESS

	LOW	MODERATE	HIGH
managing the realities of political and interpersonal sensitivities through a recognition of how to overcome organisational barriers and constraints	☐	☐	☐

AMBITION

	LOW	MODERATE	HIGH
the desire to develop further, take on additional responsibility and advance career progression	☐	☐	☐

Character

Role: _____

CHARACTER will be higher when: _____	**Minimum spend**	**Maximum spend**

● there is a need to maintain/restore corporate values of integrity and dependability
there is a long-term commitment and a desire to have a positive and sustainable
business impact
● a need for strong leadership governance and stewardship

INTEGRITY _____   LOW   MODERATE   HIGH

a leadership outlook which is deeply concerned with high
standards of ethical and professional conduct; establishing
a personal role model of honesty and truth in the workplace;   ☐   ☐   ☐
building trust with others through the willingness to address
fairness and justice.

RESILIENCE _____   LOW   MODERATE   HIGH

an inner resolve to overcome setbacks and disappointments;
persisting and persevering in the face of opposition; refusing
to allow adversity to undermine commitment; a flexibility of   ☐   ☐   ☐
approach which is prepared to adapt own approach to changing
circumstances to keep focused on key goals.

DISTINCTIVENESS _____   LOW   MODERATE   HIGH

a leadership approach which looks to make a unique impact,
setting own personal stamp to build something different and
special; an independence of mind which applies originality to   ☐   ☐   ☐
identify new possibilities to work for change and improvement.

Figure 5.3   Role trade-off

reputation", a high-profile name to reassure the investment community that you are a serious player, that will cost an additional £100 000.

What about *capability*? Again nothing comes for free. Problem-solving skills, the power of high levels of analytical thinking and decision-making to exercise sound judgement and generate innovative ideas, will cost £60 000. Interpersonal influence, the facility to persuade others, to energise and motivate a work group, to communicate and negotiate is £60 000. Results are achieved through planning, scheduling and coordination skills; these task management skills will cost another £60 000. If specific technical know-how or professional expertise is demanded, again there will be a cost, say £75 000.

How important is *career management*? High-level self-management skills and effectiveness in personal organisation and time management cost £40 000. Tactical awareness, the management of the realities of political and interpersonal sensitivities, will cost £60 000. Does ambition matter? How important is it that this individual has the desire to develop further and is motivated to take on additional responsibility? Ambition is another £50 000.

Finally, does *character* matter? If it does, don't assume it. Factor it in to your role specification. How important is *integrity*: operating around high standards of ethical and professional conduct, being a personal role model of honesty and truth, and building trust through the willingness to advance fairness and justice? Another

£80 000. Does *resilience* matter: the resolve to overcome setbacks and disappointments, the persistency to persevere in the face of opposition and the refusal to allow adversity to undermine commitment? It will cost £70 000. Finally how much should be paid for *distinctiveness*, that leadership quality which makes a unique impact, which sets a personal stamp over events to build something different and special; the independence of mind that identifies original possibilities? Again there is a cost: £80 000.

Specifying everything clearly exceeds the original budget. So we now need to embark on a series of trade-offs. For credibility, do we really need a "blue-chip track record"? We can save £50 000 if we lower this requirement and only insist on a career history with, for example, high-growth start-ups. That money can now be spent elsewhere. How much credibility, for example, can be traded against capability: are the skills to be effective in future more important than the reputation of past glories? How much character is needed in this role? And so on.

This is a high-level example with arbitrary numbers. This approach can be used flexibly, allowing you to incorporate your own organisation's frameworks to define management competency and professional expertise. But it does highlight the need for choice and priorities and, above all, the need to identify differentiating criteria in order to pinpoint a realistic role specification for short-listing imaginative candidates.

THE INVOLVEMENT OF INFORMED STAKE-HOLDERS IN DECISION-MAKING

Effective decision-making requires the input of those most familiar with the issues and most directly involved in the impact of the final decision. Typically many appointment decisions are contrived to ensure that those with most stake in the consequences of the decisions are excluded. If, for example, the Board initiates the selection process the risk is that the search committee, many of whose members have neither the time nor the insight to know the realities of the organisation, its strategy, structure, culture and politics, find it difficult to go beyond a superficial understanding of the role. Those with the keenest insight, those senior executives closest to the role, or the HR function with access to valuable data about individuals, are often excluded from the exercise on the grounds of confidentiality. The Board, reluctant to alienate the executive population by making public the decision to appoint externally, keeps the process under wraps. But optimising the decision should involve the key stake-holders of the appointment, those most affected by the decision.

- Firstly, ensure that the group of individuals with responsibility for the selection process understand the detail of the organisation, its operating priorities, structure and cultural style as well as its future challenges. If they don't, make it a priority to give this group exposure to as many different facets of the organisation and its professional and executive population as possible.
- If the process is to be managed by a search committee, ensure a well-informed and astute individual chairs it, someone with extended networks throughout the organisation, not simply with wider industry networks or connections to the headhunting profession. This individual needs to be exceptionally insightful about the organisation and its future, objective and detached from political pressures, and influential in shaping the search process and managing the ongoing dialogue to guide short-listing.
- Don't allow a search firm to set the agenda. Be well prepared and fully informed to take control of the selection process based on your own research and analysis of the resourcing options. It is in the commercial interests of the headhunters to overstate the complexity and difficulty of the assignment. Work with your professional and executive population, with their own extended networks across the industry and into other sectors to keep abreast of marketplace developments. Some organisations use this strategy effectively to create an "external talent bank", a listing of target managers from outside with which they track and keep in close contact to complement their own internal succession database.

GENERATING A RANGE OF OPTIONS

The decision-making process can be designed to search out the best alternative, and to consider all options no matter how unusual or radical to provide an optimal recommendation. Or decisions can be made to "satisfice", to deliver an acceptable solution which balances the needs of all constituents. This produces a tolerable decision, agreeing a compromise to preserve the political peace.

Many search processes seem constructed to satisfice rather than optimise, to agree the candidate who no one opposes but no one is thrilled about either. Alternatively, at the other extreme, the search committee, under pressure to appoint the individual who will reassure external stake-holders, becomes overly impressed by a "big-hitting" name. Because external recruitment is often triggered by a combination of corporate under-performance and/or the lack of capable internal candidates, the search committee is motivated to respond to short-term pressure from the business media and investors. Credibility is therefore uppermost in its mind so there is a need to bring in a player from a well-established and high-performing firm. Furthermore, because of the background of the search committee members (typically, white, male, middle-class and middle-aged with shared educational and professional career experience) and their associated social networks, short-listed candidates are likely to be drawn from an extraordinarily narrow pool.

- Revisit the role specification to keep focusing on the trade-offs. Refusing, for example, to lower the credibility requirement will constrain your resourcing options. "Compromising" on credibility may identify new candidates, surprising and unexpected individuals who may lack "heavy-duty" reputations but with the outlook, ethics and skills to make a long-lasting impact over time.
- Ensure that your own management database is set up to allow you to interrogate imaginatively the target population of internal candidates, asking "what if" questions which go beyond career resumés to explore underlying experience, skill sets and personal qualities.[18]
- Don't short-list simply on career resumés or impressive-sounding track records with big-name firms. Remember: "a good managerial record is far more a function of what business boat you get into than it is of how effectively you row".[19] You are not recruiting a company; you are recruiting an individual who can "row in your boat". Your short-listing should therefore look beyond currently successful firms to consider companies that may have struggled. The lack of organisational success for professionals and executives in these firms may be less a reflection of their personal capability and more a poor business model they have inherited. And these individuals are more likely to have faced the kind of business adversity that builds the leadership character your organisation requires. Conversely those executives who have operated only in highly successful firms may have coasted comfortably along on the organisation's success momentum but never had to personally tackle the tough challenges of corporate life.

OBTAINING ACCURATE INFORMATION ABOUT THE OPTIONS

An effective decision analysis requires a detailed insight into the relative advantages and disadvantages of the options. If there is an obvious answer, it isn't a decision. Decision-making depends on an informed evaluation of the upside and downside of the options and a trade-off between their benefits and risks.

An intelligent selection strategy should therefore scrutinise in detail the relative pros and cons of each short-listed candidate. It should find out everything there is to know about each candidate. It is extraordinary therefore how little a search committee actually gets to know about the candidates under review for key roles. It knows which companies each executive has worked for and the positions they have held. Beyond that it doesn't know much. It is working on the assumption that association with a high-performing organisation must translate into personal leadership capability. And because of the dynamics of the process it doesn't get to know much more than career history. An external search firm is typically reluctant to organise face-to-face interviews too quickly. There is too much to lose on both sides. For the short-listed candidates they don't want their interest to be known to their current organisations; that might indicate disloyalty and undermine their career options if they are unsuccessful. It would also be a setback to their self-esteem to know whom they were in competition with and whom they had lost out to in the selection contest. The recruiting organisation is also motivated by secrecy. The open disclosure of its intentions may send out the "wrong signals" to the market as well as create political ripples internally.

Given these dynamics it is not surprising therefore that the final decision rests on a relatively brief social encounter: the final interview between the short-listed candidates and the search committee. Even more extraordinary is the nature of the interview. Given what is at stake, a decision with major implications for the organisation's future, the selection interview could be expected to be a gruelling and demanding evaluation of each candidate, their credentials, their business thinking, the nature of their character and the kind of individual they are. It isn't. It has been called the "deferential interview", characterised by "guarded politeness and extensive impression management". Particularly in an external search and selection process, by the time of the final interviews no one wants to ask those difficult and tough questions which might "rock the boat". As one director commented, "we might lose the candidate and have to start again because of a squabble the candidate had with me".[20]

- *Conduct a detailed evaluation of each short-listed candidate.* Don't accept the positive recommendations of the executive search firm. It is your organisation that will suffer if you make the wrong choice. The headhunter can walk away, rationalising the assignment as "one of those things that can happen". You can't.
- *When faced with a polished interview technique, don't over-generalise* to make conclusions of leadership effectiveness. A good interviewee can "talk the walk". Social impact and communication skills are valuable leadership assets, but the interview is only a snapshot into those qualities, and not well suited to identifying other attributes. "The fact is that some people interview well and some people don't. And a person who doesn't interview well may be the best choice for the job" — this from a CEO who has personally hired and promoted about 1000 leaders.[21]
- *Utilise an objective assessment process.* An impressive track record is a reflection of the past, and a flattering version of the past; the issue is your organisation's future. Don't allow association with another successful firm to sway your judgement about candidate effectiveness. Minimise risk by incorporating data from robust assessment methods, methods which look at the individual as an individual, not as a set of accomplishments on a career resumé, which may be more a reflection of good fortune or others' efforts. Dig deep to get to know the real person, their fundamental talents and the nature of their leadership character.
- Although intensive interviewing is important, *don't over-play the "hoops and loops" strategy*, that selection tactic in which prospective recruits must meet 10 or 15 of your organisation's senior people before a decision can be made. This is often a way of diffusing responsibility for selection decision-making. (Here no one is to blame if the appointment doesn't work out.) More importantly, it typically results in compromise candidates.
- Develop a systematic process to *weigh up the pros and cons* of each short-listed candidate. No candidate will be perfect. If you used the Four C framework to prepare the role specification, review each candidate against these criteria. Decide in advance what you will and won't compromise on and don't shift your views. If no candidate meets your criteria, don't select the "least worst option".

AN ACTION PLAN TO MAKE THE DECISION WORK

The appointment decision is important. It is also important to manage the post-appointment process to help the successful candidate get up to speed as quickly as possible. This is especially important for external candidates who need to get to grips quickly with the organisation.

Key actions:

- Ensure the appointed individual *understands the responsibilities and relationships of the role*. Of course, accountabilities should have been negotiated as part of the initial selection process, but real life can be different from formal role descriptions and reporting lines on paper. How are day-to-day working relationships going to work? Where is the real balance of power? Does, for example, the chairperson expect to keep a close hand on the "tiller" or are they more hands off? Rather than allow initial assumptions (the assumptions the individual has of the organisation, and the organisation has of the individual) to continue, force the issue to work assumptions into explicit accountabilities and clear expectations.
- *Plan a thorough induction programme.* Relationships need to be established with executives, individuals who may have been in the running for the job but weren't successful, those whose loyalties and affinities may linger with the previous role-holder. External candidates may need to be guided through these sensitivities, but don't assume that internal appointments appreciate the complexities of the political dynamic.
- *Provide an infrastructure of support.* Put in place the resource to make the selection decision work. Often development seems to stop on appointment. The successful candidate is viewed as perfectly equipped to tackle the challenges of the role. In fact the development need is probably at its greatest at this point. Draw on a range of development interventions, especially coaching and mentoring, to help the appointee get up to speed and navigate the hazards of the first few months in the role.

External recruitment, particularly at the most senior levels, is often seen as the safer option. After all it broadens its scope beyond the "narrow" pool of internal talent to include executives from other organisations. External candidates don't come with baggage of past involvement in organisational failings or of political battles and adversaries. But they do come with baggage; the problem is that you don't know what the baggage is. Paradoxically, external resourcing can be the riskier strategy and, given the nature of the initial search, the way short-listing operates, the secrecy of the process, the role of a small number of players, and the lack of meaningful data, external search can be a leap into the unknown.

SELECTING AND WORKING WITH AN EXTERNAL SEARCH SELECTION PARTNER

1   *What is the breadth and depth of the consultancy base?*

Do you need to work with one of the major global players with international reach, or will a specialist boutique, focusing on a specific sector or professional group, best suit your requirements? Boutique firms, specialising by industry, will be quicker to generate a short-list of credible candidates, but may be fishing in a narrow pool, unimaginative about potential players from other sectors, and more likely to have worked recently (or will in future) for your competitors.

What is its consultancy profile? Is it drawn from a narrow group with similar backgrounds, connected through previous educational and business connections to "the club", or does it have a range of practical business and leadership experience with contacts across diverse sectors? How well connected are the search consultants with talent from, for example, different social and ethnic backgrounds?

2   *Where does its current loyalties lie?*
Which searches and appointments for
which firms has it conducted recently; were
they major customers, suppliers and
competitors of your organisation? How
might this affect their commitment to your
requirements? Executive search firms will
rightly be reluctant to disclose other client
assignments; however, it is a major risk for
your organisation to brief a search firm that
may well have highly developed
relationships with key stake-holders of your
company. After all they will in effect be
operating as a "brand manager" for your
organisation, approaching executives in the
marketplace to sell your proposition. Press
this issue if you are serious about building a
long-term relationship.

Is it working across different divisions and
business units within your organisation
under separate contracts? Do these need to
be reviewed and re-negotiated? Does it
possess an in-house consulting arm
providing, for example, executive coaching
or leadership audit services? Which
organisations is it currently working with in
this area? What additional conflicts of
interest might this create?

Remember that ultimately the loyalties of
executive search firms lie with their own
financial interests, not with your organisation.

3   *Does this firm possess genuine research
capability?*
How extensive is its database? Where does
it specialise, by sector, by level, by
professional area? Is this firm able to access
accurate intelligence about market trends,
the available supply and demand of specific
capabilities and expertise and know the
associated remuneration? How far-ranging
is its database? Is it restricted to the FTSE
500 or is it picking up talent from other
firms? To use a football analogy, is it
watching only Premiership football matches
or is it scouting for talent in the Nationwide
Conference?

How well does it know the sector in
which you operate? How insightful is it
about current trends and emerging
developments and the implications for ease
or difficulty of resourcing?

4   *What is its code of professional ethics?*
How does this differentiate the firm from
accepted industry conventions? What will it
do/won't do? What guarantees are there of
delivery; what is the firm's policy on
poaching candidates it has placed or
poaching other managers from your
organisation, suppliers and contractors?

5   *What assessment methods does it use?*
What is the first filter? A reliance on word-
of-mouth recommendation and "tittle-
tattle" across the industry? Prominence
through networking and involvement in
high-profile events? How does it access
talented individuals who keep a low
profile?[22] What process is used to filter the
first cut of possible candidates to the
short-list? Does it rely primarily on
interviews or does it have access to a
range of objective measures of cognitive
ability, personality and motivational
instruments to support its evaluations?
Which methods are used?

What referencing and background checks
does it utilise? How transparent and
defensible are they?

6   *How does it expect to be paid?*
Typically this is a percentage, 20–50 per
cent of the candidate's remuneration for
the first year, usually on a contingent basis,
no placement, no fee. The problem here is
that there is little link between the difficulty
and duration of the assignment and the
final fee. In addition there is a risk that
search firms will push for the placement of
the candidate with the highest
compensation rather than the most suitable
candidate. A flat fee agreed on the basis of
the complexity of the assignment may be a
better approach.

Robust assessment and the appointments process

Any selection decision has its risks, and the dice seem loaded to ensure that external recruitment contains greater risk. Apart from the companies and jobs which external candidates have worked for and held, relatively little is known about them. Generalising from a candidate's past association with successful firms to conclude they must be effective in your organisation is a dangerous assumption. Increasingly organisations are looking to minimise risks through the utilisation of more robust assessments of candidate suitability, evaluations that go beyond career history and track record to find out about the person behind the career resumé. Is this a credible career resumé, a pattern of outstanding business accomplishment and outcomes, a reflection of good fortune, of being in the right place at the right time, and benefiting from the achievements of talented work colleagues? Or, is it indicative of an individual with the attributes and qualities, the character and capability, to rise to the future challenges your organisation is facing?

There are three categories of assessment method:[23]

- Self-report, asking people about themselves via interviews or self-assessment questionnaires
- Observational data, based on what other people think about the individual, for example references, 360° feedback
- Test data, evaluating the individual through performance at "simulations" of work activity, for example aptitude tests, assessment centres.

We will review in detail the pros and cons of different assessment options in Chapter 8. However, in the context of the appointments process, and certainly at senior levels, most organisations rely on a mix of *references* and self-report via an *interview* to decide from the short-listed candidates.

REFERENCES

References come in a variety of forms, from open-ended (where referees simply provide free-form text), semi-structured (commenting on a few themes) to ratings of specific work behaviours (evaluation of, for example, absenteeism, punctuality). "References as they are typically used, are often a complete waste of time."[24] The difficulties are well known: who the referee is (usually nominated by the candidate with the bias this involves); social conventions of what a reference should and shouldn't look like (typically, a positive spin which either focuses on admirable qualities, ignoring any criticisms, or utilising an impenetrable code to highlight any shortcomings); and the legal dimension (the reluctance to provide a fully frank description of the individual because of the serious threat of legal claims if it results in the rejection of a candidate). As such it is highly unlikely that references will provide a meaningful and accurate description of candidates that would help discriminate across individuals and inform the selection process. Should references then be abandoned? No, quite the opposite. Background checks and a detailed investigation of candidate education, career history and achievements are becoming critical. Take nothing for granted. The solution probably relies on a greater willingness to talk directly with the candidate's organisation and with former colleagues. Larry Bossidy, ex-CEO of Allied Signal,[25] personally checked references of external candidates, calling into question two or three contacts about the individual. Direct communication, rather than reference by correspondence, also creates greater honesty and candour. This of course is a difficult tactic in the search/selection process led by the headhunter where the "rules of the game" constrain this kind of openness and transparency — another reason perhaps why a reliance on external search/selection firms is unwise.[26] "The bottom line is that you have to be persistent in checking references and getting to the heart of the matter."[27]

SELECTION INTERVIEWING: IDENTIFYING CHARACTER

Despite a mountain of evidence that the traditional job interview is the one of the least valid ways to select,[28] it is here to stay. No organisation will make an appointment without a face-to-face encounter, certainly at senior levels. The issue then is how to improve the interview process to ensure it goes beyond the typical exercise in social pleasantries and impression management. There is no shortage of interview methodologies — behavioural, competency, situational — to establish greater consistency and objectivity, and these should be utilised to develop a specific protocol for your organisation. Our focus here is around the theme of character.

Here it is important to look beyond words to actions. "I was, am a strong believer that one of the most satisfying things in life is to create a highly moral and ethical environment in which every individual is allowed and encouraged to realise God-given potential." This from Kenneth Lay, chairman of Enron![29] The facility to *talk about* moral purpose and ethics is different from *operating* with character in the face of business adversity and commercial ambiguity. William Pollard, CEO of ServiceMaster, believes in the importance of understanding each candidate's philosophy of life; "we decided to get at it by simply asking this question of every candidate: how do you determine whether something is right or wrong?"[30] This simple question he discovered yielded important insights into how those aspiring to leadership thought about themselves and the moral dilemmas they would face as future business leaders. Figure 5.4 outlines a summary protocol to indicate how an interview exploring leadership character might be explored and conducted.

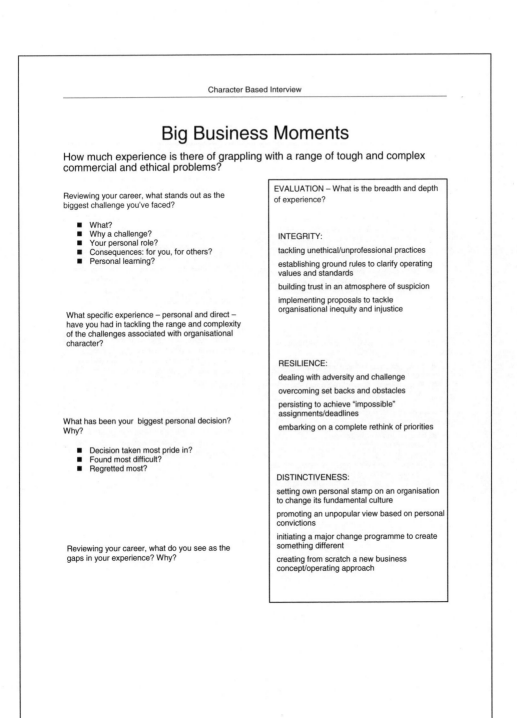

Character Based Interview

Big Business Moments

How much experience is there of grappling with a range of tough and complex commercial and ethical problems?

Reviewing your career, what stands out as the biggest challenge you've faced?

- What?
- Why a challenge?
- Your personal role?
- Consequences: for you, for others?
- Personal learning?

What specific experience – personal and direct – have you had in tackling the range and complexity of the challenges associated with organisational character?

What has been your biggest personal decision? Why?

- Decision taken most pride in?
- Found most difficult?
- Regretted most?

Reviewing your career, what do you see as the gaps in your experience? Why?

EVALUATION – What is the breadth and depth of experience?

INTEGRITY:

tackling unethical/unprofessional practices

establishing ground rules to clarify operating values and standards

building trust in an atmosphere of suspicion

implementing proposals to tackle organisational inequity and injustice

RESILIENCE:

dealing with adversity and challenge

overcoming set backs and obstacles

persisting to achieve "impossible" assignments/deadlines

embarking on a complete rethink of priorities

DISTINCTIVENESS:

setting own personal stamp on an organisation to change its fundamental culture

promoting an unpopular view based on personal convictions

initiating a major change programme to create something different

creating from scratch a new business concept/operating approach

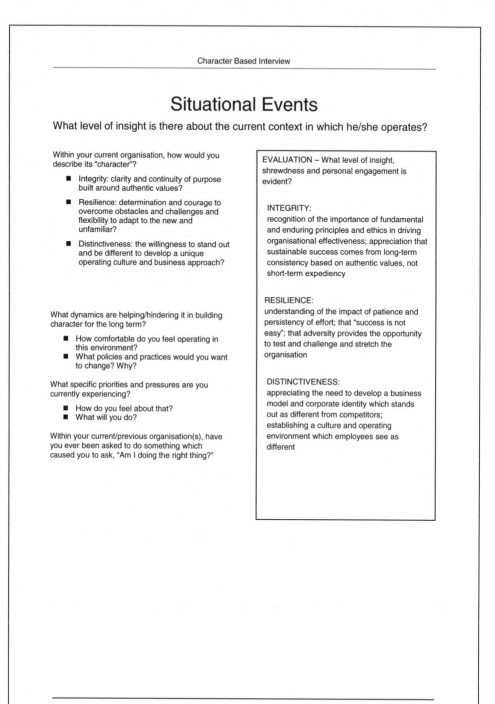

Character Based Interview

Situational Events

What level of insight is there about the current context in which he/she operates?

Within your current organisation, how would you describe its "character"?

- Integrity: clarity and continuity of purpose built around authentic values?

- Resilience: determination and courage to overcome obstacles and challenges and flexibility to adapt to the new and unfamiliar?

- Distinctiveness: the willingness to stand out and be different to develop a unique operating culture and business approach?

What dynamics are helping/hindering it in building character for the long term?

- How comfortable do you feel operating in this environment?
- What policies and practices would you want to change? Why?

What specific priorities and pressures are you currently experiencing?

- How do you feel about that?
- What will you do?

Within your current/previous organisation(s), have you ever been asked to do something which caused you to ask, "Am I doing the right thing?"

EVALUATION – What level of insight, shrewdness and personal engagement is evident?

INTEGRITY:
recognition of the importance of fundamental and enduring principles and ethics in driving organisational effectiveness; appreciation that sustainable success comes from long-term consistency based on authentic values, not short-term expediency

RESILIENCE:
understanding of the impact of patience and persistency of effort; that "success is not easy"; that adversity provides the opportunity to test and challenge and stretch the organisation

DISTINCTIVENESS:
appreciating the need to develop a business model and corporate identity which stands out as different from competitors; establishing a culture and operating environment which employees see as different

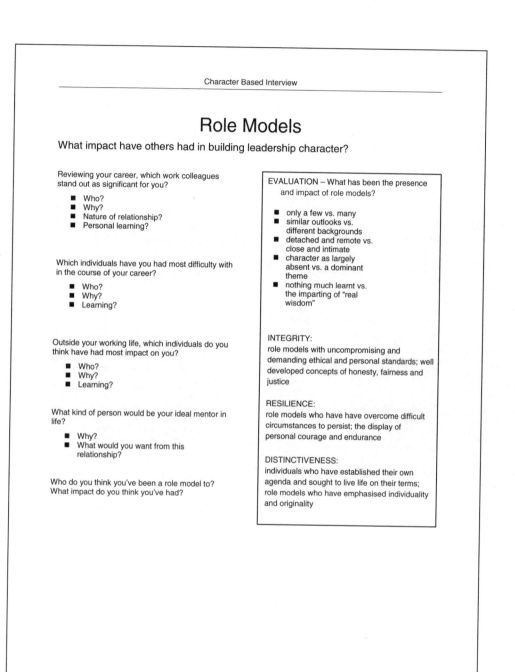

Character Based Interview

Role Models

What impact have others had in building leadership character?

Reviewing your career, which work colleagues stand out as significant for you?

- Who?
- Why?
- Nature of relationship?
- Personal learning?

Which individuals have you had most difficulty with in the course of your career?

- Who?
- Why?
- Learning?

Outside your working life, which individuals do you think have had most impact on you?

- Who?
- Why?
- Learning?

What kind of person would be your ideal mentor in life?

- Why?
- What would you want from this relationship?

Who do you think you've been a role model to? What impact do you think you've had?

EVALUATION – What has been the presence and impact of role models?

- only a few vs. many
- similar outlooks vs. different backgrounds
- detached and remote vs. close and intimate
- character as largely absent vs. a dominant theme
- nothing much learnt vs. the imparting of "real wisdom"

INTEGRITY:
role models with uncompromising and demanding ethical and personal standards; well developed concepts of honesty, fairness and justice

RESILIENCE:
role models who have have overcome difficult circumstances to persist; the display of personal courage and endurance

DISTINCTIVENESS:
individuals who have established their own agenda and sought to live life on their terms; role models who have emphasised individuality and originality

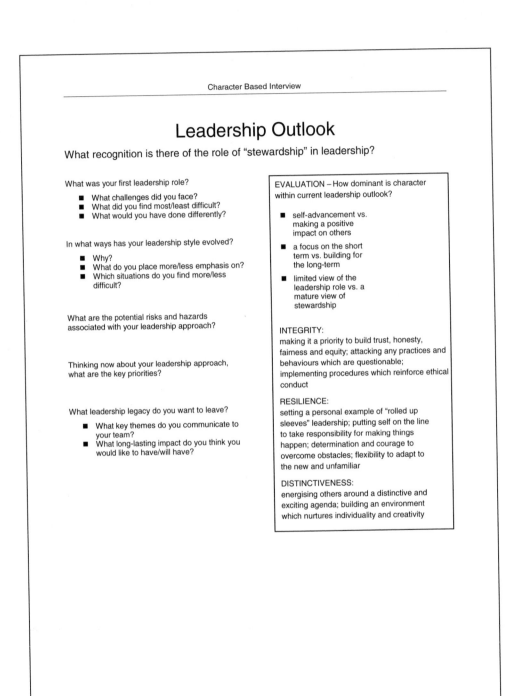

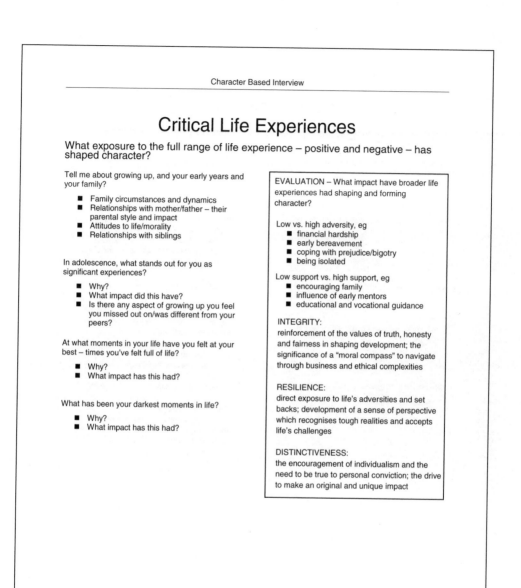

Character Based Interview

Critical Life Experiences

What exposure to the full range of life experience – positive and negative – has shaped character?

Tell me about growing up, and your early years and your family?

- Family circumstances and dynamics
- Relationships with mother/father – their parental style and impact
- Attitudes to life/morality
- Relationships with siblings

In adolescence, what stands out for you as significant experiences?

- Why?
- What impact did this have?
- Is there any aspect of growing up you feel you missed out on/was different from your peers?

At what moments in your life have you felt at your best – times you've felt full of life?

- Why?
- What impact has this had?

What has been your darkest moments in life?

- Why?
- What impact has this had?

EVALUATION – What impact have broader life experiences had shaping and forming character?

Low vs. high adversity, eg
- financial hardship
- early bereavement
- coping with prejudice/bigotry
- being isolated

Low support vs. high support, eg
- encouraging family
- influence of early mentors
- educational and vocational guidance

INTEGRITY:
reinforcement of the values of truth, honesty and fairness in shaping development; the significance of a "moral compass" to navigate through business and ethical complexities

RESILIENCE:
direct exposure to life's adversities and set backs; development of a sense of perspective which recognises tough realities and accepts life's challenges

DISTINCTIVENESS:
the encouragement of individualism and the need to be true to personal conviction; the drive to make an original and unique impact

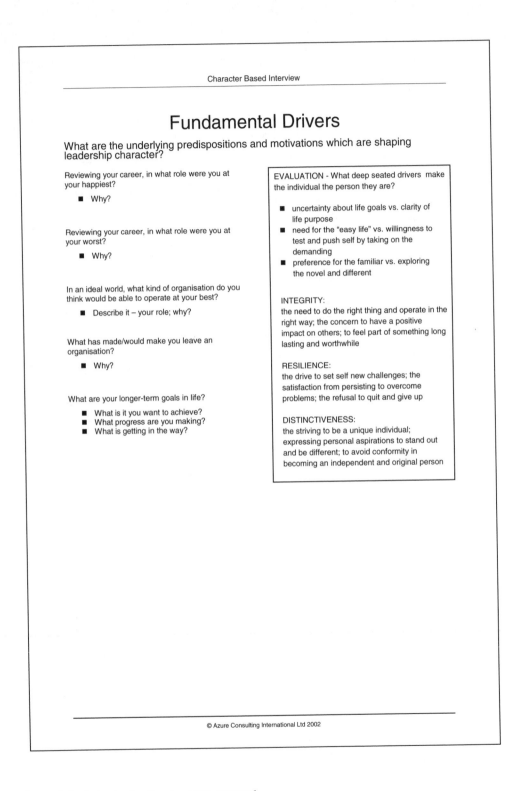

Figure 5.4   Interviewing for character: protocol

Next steps

How is the current appointments process "working"?

- What level of activity was there over the last 12 months? What metrics are in place: speed, cost, impact and so on, to indicate the efficiency and effectiveness of the current appointments process?
- What formal policies and informal practices are in place? How are they helping or hindering the organisation make good selection decisions?
- Where in the current appointments process are the obvious hold-ups, blockages and barriers?

What are the anticipated priorities?

- Which roles can be easily be anticipated to require attention over the next few months? What options need to be considered now to prepare for this vacancy?
  - Straightforward replacement from within?
  - Realignment of the role to shift the emphasis?
  - Fundamental reconfiguration to update accountabilities and change reporting lines and relationships?
- How are emerging business plans, plans with a direct impact on structures, roles and the redeployment of employees, professionals and executives connected to resourcing activity? How are plans from different business units coordinated to identify overall organisational priorities?
- What analysis needs to be conducted to highlight "critical" roles, positions requiring strategic resourcing rather than tactical filling?

What supporting infrastructure needs to be in place to speed the appointments process?

- How well are accountabilities mapped out for managing the appointments: who has discretion to initiate the process; who for first-round recruitment and selection; who for final decision-making; what is the relationship between the recruiting manager and human resources?
- Is there a high-level template for agreeing role specifications across different operating units and work areas?
- What policies and practices exist for advertising internally; how is the first-round short-listing of candidates informed by professionals and executives identified in succession and talent reviews?
- How accessible is data about internal candidates? How easy is it to interrogate your database to identify short-lists of candidates against different permutations of criteria: experience, expertise, capability and so on?
- What assessment methods need to be deployed to improve the rigour of selection decisions? How should the interview process be tightened to provide a more robust evaluation of candidate capability and character?
- What relationships exist with the range of external advisors and providers? What contracts are currently in place; which need to be reviewed and renegotiated?
- What induction processes are in place to get appointees "up to speed" quickly?

How should CEO succession be managed?

- What process is in place for planning and managing CEO succession? Who has overall accountability? How well are these responsibilities being discharged? How much time and effort is this activity receiving?
- Given your current business position, what key themes will guide the selection of the CEO successor? An individual outside the current established order who can attack complacency, refocus the management structure and revitalise organisational culture? Or someone with an in-depth understanding of the organisation and how it operates, who will work with the current management team? An individual with the mind-set to keep the current strategy on course? Or someone who will undertake a major review to point the organisation in a new direction?
- Which individuals within the internal succession pool can best meet this requirement? What needs to be done now to begin preparing these individuals for the possibility of CEO succession?
- Do we need to accept that the next CEO will come from outside? What are the likely options? What measures should be undertaken to open up new options and pursue alternatives?

Notes

1. Robyn Brown of Stanton Chase in Australia makes the point that we need to move away from the label of succession to think of proactive resourcing and development as "success management".
2. J. Collins and J. Porras, *Built to Last*, 1993.
3. The Kingsmill report, "Accounting For People", November 2003, has highlighted the importance of measuring and reporting on organisational effectiveness in human capital management. We see the various metrics outlined in this book as establishing greater discipline in summarising succession management activity and impact to inform stake-holders of the organisation's health.
4. Malcolm Gladwell, *The Tipping Point*, 2000.
5. This account should be read in full in *The New New Economy*, T. McEachen and C. O'Brien, 2002.
6. An IBM insider comment at the time of the appointment of Lou Gerstner quoted in Kets de Vries, *Leaders, Fools and Imposters*, 1993.
7. A Booz Allen Hamilton survey notes that, while outsiders excel in the initial phase of their tenure, by the second half the organisation experiences a slump in performance. It looks like outsiders have an initial phase which stimulates energy and creates a certain "feel-good" factor which they find difficult to sustain. "Serial" CEOs under-perform first-timers, both outsiders and insiders.
8. This is an observation made in Jim Collins's analysis of the leadership of those companies that didn't make the transition to greatness (*Good to Great*, 2001). It is also a theme in Ket de Vries' assessment of the trauma of leadership succession (*Leaders, Fools and Imposters*, 1993).
9. Quoted from *I'd Like the World to Buy a Coke: The Life and Leadership of Roberto Goizueta*, David Greising, 1997. (Coca-Cola's succession problems were no doubt intensified by Goizueta's illness.)
10. "Wall Street Journal", 30 September 1996. Ben & Jerry's has now been acquired by Unilever.
11. J. Collins, *Good to Great*, 2001.
12. Stephen Bartholomeusz, "The Age", 13 November 2003.
13. R. Khurana, *In Search of the Corporate Savior*, 2002.
14. James Bagnall, "The Ottawa Citizen", 7 November 2002.
15. *Sunday Times*, 18 January 2004.
16. Rakesh Khurana, *In Search of the Corporate Savior*, 2002; a detailed and comprehensive analysis of how the search and selection decision-making process operates in reality.
17. "Taking Charge: What Makes CEO Succession Work", Judge Institute of Management Studies report for Saxton Bampfyde International, 1996.
18. Database management to support succession management will be explored in Chapter 9. The point

here is to ensure that your own internal succession intelligence is insightful in locating imaginative candidates from within. Indeed an important trend we identified in our research is the move by an increasing number of organisations to deploy in-house the kind of research and database management capability which traditionally external search firms have utilised.

19. James O'Loughlin, *The Real Warren Buffett*, 2003.
20. *In Search of the Corporate Savior*, 2002.
21. Larry Bossidy, "The Job No CEO Should Delegate", *Harvard Business Review*, 2001.
22. Hamish Davidson, Chairman of Veredus Executive Resourcing (October 2003) identifies the secrets of being headhunted. "To be noticed you need to network — and network with the right people...Get yourself noticed through raising your profile. Try and get asked to speak at conferences." This is short-listing by connection and credibility, no doubt important "rules of the game". But a more imaginative resourcing strategy might seek out those individuals off the "radar screen", professionals and executives who are motivated to get on and do a good job rather than talk to others about the good job they are doing.
23. A. Furnham, *The Incompetent Manager*, 2003.
24. A. Furnham, *The Incompetent Manager*, 2003.
25. Larry Bossidy also utilises 360° feedback reviews for internal candidates to gain a better insight from peers and subordinates of the strengths and limitations of candidates.
26. Al Dunlap, for example, managed to slip through the checks of two prestigious headhunter firms.
27. L. Bossidy and R. Charan, *Execution*, 2002.
28. A. Furnham, *The Incompetent Manager*, 2003.
29. Quoted from Mihaly Csikszentmihalyi, *Good Business, Leadership, Flow and the Making of Meaning*, 2003.
30. C. Pollard, *The Soul of the Firm*, 1996.

6 Identifying Business Risk: How Resilient is the Organisation?

"The word risk derives from the early Italian, 'riscare', which means to dare. In this sense risk is a choice rather than a fate." Peter Bernstein, *Against the Gods*

"Risk comes from not knowing what you are doing." Warren Buffett

Good selection decisions stem from previous organisational activity in anticipating and planning resourcing opportunities and threats, and reviewing the capability of the current professional and executive population, and proactivity in the development of key individuals.

Conventional succession planning has many limitations as a tool in assessing business risks but it can't be completely ignored. For one thing key stake-holder groups have an expectation of an "organogram", mapping out coverage against the current management structure. But an analysis of succession within existing roles, reporting lines and relationships lacks the insight and flexibility to track key resourcing trends. Alternative formats need to be utilised to be more imaginative in identifying business opportunities and risks, formats which open up a wider debate about the organisation's structure and strategy.

NEW STRUCTURES IDENTIFY SUCCESSION EXPOSURE

The Board has concluded its weekly meeting. The CEO and her key lieutenants remain in the room after most of the other directors have left.

Operations Director: "Are things as bad as they look?"

Finance Director: "They are not good, that's for sure."

CEO: "I think the fundamentals are fine. The basic strategy is strong. Our product range is competitive. But I agree that we're not pulling our weight out there in the market."

Operations Director: "My instinct is to review how we're organised. We need to shift the relationship between Head Office and the businesses. Right now the guys out there keep looking to the centre to sort out the problems when they should be taking the lead to push on."

CEO: "I agree. This structure is holding us back. We need to draft some new accountabilities."

A week later:

Operations Director: "We've got a problem here. Looking at this new structure who do we have to stand up and fill these roles?"

Personnel Director: "We've created big roles but we don't have the people to fill them."

CEO: "Let's keep the lid on this one until I sound out the headhunters and explore some options."

Challenges and dilemmas

If the appointments process is the moment of organisational truth, then business risk assessment increases the chance of "corporate honesty". It is no accident that a dynamic in the transition for those organisations that went from "good to great" was a "brutality with the facts".[1] Those organisations that made the breakthrough from good to greatness, rather than congratulate themselves on their current performance, kept asking the difficult questions, raising the unpopular issues, and demanding uncomfortable answers. As a battle-ground of succession management, business risk assessment should be the dialogue for your organisation to be "brutal with the facts" about its resourcing capability. It should ask not only how well placed you are to protect your current position, but also how well equipped you are to advance into new business territory. A casual review of a "succession plan" hastily compiled to comply with a regulatory requirement is unlikely to provide the answers. Business risk assessment represents that set of activities which connects talent management — the identification and development of next-generation professionals and leaders — with the appointments process. The short-listing of capable candidates to open up selection options does not arise by accident. Shrewd resourcing decisions and the ongoing "ratcheting up" of leadership capability stems from a clear-headed evaluation of the business opportunities and risks which face the organisation.

At best, business risk assessment is the management tool that provides the critical scrutiny to identify potential vulnerabilities from the current and emerging challenges facing your organisation. In a world in which "only the paranoid survive",[2] business risk assessment is the early warning system that highlights those problems which might constrain or threaten your organisation. The aim is to "avoid problems not have to solve them". It is also the mechanism to review business options and how the organisation should organise itself based on a frank assessment of professional and leadership capability. Is the current structure supporting your strategy? Which roles within the structure are critical and at the heart of our business game plan? Are the incumbents within these roles maximising their contribution or failing to exploit the full potential of the role? Do you have back-up coverage in the event of the loss of the current role-holder? What is the breadth and depth of professional and leadership talent available to provide continuity for the future?

Competing on this battle-ground requires more than the construction of an organisational chart of coverage and exposure. It also requires the following:

- A mechanism to link the business planning function with resourcing priorities. Business proactivity asks: do we have the capability to excel against our ambitious business goals? Business paranoia asks: where might we be vulnerable to our competitors? The Human Resources function needs to help provide these answers; increasingly the risk and audit functions, faced with greater pressure from regulatory bodies to map out a clear line of accountabilities from CEO downwards, are also involved in shaping this discussion.
- Agreeing a format to summarise information about roles and individuals to highlight organisational risks and vulnerabilities. The challenge is to find a framework and process that has sufficient flexibility to accommodate changes in structure with the detail to pinpoint specific issues that need to be resolved. This is a big challenge. The remuneration committee has the expectation of a classic chart mapping out succession coverage. But everyone else acknowledges this is a succession fairy tale, telling a story

that no one quite really believes. What alternative formats are needed to provide a more realistic assessment of resourcing opportunities and risks?

- Ensuring that the exercise goes beyond an annual chore of form filling and one-off review to become an ongoing theme on the management agenda. The immediate challenge is top-level management commitment and time. In fact, the underlying and real challenge is an understanding and acceptance of the role of leadership. Is leadership largely about short-term delivery to meet this quarter's targets or does it require a recognition of longer-term stewardship?

- Balancing consistency of organisational approach to allow meaningful comparisons to be made across different business and functional areas while avoiding the corporate strait jacket. Often specific work units cannot relate to the corporate "succession cycle", seeing it as out of synch and touch with their business priorities and lacking relevance to the challenges of their hard-pressed managers. The challenge is to facilitate a trade-off between corporate requirements, providing the top team with a high-level summary of business information while supporting different organisational units in tackling the acute resourcing problems they face in retention and recruitment.

SUCCESSION INTELLIGENCE

Monday morning and it is the first day at the office for two recruits. One, the new Finance Director, is spending the morning with two of her most senior team. She pulls down the current management accounts and her expert eye scans through the figures, taking in the pattern to review trends and spot any anomalies. Occasionally she scribbles down some notes, but for the most part she is getting to grips with the material easily. She knows that her first Board meeting is on Friday and it is important that she provides an authoritative grasp of the company's financial position. So every now and again she one of her colleagues for more detailed analysis —by region, by product — to interrogate the data and highlight specific issues. After four hours she congratulates her colleagues on their good work, impressed with the speed and efficiency with which they've worked. Although there are a couple of issues to be checked and double-checked, she feels confident she is on top of the organisation's financial status. Overall, things look fine but there are a couple of worrying indicators she wants to explore with the Operations Director in advance of Friday's debrief.

Further down the executive suite, the other new recruit, the HR Director, is having a bad morning. He knows that on Friday afternoon there is a planned update to the Organisation and Management Review. Although there is no great pressure — after all he has just joined — he still wants to make strong impression to establish his credibility. By Monday afternoon, however, he is worried. "The trouble is there is no data," he says to his PA. Unlike his new counterpart in Finance with access to a standard set of print-outs, following agreed conventions and all familiar to the Board, the HR Director knows he has nothing to work with. There is no financial equivalent of the "succession plan". Instead his PA has pulled out a few organisational charts dated from last year. Glancing at it he sees that the structure is hopelessly out of date and that many of the candidates named as potential successors have either left or been moved sideways. "Could we pull down the data for the top 100 execs?" he asks. She disappears to return 30 minutes later with two colleagues, holding armfuls of folders. "This is mainly CV stuff, but I do know that the execs went through an individual assessment exercise last year with an external consultancy. The trouble is I don't know where the reports ended up."

The HR Director knows he will "wing" it on Friday. He also knows that unlike the Finance Director he won't have to face the critical scrutiny of the Board. He won't have to provide an update against target (there are no targets); he knows he won't face a demand for immediate action. He also knows deep down that the Board doesn't really care.

Working backwards: metrics of business risk assessment

There are three overall themes (see Figure 6.1) which need to be tracked in evaluating the business risks associated with the leadership and professional capability of the organisation.

Coverage measures are the classic metrics of succession management. Applied across the entire organisational structure they are crude and unstable indices, more likely to obscure rather than illuminate any meaningful organisational reality. Nonetheless, for *critical* roles, those roles that are fundamental to the organisation's purpose, *"contingency coverage"* highlights immediate organisational back-up. What percentage of critical roles have at least one back-up successor, a nominated individual who could step into the breach in the event of a role-holder being hit by the proverbial bus? If, for example, your CEO or Finance Director falls seriously ill, is there a credible internal player who could assume their responsibilities, at least temporarily, and minimise external concerns about the organisation's future? Contingency coverage, apart from summarising likely business disruption, also provides a good insight into business confidence. Low contingency coverage is a worrying sign that the current leadership is dissatisfied with the capability of its direct reports, a perception that even as short-term stand-ins they would be unable to provide adequate leadership.

"Bench-strength" coverage is an analysis not so much of "succession emergency", but more an indication of the strength of the leadership pipeline at senior levels. What percentage of critical roles have medium-term coverage, at least two nominated successors,

Coverage	Resilience	Capability
Contingency % of critical roles with "back up coverage" ● minimising business disruption	**Safety** % of nominated successors to critical roles as a % of the available target population ● breadth and depth of leadership capability	**Excellence** % of target population showing exceptional capability ● depth provides "cutting-edge" business leadership
Bench-strength % of critical roles with medium term coverage ● ensuring continuity of business purpose	**Diversity** % of the target population capable of providing: a robust response to adversity; responsiveness to market opportunities; the wilingness to rethink the future ● flexibility to meet business challenges	**Constraint Factor** % of target population mediocre or worse ● holding back organisational progress

Figure 6.1   Metrics of business risk assessment

who could with proactive development be serious succession candidates within, say, 18–24 months? The "bench-strength" index is a summary of business continuity, indicating the organisation's capacity to maintain and renew its strategic momentum. Low bench strength highlights a significant risk, a statement that in all probability the future of the business will not come from within. Alternatively it is a reflection of "succession conflict", a fundamental difference between the Board and its view of what is required and the organisation's emerging talent. Here there is a fundamental organisational misalignment, manifest in the difficulty to agree successors. With greater consistency about leadership requirements and maturity of discussion, apparent gaps in bench strength can sometimes be resolved.

Resilience is a broader concept, measuring those business risks associated either with dependency on a small number of individuals, or a reliance on "one-dimensional" leadership, namely, leadership that is good at one thing but lacking the flexibility to adapt to shifting business circumstances. "*Safety*" measures provide an index of leadership breadth within the succession population. Is the group of nominated successors restricted to a handful of the executive population or is succession coverage spread across a substantial number of the available succession pool? What percentage of the "available" population is seen as providing succession coverage for critical roles? If, out of a target population of 200 executives, only ten individuals (5 per cent) are seen as providing succession coverage for the 35 roles at the next organisational level, then this is not safety but dependency on a few individuals.

Diversity ratios are informative in evaluating how well your organisation is "future proofing" itself. Diversity is an analysis of the variation of organisational capability, expertise and leadership style within the professional and executive population. If all emerging successors have exactly the same experience and outlook as the current leadership group your organisation is running a major risk, as it is assuming that the future will be the same as the present.

This throws up yet another succession dilemma. Do current leaders accept that their successors may, and in all likelihood should, be different from them? Psychologically this is a difficult challenge. Human nature is such that like attracts like. The individuals we value and want to continue our legacy should resemble us in our background and approach. But organisational survival and success, stripped down to its basics, is a Darwinian survival of the fittest, a competition for customers based on the capability to access resources more efficiently than rivals. "If a species is diverse it can survive and prosper. If a species is homogeneous it is vulnerable."[3] "Evolutionary progress" for the long term is about diversity, about variation in the "gene pool" which opens up new options to compete. Some of these options will fall by the wayside, unable to find a niche in which they can thrive. Other options will thrive and provide the basis for different evolutionary forms, better adapted to new environmental conditions. In organisational terms, diversity is the source of renewal and change. But in the short term, at least, it comes at a price. While its opposite, uniformity, makes for an easy life, diversity can be uncomfortable, raising the prospect of the conflict of different and opposing views. For the organisation where the strategic outlook is "Play the Same Game", succession resilience comes through a similarity of operating approach, a shared mind-set of exactly what is required to compete for the future, that is, more of the past. Here the risk is that the organisation's business environment shifts but the corporate gene pool is so narrow that it cannot adapt to these changes. "Like breeds like" and the organisation becomes populated with "clones", executives who think and behave the same as each other, emulating the operating style of the top team.

The final category of measures in tracking and evaluating the impact of activity in business risk assessment is *capability*. Reviewing the target population, what percentage of individuals are seen as excellent, as outstandingly successful appointments you would make again without a moment's hesitation? These are the individuals who are exceeding the requirements of the role, coping easily with current demands and pushing ahead to take on new challenges. This will be a critical index for those organisations operating, for example, at the leading edge of scientific and technical innovation, but important for almost any company looking for that small gain which will tilt the balance in its competitive favour. Threshold competency — that is, a leadership population which is OK — will not be enough. It is outstanding capability to form "cutting-edge" leadership and professional expertise which will make the difference. This doesn't imply that you need exceptional individuals in every role at every level; that is a highly expensive resourcing strategy. But you do need "enough" excellence in the right place at the right time to make a difference. Indeed this might be the smartest resourcing strategy of all: knowing which roles will provide the greatest leverage of all and ensuring they are filled with the organisation's best talent. Too often an organisation's best talent is squandered in deploying exceptional individuals on the wrong kinds of organisational problems (attempting to rescue a business unit in terminal decline or salvaging a misguided IT programme which has become a sunk cost rather than a future investment), rather than directing them towards those organisational challenges where talent can make a genuine difference.

If the percentage of professionals and executives displaying excellence, the proportion of the population operating at the "top end", is a key metric of resourcing strength, then the converse, the percentage of individuals at the "bottom end", those who are mediocre or worse, highlights the *"constraint factor"*. These are the individuals whose capability and/or motivation is questionable but with the power to hold the organisation back from making rapid progress. It is this group of managers who are not only the weak link in driving initiatives to retain and develop talent but are the blockages to the "pipeline" of your organisation's emerging leadership. What may be even more illuminating is the "ratio of excellence to constraint factor" for the target population. As a massive generalisation, one based on intuition rather than any empirical research, I would suggest that where the proportion of excellence to constraint factor is less than 3:1 (that is, where there are fewer than three excellent individuals to one constraint factor individual), the corporate equivalent of Gresham's Law ("bad money drives out good money") starts to apply. Excellent leadership, frustrated by the efforts of poor and mediocre management, leaves. Analysing leadership audit data around the "average" may therefore distort the leadership profile.

Classic succession planning

ORGANISATIONAL CHARTING

In traditional succession planning (see Figure 6.2), documentation is circulated to senior executives for their initial evaluation. As well as overviewing general themes within their sphere of organisational responsibility, successors (immediate back-up and medium term) are nominated against key roles. Additional follow-up interviews with the HR function and/or external consultants may also be conducted. This material is then collated to

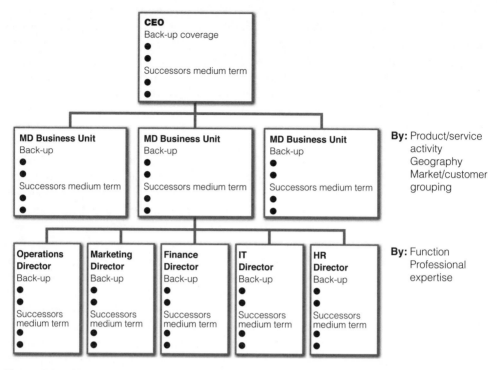

Figure 6.2   Classic format for succession planning

produce an organisational "snapshot" of succession coverage and exposure (see Figure 6.3). This document becomes the focus of a collective review to trigger debate and inform actions. How useful is this approach? The quick answer is "not very". But stake-holder groups have an expectation of the classic succession plan, the depiction of succession coverage within the current management structure. The non-executive Board wants to review a piece of paper which reflects management accountabilities within the organisational structure and to see "names on doors". Increasingly, regulatory agencies, notably in the financial services sector, but becoming more common in other industries as corporate governance initiatives gain momentum, also want sight of the formal succession plan.

MAPPING THE SUCCESSION PICTURE

Rarely, but occasionally, the succession map can be a useful visual summary indicating the "succession flow" at different levels and across different business units to stimulate a dialogue about specific roles and individuals and where action needs to be taken. Figure 6.4 highlights an example succession map indicating the conventional issues.

Exposure

This stands out starkly. There is no back-up replacement and no emerging successor. The debate should focus on: has the role been designed in such a way as to make future resourcing, either succession from within or external recruitment, impossible? Are the size of the role and the configuration of requirements so problematic that no one could be

Business Resource Review

Current and future structure: priorities

1 Overall Evaluation

Does the current structure support the strategic aims of your business unit?

How well does it meet the criteria of:

Customer responsiveness? Low cost and process efficiency?
Sustainability over time?

2 Current Opportunities and Risks

Are you maximising opportunities with other business units? With Head Office?	Gaps: which activities which are not receiving sufficient attention?	Overlaps: which activities have the potential for duplication?

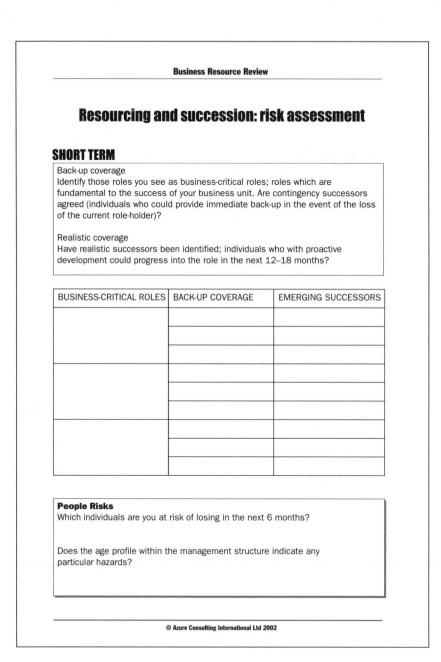

Business Resource Review

Resourcing and succession: risk assessment

SHORT TERM

Back-up coverage
Identify those roles you see as business-critical roles; roles which are fundamental to the success of your business unit. Are contingency successors agreed (individuals who could provide immediate back-up in the event of the loss of the current role-holder)?

Realistic coverage
Have realistic successors been identified; individuals who with proactive development could progress into the role in the next 12–18 months?

BUSINESS-CRITICAL ROLES	BACK-UP COVERAGE	EMERGING SUCCESSORS

People Risks
Which individuals are you at risk of losing in the next 6 months?

Does the age profile within the management structure indicate any particular hazards?

© Azure Consulting International Ltd 2002

Figure 6.3   Compiling a "succession plan"

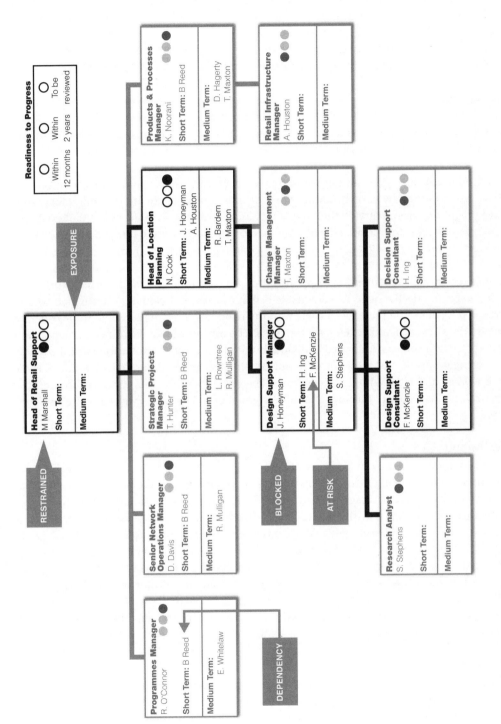

Figure 6.4   Mapping the succession picture

effective in this role? This can arise when the current incumbent has redefined the role around their own personal preferences to reflect their distinctive experience, skills and leadership priorities. If so, can this role and its positioning alongside other roles within the organisation be redefined to open up new resourcing options? Or have we been unimaginative in identifying potential successors? Do we need to look beyond the obvious pool of credible candidates to be more radical about who should be considered?

Dependency

This pinpoints those individuals who have been nominated as successors for many roles. A superficial examination of succession coverage might indicate an organisation with the breadth of capability to provide future leadership. But if this coverage is based on a small number of individuals to provide future leadership, the organisation is vulnerable. This is a common succession problem. Organisations often find themselves directing attention and effort around a narrow and shrinking group of individuals. These are the individuals who have progressed, demonstrated their credibility and capability, with the character and career management skills to operate effectively at senior levels. It is these individuals, the "usual suspects", who are rounded up to contribute to strategic reviews, to form start-up teams for new ventures, to be part of task forces addressing specific problems, and so on. These challenges open up tremendous opportunities for development, and consequently this group gains in effectiveness. The downside is that as these individuals become increasingly stretched through the increase in their working demands, they are less able to provide the quality time to coach and develop their reports. The organisational outcome is a "succession vicious circle". The most talented individuals are given greater responsibility and become increasingly capable, but are less able to nurture the next generation of talent. Some of these over-worked and fatigued individuals leave. The circle then becomes more vicious and the organisation has to keep drawing on a smaller group of individuals. Eventually the well runs dry.

Restrained

Here, an individual is obviously ready to progress and make a larger organisational contribution but is being held back by the lack of an obvious replacement to move into his or her role. This again represents a business risk. Either the organisation promotes this individual, leaving itself with the headache of finding a successor from elsewhere, or it embarks on a "holding exercise", making positive-sounding noises to the individual, while exploring other options. This of course runs the risk of losing a key individual who is not prepared to wait to progress their career. Another perspective, of course, would be to ask: why is this individual seen as ready to progress to take on greater responsibility if they haven't developed any of their own people? As a tactic to indicate a commitment to succession management, some organisations require candidates for career progression to provide evidence that they have found a suitable replacement for their own roles.

Blocked

In this scenario a talented individual is ready to take on greater responsibility and make a bigger contribution. However, progression is being blocked by an individual who isn't ready to move. The business risk again is that a talented manager or professional sees their career aspirations as thwarted and more likely to be fulfilled elsewhere, and leaves the organisation. An imaginative response would look at the big picture and identify new ways of organising work activity to accommodate the individual's skill set. This manoeuvre, if unchecked, can also result in a "patchwork quilt" of bespoke roles, tailored around individual motivation and preference, distorting the overall shape of the organisation, and undermining broader resourcing plans and priorities.

At risk

Here, more than one individual is seen as ready to progress but only one can. The risk for the organisation is that, in deciding to promote one individual, the other individual, seeing their career options closed down, leaves. Both individuals are talented but within the constraints of conventional progression within the current structure only one individual can advance. Again the organisation needs to think creatively about its resourcing options. Alternatively, it accepts that turnover is an inevitable consequence of managing succession proactively. High levels of turnover created by the departure of talented individuals who don't see or don't want to see a long-term future within the organisation is an indicator of a business in trouble. But the lack of any professional and executive turnover is a sign of a culture of complacency, of a lack of stretch and challenge, and an organisation that is in danger of living on its comfortable past.

THE PROBLEMS OF ORGANISATIONAL CHARTING IN THE REAL WORLD

These succession problems within the previous scenarios are based on a static organisational structure, and as such, are artificial. The resourcing reality is very different. A major difficulty with this classic approach is that it revolves around the assumptions of organisational stability, of continuity of management structure, that future resourcing will be met through straightforward replacement into existing roles, and that individuals' career progression will follow the existing hierarchy. Increasingly, these are unsustainable assumptions. However, this approach does provide a structure to form the beginnings of a debate about resourcing risks and vulnerabilities. Even a cursory "eye-ball" review of the classic succession plan should provide a rudimentary organisational "health check". This kind of first cut review should overview coverage and exposure, highlighting your organisation's overall resourcing health and identifying specific pressure points. Exposure is a constraint to an organisation's overall business options. Flexibility and freedom of manoeuvre are critical organisational assets. Succession exposure puts the organisation on the back foot, forcing it to make compromises around a handful of dominant and powerful individuals. At Enron, Jeff Skilling saw the departure of Rich Kinder in 1996 and knew that chairman Ken Lay couldn't contemplate the loss of another Enron top executive. Seizing the moment, Skilling presented the case to Lay that he should be promoted, otherwise he too would leave. Lay, with few cards to play, agreed to Skilling's request and Skilling progressed to President and CEO at the age of 43. The departure of Kinder, regarded as the best operations man in the energy business, was a decisive moment in shaping Enron's future.[4]

If exposure closes down resourcing options, coverage opens up possibilities. Coverage provides choice from a number of able candidates equipped to take on greater leadership responsibility, with the reassurance that other solid players can rise to the challenge of providing back-up to take on existing organisational tasks. Coverage allows your organisation to take an objective decision based on merit rather than be forced into ad-hoc and expedient appointments.

Succession coverage has its risks. Turnover may increase as those talented individuals no longer viewed as in the running for key roles leave to pursue career opportunities elsewhere.[5] But it is a price worth paying. Above all, genuine succession coverage drives out complacency and arrogance, those constant enemies of continuing business success, to reinforce a culture of performance and achievement.

If classic succession charting can be criticised as an attempt to preserve the present in the face of change and uncertainty then its next problem is the typical process in which successors are nominated and then compiled into a simple organogram. Time and time again we have seen succession charts listing the names of potential successors, but when "push comes to shove" and a resourcing decision needs to be made, the nominated successors are rarely seen as ready to move into the role. It isn't just the degree of subjectivity and bias that can be the problem, significant though that can be;[6] it is the fact that the organisation doesn't have the data it needs in the first place to summarise considered and meaningful information. This "information vacuum" becomes filled by "succession tittle-tattle" and informal washroom conversations.

Classic succession charting is unlikely to advance an insightful dialogue about the reality of the organisation's risks and opportunities or encourage imaginative thinking about resourcing options and solutions. Even worse classic succession may compound the problem, crystallising management thinking to see the future as "more of the same", as about the progression of the same kinds of leaders within the same kind of structures. It is hardly surprising then that these charts, once they have achieved their primary objective of impression management to the Board or to a regulatory agency, are quickly filed, never to see again the light of organisational day for the next 12 months. It is rare indeed for this chart to be a "living and breathing" document which shapes and directs month-to-month resourcing and development actions (see Figure 6.5).

The agreement of back-up coverage for critical roles is an important discipline. If nothing else, it reassures stake-holders that options have been reviewed and plans are in place to respond to the "slings and arrows" of organisational life. Depending on the stability of the organisational structure, extending this exercise to highlight potential successors over the next 18 months or two years may in some circumstances be useful, helping answer the following practical questions:

- Who could we move into this key marketing position when the current role-holder retires in 12 months' time?

Useful	Problems
● as a response to the conventional expectations of key stake-holders (e.g. regulatory bodies)	● succession recommendations which make little impact on subsequent resourcing decisions
● when drawing up a map to visually display coverage at senior levels	● an assumption of organisational stability which flies in the face of the realities of business change
● to pinpoint and track the "succession flow" under stable organisational conditions	● the "crystallisation" of the current resourcing pattern rather than opening up a creative dialogue about options
	● a static picture which rarely drives meaningful action

Figure 6.5   Applications and problems with conventional succession charting

- If we move this individual into a new finance role, who is in the frame to succeed them?
- What do we do with this key individual who isn't quite ready to progress, but if we don't do something, will in all likelihood leave?

Succession planning for critical roles

If a full-blown succession chart, covering the entire echelons of the top two or three levels of the organisational structure is largely a waste of time and more often than not an exercise in impression management for the benefit of external constituents, then it may be more helpful to pinpoint those specific areas of the organisation where a detailed evaluation of coverage and exposure will inform specific actions. Significantly this exercise may open up the succession agenda to look beyond senior levels in order to highlight roles further down the hierarchy which, although not viewed as especially important in the formal rankings of job evaluation, are in fact key to your organisation's future.

Are all roles equally critical to the business? Probably not, whatever your executives might say. Some roles are losing their significance to the business and others are emerging as more critical. The aim is to identify this shift quickly to anticipate and plan resourcing requirements. If business success is achieved by "running through the valley of death faster than your rivals",[7] then spotting quickly which roles need greater corporate attention might help you get a head start. There are two themes which outline *criticality*:

- *Centrality to business.* These are the roles which meet the following criteria:
  - *Pivotal* to your corporate strategy — roles that are fundamental to the execution of your current business game plan. Without these roles your strategy will falter.
  - *Leverage vis-à-vis* your competitors — roles that are growing in significance to your competitive advantage; those roles where outstanding performance will create "clear blue water" between you and your business rivals.

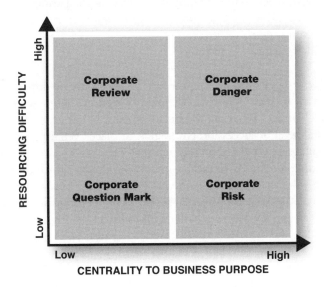

Figure 6.6 Identifying critical roles

- *Intrinsic* — roles that are bound up in a complex matrix of organisational know-how, functional coordination and reporting relationships with different stake-holder groups, internal and external. These are the roles which couldn't, for example, be outsourced easily without creating massive disruption.
- *Resourcing difficulty*. These are the kind of roles which meet the following criteria:
  - *Scarcity of supply*. These are roles that will be difficult to resource because the available pool of talent (for example, a specific aspect of technical know-how or industry-specific knowledge) is extremely limited.
  - *Complexity of resourcing mix*. Some roles require an unusual mix of business experience, leadership and/or professional skills and technical know-how, a set of components which, in combination, narrow resourcing options. It isn't that each individual component of the role is necessarily rare in the marketplace; it is the organisational permutation of different role requirements which makes it unusual.
  - *Unpopularity*. These are the roles no one wants to take on. These are the roles where the odds of success are either so low or are associated with such difficult and demanding organisational tasks, assignments that can only result in a personal and political backlash, that they represent "career black spots".

Work with key stake-holders to agree the scope of the target population of roles. Although this exercise can be conducted individually, it is probably best facilitated with a group of executives who represent a range of different organisational work areas and who have an overall perspective on strategic priorities. Emphasise that the *exercise is to focus on roles* not to review individual role-holders, their performance or potential.

Ask each participant to consider the roles within their area of responsibility and plot them on the matrix shown in Figure 6.6. The initial results of this exercise will be fairly predictable, with a bias towards roles being assigned to the top right-hand quadrant — high centrality to business and high resourcing difficulty. If this mapping is massively skewed, be prepared to repeat the exercise, asking participants to assign a quarter of their roles to each quadrant on the matrix. This will be unpopular. Persevere, explaining that the aim is not to provide absolute evaluations but to prioritise and highlight resourcing priorities where organisational attention needs to be directed.

Then review the classification of roles:

- *Corporate danger* (high centrality to business – high resourcing difficulty)
  Is there a pattern to these roles? Are there any surprises? Why do these roles represent such corporate danger? What are the business risks? What actions need to be taken in response? What level of succession coverage is in place? What measures need to be put in place to explore external resourcing options?
- *Corporate risk* (high centrality to business – low resourcing difficulty)
  These are the roles critical to the organisation's future but which can be resourced relatively easily, at least in the short term. How confident are you in the assessment of succession coverage? Or are you making ill-founded assumptions about the ease of resourcing? What actions need to be taken to ensure potential successors are being developed and a pipeline of talent is maintained?
- *Corporate review* (low centrality to business – high resourcing difficulty)
  Despite their relatively low significance to the organisation, these roles represent potential problems due to the lack of available talent. These may be highly specialist,

technical roles which cannot be resourced easily from the external market. As such, an imaginative strategy may be to integrate these roles more closely within the overall structure. Alternatively, are these the kind of functions and tasks which might be better outsourced or resourced from a mix of interim, contract and consultancy supply?

- *Corporate question mark* (low centrality to business – low resourcing difficulty)
  These roles, if not continually questioned and challenged, have a habit of expanding and growing within organisations. Although they may only make a peripheral contribution to the organisation, their lack of business accountability makes them an attractive option for those individuals who prefer an easy life. Allowed to continue these roles will undermine a performance culture and constrict the organisation's financial well-being. These roles identify candidates for a fundamental resourcing review. It is unlikely that the organisation gains much, if any, competitive advantage from their positioning within the structure.

The objective of this exercise is to go beyond succession for all roles at all levels to identify those that have *most strategic impact and where resourcing and development needs to concentrate its effort.* For example, Williams-Sonoma, the household goods firm, estimates that "people in only five job families determine 80 per cent of the company's strategic priorities" and Unicco, the integrated facilities services management company, reckons that only three job families are integral to its strategy, jobs employing less than 4 per cent of its workforce.[8] Rather than being absorbed within the annual round of succession planning, these critical roles need to be the focus of ongoing succession activity. These are the roles where regular reviews of coverage need to be conducted to ensure that plans are in place to maintain the future supply of relevant professional and leadership talent.

Organisational structure, clusters and resourcing priorities

GIULIANI'S RESOURCING STRATEGY

Rudi Giuliani,[9] elected mayor of New York in 1993, setting out a new operating agenda for the range of governmental agencies and departments within the city, knew he had to think beyond conventional structures in planning and implementing an appointments process for his new government. Starting with the premise that he wanted at least three candidates for each of the key roles to be filled, his staff organised the different government agencies and senior roles into "clusters", grouping those governmental activities which shared similar themes. This meant that candidates could be short-listed for a number of different roles but within the same cluster. The objective was to open up the appointments process to be imaginative in short-listing a variety of suitable candidates rather than be constrained by formal job titles and career resumés.

GOING BEYOND "NAMES ON DOORS"

While "names-on-the-door" succession charts may fail to provide a real insight into business risks and opportunities, based as they are on a set of roles and reporting relationships which shift frequently, structure cannot be ignored. Structure is how an organisation decides to organise the collective efforts of its workforce and how it links its overall strategic aims to the day-to-day working realities of front-line staff.

For the sole trader, strategy is translated into today's to-do list. There is no structure; there is one individual performing a range of functions in response to the demands of customers. But as the business expands and additional staff are employed, the sole trader needs to identify the best way to organise and coordinate the workforce. In other words, they need to find a structure to suit their business requirements. Structure is the design template which maps out how the organisation decides to plot out accountabilities and reporting relationships, to coordinate and integrate activity and clarify decision-making responsibility. Structure therefore should drive resourcing and succession requirements. A good organisational structure reflects the dominant challenges of current and emerging strategy, providing clarity of role responsibilities and reporting relationships, and directing and optimising employee time and effort efficiently. A bad structure is a jumble of vague accountabilities, overlapping responsibilities, and haphazard reporting lines, limiting the possibility of any kind of meaningful strategic resourcing. Instead resourcing becomes a set of tactical stopgaps, ad-hoc compromises and expedient selection decisions.

THE DILEMMAS OF ORGANISATIONAL DESIGN

Organisational design seems to be more of an art than a science, a set of intuitive judgements involving a series of trade-offs across those fundamental paradoxes of centralisation vs decentralisation and specialisation vs generalism.

Centralisation is a structural solution which establishes control from the centre to ensure clarity and continuity of purpose, issuing policies and procedures to maintain consistency of operating approach through the enterprise. Centralisation retains a tight grip on decision-making authority to exert control over how things get done. But centralisation can easily become slow, unwieldy and inflexible, making it difficult for different business activities to respond swiftly to the distinctive requirements of their markets and customers. *Decentralisation* devolves power from head office to provide operating units with greater freedom. Business units, rather than waiting for head office to give the go ahead, have the autonomy to make their own decisions. But, as decentralised business units assemble their own support functions rather than accept the head office prescription, mini empires grow and cost increases. At this point the organisation, alarmed at rising costs as well as the emerging divergence of business approach which threatens to undermine overall corporate identity, pulls back decision-making power to the centre. And the pendulum between the pros and cons of centralisation swings back and forward between the advantages and disadvantages of decentralisation.

Specialisation has an enormous appeal. Organising work activity around specific tasks, allowing employees to focus on what they do best and draw on their experience and expertise, develops greater overall proficiency. Applying this logic, organisations continue to break work activity into smaller and smaller tasks, creating increasingly narrowly defined roles. At this point the great challenge of integration kicks in as organisations find it increasingly difficult to coordinate different strands of specialist activities. Specialisation constrains the flexibility of work allocation and scheduling needed to maximise productivity. Highly trained employees proficient in only one task, familiar with only one product or adept in dealing with only one customer group, provide high levels of productivity when it is all steam ahead, but lack flexibility in shifting focus to adapt to the ups and downs of demand. Here, specialisation becomes an expensive resourcing option. Unhappy with the logistical constraints of specialisation, the organisation shifts to *generalism*, setting up multi-skilled teams, trained across a range of different product and customer transactions. Generalism provides that degree of responsiveness and flexibility to avoid the typical delays and hand offs that specialisation across different work units and departments creates. But generalism comes at the price of resourcing difficulty. Recruiting, training and rewarding staff equipped to take on a broad range of work responsibilities, while also maintaining high standards of quality and service, is no easy feat. The drawbacks and gains of specialisation need to be traded against the upsides and downsides of generalism.

ORGANISATIONAL DESIGN OPTIONS

The ongoing organisational challenge is to find the best structural compromise which best balances these tensions. How? By deciding how best to configure four different streams of activity (see Figure 6.7):

- *Strategic*: every organisation needs to look beyond its immediate priorities to establish a game plan, a forward-looking road map to indicate how and where it will and won't compete. For a global enterprise this represents a major exercise involving significant amounts of executive time. For the sole trader this might be a few bullet points on a single page of paper. But any organisation, however large or small, needs a purpose, committing resources to thinking through its ambitions and future intentions, and plotting out a game plan to determine how it will compete to advance this purpose.

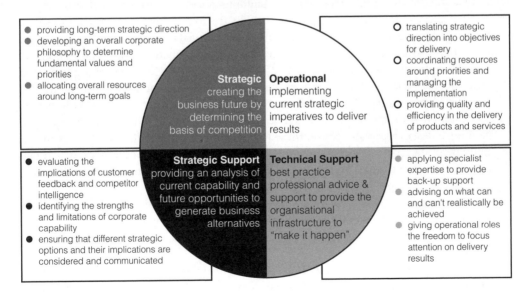

Figure 6.7   Four themes of organisational activity

- *Operational*: this is the set of activities which translates current business priorities into the delivery of its products and services to customers. This is the mainstream of organisational life, the managerial processes and practices that ensure that strategic imperatives are implemented and communicated to direct production, sales, service and administrative priorities. Strategy does not make money; it is only a concept and set of ideas. It is only when Strategy informs what front-line staff do and don't do and how they do it and don't do it, that it has any business reality. Operations provide that day-to-day reality.
- *Strategic Support*: these are the activities which inform and shape the process of strategic decision-making. Not directly involved in day-to-day operations nor required to make the big business decisions, Strategic Support provides the intelligence to guide strategic review and planning. This activity incorporates marketplace scanning and customer research, the analysis of competitor activity and tracking the impact of wider political and social trends to evaluate the organisation's strengths and weaknesses. It also includes financial analysis and risk management to inform the organisation's assessment of its prospects and opportunities and its shortcomings and vulnerabilities. It is Strategic Support which provides the "eyes and ears" for the organisation to keep it alert to its dangers and opportunities.
- *Technical Support*: this provides the organisational infrastructure to support operational requirements. If Strategic Support facilitates the Strategic function, then Technical Support makes it easier for operational activity to focus on product and service delivery. Technical Support comprises the professional advice, support and best practice innovation to ensure that operational activity is running at optimum levels. It incorporates a miscellany of activities ranging from mailroom, payroll, car fleet, premises, network support, and much more. Technical Support takes on the peripheral but necessary functions to make the organisation tick, allowing Operations to do what it does best: delivering quality products and services to customers efficiently.

These four streams of activity represent the building-blocks of organisational structure. As Figure 6.8 depicts, there is an ongoing tension across the four themes. Each group focuses on its own priorities (and importance), locating any organisational problems with other activities, never of course within itself. So, for example, the Strategic function blames Operations for poor implementation. Operations argue that ill-conceived strategies can't be implemented. Strategic Support views Technical Support as an unnecessary cost (and a set of activities that could be outsourced easily). Technical Support sees Strategic Support as preparing initiatives without thinking through the practical implications for the organisational infrastructure.

Building a design template around these four streams of organisational activities throws up many permutations.[10] The challenge then is to find that structural template which best configures these activities to optimise the trade-offs between centralisation and decentralisation and specialisation and generalism.

- In which of these four functions do we need to excel? Where will excellence give us the greatest advantage? Which activities do we need to undertake ourselves? Which could we outsource?
- How should we organise these four activities to direct our business effort most effectively? Which functions should we centralise; which should be decentralised? Which will gain most from specialisation; which from generalism?

	Strategic	Strategic Support	Operational	Technical Support
Strategic's views of...		Conducting extensive analysis which fails to provide meaningful recommendations Attempting to hijack strategic decision making with ill-conceived innovations	Going "AWOL" and failing to translate corporate direction consistently An expediency in achieving results which undermine long-term purpose	Creating technically excellent solutions which constrain strategic flexibility Demanding unrealistic increases in budget
Strategic Support's views of...	Imposing constraints on radical strategic innovation Ignoring the conclusions of well-founded analysis		Dismissing futuristic thinking as irrelevant to business priorities Failing to provide timely data to inform competitor and market intelligence	Ignoring market-place feedback which indicates what customers want Professional perfectionism out of touch with business realities
Operational's views of...	Imposing an inflexible strategic game-plan Setting performance targets which lack an understanding of business pressures	Confusing mainstream management with complex business planning directives Ignoring front-line feedback about what is important to customers		Failing to provide pragmatic solutions quickly enough Developing technically innovative solutions which lack business relevance
Technical Support's views of...	Setting budgetary criteria which constrain best practice innovation Failing to provide a consistent set of corporate priorities to plan "infrastructure changes"	Introducing initiatives which ignore professional and technical best practice Implementing "quick-fix solutions" which create longer-term problems	Introducing ideas which lack awareness of the constraints within which we operate Formulating plans which ignore the implications for the organisational infrastructure	

Figure 6.8   Typical organisational tensions

- What overall configuration of these four streams of activities will provide the most optimal structural trade-off to direct optimum effort around our business goals?

The response to these questions will drive the resourcing and succession agenda. A "hub-and-spoke" organisation, designed around a strategic core, outsourcing all other activities to a variety of business partners, will have a different set of succession priorities from that of a company "firing on all cylinders", organising itself to compete vigorously across all four strands of organisational activity.

Figure 6.9 maps out two examples. In configuration 1, the organisation is dominated by a powerful head office in which functional expertise at the centre shapes strategy and drives operational activity. At best, this configuration is a highly focused and cost-effective way of directing organisational time and effort. Centralised specialist support provides direction for operational activity, organised around geographic, product or customer groupings. For "simple" businesses this is a workable structure but one that is likely to become sluggish and unresponsive with greater complexity and size. In resourcing terms it is obvious where potential succession blockages may occur. Talented individuals within Operations will find it difficult to advance to positions at the centre. The centre then becomes reliant on external resourcing, bringing in strategic and support leadership from outside, leadership which over time potentially becomes disconnected from operational realities, risking the "corporate core". This structural template becomes a "them and us" resourcing solution, "them" at the centre and detached from operating priorities, and "us" alienated from influence and decision-making. In terms of playing "succession roulette", this is betting on the future with only a few chips; the reliance on a small number of individuals at senior levels to "call the organisational shots". For some organisations, this may be an efficient organisational design and resourcing strategy. For ambitious organisations, working to a long-term game plan, looking to build in resilience, and future-proof itself from adversity, this is a potentially risky approach.

In configuration 2, the centre provides an overall "strategic steer" but its control is reduced. Each operating unit has greater strategic control over its destiny, with Strategic

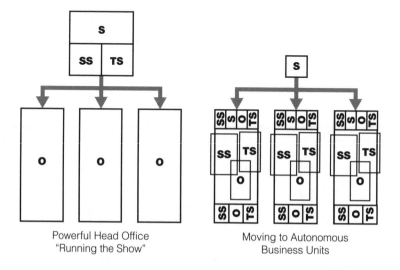

Powerful Head Office
"Running the Show"

Moving to Autonomous
Business Units

Figure 6.9   Structural caricatures

Support and Technical Support providing more responsive services to meet each unit's distinctive requirements. This opens up a broader set of resourcing options, providing greater flexibility of career opportunities. (As a substitute for ineffective support from the centre, slow and inflexible back-up, this structural template is, however, a potentially expensive resourcing option with a risk of duplicating effort across different operational units.) But if the game plan is to begin shifting towards autonomous business units this is a price worth paying. In the game of "succession roulette", more chips need to be played and spread across more bets, but this is a design solution more likely to build organisational resilience.

FACILITATING A STRUCTURAL DEBATE

Managing succession not against specific roles, but by reviewing professional and executive talent against *clusters* of organisational activity, should:

- *Trigger a debate about your organisation's configuration of roles* within the overall structure. How effective is your structure in directing executive and professional time and effort? How might this need to shift in future to maximise the trade-offs between low cost, consistency and standardisation vs speed, flexibility and responsiveness? Should Strategic activity, for example, be retained tightly at the centre or pushed down to business units? Should Technical Support be pulled back as a centre of excellence and all other activity outsourced? Without this fundamental discussion about the future configuration of activities — those which need greater investment, those which could be outsourced easily — it is difficult to see how a meaningful resourcing game plan can be formulated.
- *Generate new insights into resourcing options.* Conventional succession charting lists successors against specific roles. This perspective, seeing succession against broad-based organisational activities, encourages a much looser and more flexible approach. Reviewing your current structure, how easy or difficult would it be to group roles against the four themes of Strategic, Operations, Strategic Support and Technical Support? Which roles could be easily assigned to one of the four groupings? Which represent combinations of these themes or are more difficult to classify? Does specific technical know-how make it difficult to represent your current structure in this way? What are the implications for how you should manage succession? For some organisations highly specific technical and professional streams of activity need to be retained. For others, this approach reinforces tight functional silos, blocking leadership progression through the middle and senior levels.

The aim is to open up a broader succession debate, identifying talent which may be locked in by career resumé, to review imaginatively options for progression. This perspective on succession, however valuable in debating the shape, scale and scope of the organisational structure and the implications for the nature and size of critical roles, will not force the critical issue: are your business fundamentals correct? The issue is not simply *how* you should be organised, but *what* you should be organising to achieve.

Business risk assessment by capability

THE CAPABILITY ARGUMENT

In the mid-1990s, Hamel and Prahalad[11] set the scene for a shift in emphasis in strategic thinking. Traditional strategic planning techniques, they argued, and specifically concepts such as "strategic fit" — the matching of existing resources to opportunities — were limited. Looking out to the marketplace to identify gaps in the market where your organisation's existing strengths in products and services could be exploited, will constrain strategic options. Instead organisations should think beyond their current product and service portfolio to identify their *"core competences"*. These have been defined as "the collective learning" of the organisation and how the organisation integrates and coordinates its knowledge and technology. The strategic focus shouldn't be where you can optimise your current product and service proposition; rather, how can you "leverage resources to achieve the seemingly unattainable"? Honda, instead of simply defining itself around its car manufacturing expertise, identified its underlying excellence in engine development, a shift in mind-set which helped it to move into markets as diverse as motorbikes, lawn mowers and boats. Very different product and marketing challenges, but all unified by Honda's strengths in engine expertise. In essence, if you can look beneath the surface of what you currently do to identify the fundamentals of what you are truly good at, are imaginative at how these strengths can be exploited and have the confidence to think big thoughts, you can open up new strategic possibilities.[12]

Should the assessment of business risk then move away from organisational structures to look at core competency? For many organisations, undoubtedly yes. Although the management structure is or should be a reflection of business priorities, reflecting the focus of current products and services and directing attention to key customer and market groups, it will change. An assessment of business risk therefore needs to look beyond the current configuration of accountabilities, reporting lines and relationships to identify the fundamental capabilities around which the organisation is competing.

A THOUGHT EXPERIMENT IN COMPETITIVE ADVANTAGE

Sustainable strategic success arises not so much from one-off product brilliance, but from capability to manage the three Rs of business life, the three fundamental attributes of *resilience, responsiveness* and *rethink*.[13] *Resilience* is that attribute which allows any organisation to deal with the tough times, the corporate mind-set which:

- keeps scanning the business environment to identify signs of competitor threat or customer dissatisfaction
- scrutinises productivity and cost to highlight emerging inefficiencies
- possesses the courage to ask itself difficult questions and to provide honest answers about itself, and what is and isn't working
- tackles emerging problems quickly before they become major issues rather than passing the issues up and down or from function to function
- keeps driving on process efficiency and improving administrative disciplines
- knows how to "batten down the hatches" to control costs when under business pressure.

Responsiveness is that quality which enables the organisation to think on its feet to identify and seize new possibilities quickly in advancing its market position to push its growth strategy forward. If resilience could be caricatured as a paranoid fear of the business future, seeing threats around every corner and obsessive in its relentlessness to focus operational activity and control costs, then responsiveness is that caricature of a hyperactive, upbeat, outward-facing and optimistic perspective. Responsiveness is that entrepreneurial quality which sees every business challenge as an opportunity. It:

- tracks competitor trends and market research data to identify new commercial opportunities
- spots opportunities for partnerships to leverage mutual interests with other organisations
- has the speed of movement and decision-making discretion to accept that mistakes will happen in pursuing new possibilities
- has the facility to deploy talent quickly to "kick start" new initiatives and set up new ventures.

Resilience and responsiveness seem to be those basic organisational attributes required to play the business game. But the game is a long one, and *rethink* is required to provide that re-energising and reinvigorating force to redefine the fundamentals. Rethink accepts that the business future will not be more of the same but that it will be very different. It is rethink which:

- challenges current assumptions about how the organisation competes, questioning and re-examining the dominant business model to evaluate its relevance for the future marketplace
- generates future scenarios of what the business future may look like
- proposes radical proposals and pushes forward with innovative ideas and is willing to attack the current "sacred cows" of established products and services
- encourages an operating culture in which initiative, independence of mind and originality of thought are encouraged and reinforced.

It is the balance of resilience, responsiveness and rethink which is at the heart of business risk. Resilience looks to avoid risk through retrenchment and a return to familiar fundamentals. Responsiveness accepts that risk is an inevitable feature of exploring new possibilities. Rethink sees that the greater risk in sustaining corporate success lies not in doing something very different but in keeping doing the same thing. But rethink also has the potential to go for broke and embark on those risky activities that undermine the organisation's core.

A quick exercise. Working with informed colleagues, use the format in Figure 6.10 to ask: who within this organisation has that mix of credibility, capability, career management and character to provide meaningful leadership right now in each of these three "Rs"? Work through each member of the top team, evaluating their overall contribution against resilience, responsiveness and rethink. This will be a simplistic evaluation but should pinpoint each individual's dominant strategic outlook and attitude to risk. How are these different dynamics being played out within the top team? Which views are prevailing; which aren't? What does the overall balance indicate about the likely strategic direction of your organisation and how and where it will compete in future?

	Resilience	Responsiveness	Rethink
Top Team			
Senior Executives			
Emerging Leadership			

Figure 6.10   A thought experiment

Then extend this process down to the senior executive population. Ignore formal job descriptions. Focus on individuals, their skill set, technical know-how, operating approach and leadership outlook. What does this exercise indicate? Is there a diversity of approach across the three themes? Then ask: of the emerging leadership and professional population, who represents these organisational capabilities?

Reviewing the initial findings, what are the likely implications for the organisation?

- A risk aversion, more concerned to protect the past than explore the future and a danger of losing out to more entrepreneurial competitors?
- An impetus to rush recklessly into new markets which will threaten the organisation's profitable core activity?
- Embarking on grandiose business plans which can only jeopardise the organisation's future?
- Or, an informed and robust attitude to risk management which is able to consider different strategic options maturely, recognising when to hold back, when to push forward and when it needs to re-examine its fundamental direction?

Strategic resourcing and business challenge

A STRATEGIC VOCABULARY FOR SUCCESSION MANAGEMENT

The three Rs might be useful as a "thought experiment", to consider the balance of different business capabilities and stimulate discussion about the organisation, its strategic future and the range of leadership capabilities it possesses or needs to acquire. But a thought experiment is likely to be little more than that, and too broad brush to operate as a meaningful succession planning tool.

Faced with the pressing challenge of making succession work for a financial services organisation undergoing a major strategic transition in the late 1980s, we looked for a strategic vocabulary to inform succession management, to make explicit the link between business strategy and management capability. Our experience mirrored the observation that, "the schism between succession planning and business strategy is one of the primary reasons that succession plans fail".[14] The challenge was to create a language which connected the strategic debate with organisational capability and leadership style to formulate a business terminology which would inform Board discussion about the realities of leadership succession. A key theme in our research was the concept of "strategic choice", the importance of prioritising to direct organisational resource and leadership attention. The vague mission statement of "being world class through world-class leadership" for us missed the point. Businesses succeed through strategic choice and through clarity of business priority, recognising the key points of competitive leverage, and knowing how to align organisational effort around these priorities. "Without focus, the resources and energy of the organisation will be spread a mile wide and they will be an inch deep. If you are wrong you will die. But most organisations don't die because they are wrong; most die because they don't commit themselves."[15] Our research programme was about making explicit the link between the organisation's strategic focus, the capabilities which would make the business difference and the specific leadership capabilities and outlook which would ensure exceptional levels of execution (see Figure 6.11).

Our starting-point was the cliché that every business needs three types of individuals: the *"dreamer"* to get the firm off the ground with an imaginative insight into the future market; the *"salesperson"* to take the concept into the market, promote it and *"do the deal"*; and the *"son-of-the-bitch"* who is prepared to tackle and trouble-shoot those problems constraining business success. A simplistic analysis, but one which begins to capture some important insights:

- Different organisations can be successful in pursuing very different strategies.
- Different strategies have different implications for leadership and professional capability and operating ethos.
- Organisations, particularly those "Betting Big for the Future", need a range of different business leadership outlooks. Strategic focus needs to be balanced with leadership diversity.
- Organisations at different points in their evolution will need a different leadership mix and focus.

Reviewing a variety of different strategic models,[16] two themes kept recurring: a focus on internal operations vs alertness to the external business environment, and a preference for periods of business change vs business consolidation. See Figure 6.12.

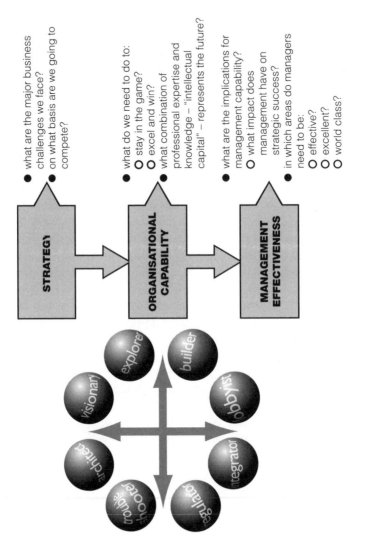

STRATEGY
- what are the major business challenges we face?
- on what basis are we going to compete?

ORGANISATIONAL CAPABILITY
- what do we need to do to:
  - O stay in the game?
  - O excel and win?
- what combination of professional expertise and knowledge – "intellectual capital" – represents the future?

MANAGEMENT EFFECTIVENESS
- what are the implications for management capability?
  - O what impact does management have on strategic success?
- in which areas do managers need to be:
  - O effective?
  - O excellent?
  - O world class?

Figure 6.11   Strategy, capability and management effectiveness

VISIONARY

Trend Spotting
Scanning the business
environment to identify
significant moves in
social, economic,
technological activity

Research Capability
Translating leading edge
ideas from the
academic/technical
research into workable
business concepts

New Product
Development
Moving promising new
concepts into tangible
products and services

EXPLORER

**Managing the Growth
Momentum**
Determining the products
and markets which
represent areas of
potential growth

Identifying Alliances
Searching out other
organisations where
partnerships and
alliances will be mutually
profitable

Deal Management
Negotiating commercial
arrangements to expand
the organisation's sphere
of operation

BUILDER

Customer Analysis
Analysing customer
feedback to determine
perceptions of the
product/service
proposition

Customer Reach
Promoting product
developments and
enhancements with
effective advertising and
pricing

**Distribution
Management**
Managing the mix of
distribution channels to
reflect customer
requirements

LOBBYIST

Reputation Management
Presenting corporate
interests positively to key
stake-holder groups

Political Influence
Setting an agenda within
the political decision
making environment

Regulator Relations
Exerting influence with
regulatory bodies to
maximise the
organisation's space for
manoeuvre

ARCHITECT

Technological Impact
Recognising the
relevance of
technological
developments on
organisational activity

Work Flow Redesign
Translating technological
innovation into improved
processes and systems

Change Leadership
Planning and
implementing major
changes in organisational
structure and practice

TROUBLE SHOOTER

Early Warning Systems
Measuring corporate
activity to determine
activity to identify
potential problems

Corporate ReFocus
Re-allocating
organisational resources
around core business
aims

**Productivity
Management**
Tackling high cost-low
value activities to raise
levels of productivity

REGULATOR

Management Information
Developing relevant
indicators to monitor
corporate activity and
outcomes

**Administrative
Consistency**
Installing standard
operating procedures to
improve process
efficiency and
standardisation

Financial Control
Establishing financial
discipline throughout
corporate activity

INTEGRATOR

Resourcing
Ensuring the ongoing
supply of employee
capability

Culture Management
Implementing processes
to reinforce corporate
values and ethics

**Knowledge
Coordination**
Facilitating the sharing of
resources, ideas and
information throughout
the organisation

Figure 6.12   Business types and organisational capability

RECURRING BUSINESS THEMES

INTERNAL OPERATIONS VS EXTERNAL ENVIRONMENT

Just as each country has its internal domestic and external foreign policy, companies must attend to external events in the marketplace as well as control their internal systems and processes. This is a difficult balance to maintain. On the one hand, organisations must ensure sufficient resources are devoted to the development of products and services and the exploration of new markets. On the other hand, time and energy must be directed towards improving the efficiency and productivity of the internal operations. For some companies this balancing act becomes too difficult and they lose their way. In the language of personality dynamics, organisations either become extroverted or introverted. Extroverted, by focusing energies exclusively on the external marketplace, which places a strain on the organisation's internal systems and processes, or introverted, by concentrating on internal efficiency and losing sight of shifts and trends in the business environment.

BUSINESS CHANGE VS BUSINESS CONSOLIDATION

Business change vs business consolidation represents the second major dimension defining business outlook. "Change is the only constant" is now a management cliché. However, it does highlight the emergence of a dominant trend. The combination of competitive pressures, technological developments, and not least, shifting social, economic and political forces has meant that flexibility and responsiveness are critical requirements in business success. During periods of challenge and crisis, for example, the formation of a new business or tackling the decline of an existing one, an organisation's ability to move quickly to exploit change is essential. While change may be an ongoing theme in organisational life, nevertheless, it must be viewed simultaneously with its mirror image, stability. Change can result in chaos and confusion, therefore organisations also need managers who can ensure stability and consolidation. When the business has expanded rapidly, and secured its market position, the challenge is to safeguard initial success through longer-term planning and coordination, and the "routinisation" of previously ad-hoc policies and processes.

Within this framework of two dominant dimensions we identified eight discrete patterns of strategic orientation, a model we described as *business types* (see Figure 6.13).

Over the last ten years this model has been used in a range of different applications:[17]

- As a *strategic thinking tool*, identifying those capabilities which are strategic assets or liabilities and as a framework to conduct competitor intelligence exercises.
- In *role profiling* to highlight the focus of executive roles and establish the strategic emphasis of senior level positions.
- In *management audits* to assess the breadth and depth of business leadership available to the organisation in facing up to its future challenges.
- *Individual assessment and executive coaching* to help senior managers take stock of their experience, capability and operating priorities.

"The best way to predict the future is to invent it."
John Sculley, Apple

"The bottom line is in heaven."
Edwin Land, Polaroid

Corporate Life Cycle	Strategic Thrusts	Challenges and Demands	Strategic Hazards
• very early stages of the start-up of a business • during a period of major renewal when the company is redefining its position in the market place	• opening up new markets by creating new technology • commitment to the development of breakthrough and innovative products and services in the market • recognising future consumer needs and creating a vision of the potential of next generation products and services	• developing ideas about future products and stimulating and exciting others to respond • educating customers about the value of innovative products • putting resources into product development and ensuring that the infrastructure is in place to deliver • protecting innovation against pirates and "me too" copies • preparing the next generation of products and services	• designing products that technology can provide rather than those that cater to genuine customer needs • introducing impractical, futuristic products that are too far ahead of their time • embarking upon high risk mega-projects that require huge resources over a long pay-back period • overlooking the importance of marketing through a concentration on technical issues

"We're on a pirate ship at sea ... I'm your captain. We're going to go out and raid all other ships on the ocean."

Ted Turner, Cable News Network

Corporate Life Cycle	Strategic Thrusts	Challenges and Demands	Strategic Hazards
• the company has built up an established customer base and is strong enough to pursue growth • profit is secured, but capital is needed to exploit opportunities for further expansion • products are successful, but awareness of the need to investigate diversification possibilities	• drive to multiply the size and scope of existing operations • exploring the most effective means to build market share • acquiring and threading together complementary businesses to create a strong unified enterprise	• growing the business without making significant and costly errors which will hinder the company in future • locating and capitalising on business opportunities when time is tight • ensuring the internal operation can maintain and support a growth strategy	• straying away from familiar businesses and acquiring product lines and companies which cannot easily be integrated • urge for quick growth results in reckless and haphazard schemes which incur debt and decimate resources • losing interest in the details of the market they are operating in through an excessive focus on financial return • failing to develop the organisational control systems and structures to support growth

"We live or die by the sales we get through the door."
Ken Cusack, MD Sorbus UK

"There aren't any categories of problems here. There's just one problem. Some of us aren't paying enough attention to our customers."
Tom Watson Sr., IBM

Corporate Life Cycle	Strategic Thrusts	Challenges and Demands	Strategic Hazards
● moving the business from rapid growth to healthy long-term maturity ● evolving the organisation in a manner which builds up stable market share by ensuring that customers receive consistently excellent service	● developing the specialist production and distribution capability to maintain long-term capability ● repositioning products through innovative marketing, sales and distribution management ● building up market share through increasing professionalisation of production and sales	● creating new ways of enhancing existing products and services ● improvements in customer service ● rethinking the most efficient means of production and distribution to reduce unit costs and enhance quality ● putting in place imaginative marketing, advertising and distribution systems which maintain customer interest	● expansion of product lines and outlets too broadly and indiscriminately such that product lines are no longer complementary and cohesive ● drift towards the packaging and design of products rather than emphasis on competent manufacture or leading-edge R&D ● introduction of administrative staff to support the sales function leads to excessive paperwork

"He had hovered near the centre of power in both the Soviet and American governments ... He courted kings and princes, and counted among his 'dear friends' the rich, the powerful and the celebrated."

"The Real Armand Hammer" – Ex-Chairman, Occidental Petroleum

Corporate Life Cycle	Strategic Thrusts	Challenges and Demands	Strategic Hazards
● business is well established and is planning its long-term future by securing prestige and influence within the industry ● when the market is threatened by increasing regulation and governmental constraints	● forging alliances with other companies and using this to shape political decision-making affecting the industry ● ensuring that the market allows continued growth by blocking rules and regulations which restrict a company's room for strategic manoeuvre ● utilising regulation to the disadvantage of competitors, especially those from other geographical markets	● developing a network across the industry which encourages the free flow of information ● presenting the company's viewpoint at key moments (press conferences, governmental consultation) ● maintaining relationships with key players in the media, industry trade bodies and government departments which ensures the company's views are influential	● losing sight of the key issues facing the business through involvement in impractical negotiations and grandiose schemes ● concern with reputation and image rather than reality and substance leads to a failure to address pressing commerical priorities ● overlooking the detailed running of the business by spending too much time liaising with external bodies

"To reinvent their companies, managers must throw out their old notions about how businesses should be organised and run. They must abandon the organisational and operational principles and procedures they are now using and create entirely new ones."

M. Hammer and S. Champy, *Reengineering the Corporation*

Corporate Life Cycle	Strategic Thrusts	Challenges and Demands	Strategic Hazards
● primary business is showing signs of decline through a lack of investment and creativity ● loss of competitive position through a failure to implement new technology and introduce new organisational working practices	● refocusing attention on internal operations, and the redeployment and restructure of organisational resources ● implementing radical measures throughout the entire company by a complete rethink of the way it operates ● using technology capability to redesign new business systems	● taking stock of overall operational strengths and weaknesses, and overhauling the systems and processes which underpin the delivery of products and services to customers ● implementing a solution which transforms the way in which the organisation operates through leading-edge technology, with innovations in organisational structure and working practices	● overly optimistic about technology potential ● tendency to think that the introduction of new systems and processes will be sufficient, and overlooks the importance of changing employee behaviour ● fails to address the realities of change management by neglecting the perceptions of front-line staff ● loses sight of the needs of customers; belief that responsive and reliable processes will be sufficient to meet their needs; ignores need to rethink products and markets

"We have got to take the gloves off and have a bare-knuckle fight on some of the things we have to do, because we have to have an effective and prosperous industry."

Sir Terence Beckett, CBI, 1980

Corporate Life Cycle	Strategic Thrusts	Challenges and Demands	Strategic Hazards
● the strategy of "being all things to all people" is no longer working, and there is a need to focus on the core business ● organisational expansion has led to a growth in business activities whose relevance to central corporate strategy is unclear	● selecting the strategic parts of the business and working to ensure their long-term survival, and cutting away the units that are not needed ● turning around those parts of businesses with a long-term strategic future through a willingness to think the unthinkable ● attacking problems of high cost and low productivity in internal operations	● focusing attention on the core of the business through the questioning of accepted and traditional views ● managing with limited resources under tight time pressures ● establishing a performance-focused culture by tackling lethargy, complacency and hostility ● implementing short-term solutions to assure survival while maintaining a long-range perspective	● tendency to decide what has to be done and think later ● getting caught up in solving short-term problems and overlooking the broad strategic picture ● focus on immediate efficiency and cost misses opportunities for careful growth of specific products

"It was crammed with minutiae. It told operators exactly how to draw milk shakes, grill hamburgers, and fry potatoes. It specified precise cooking times for all products and temperature settings for all equipment. It fixed standard portions on every food item, down to the quarter ounce on onions and the thirty two slices per pound of cheese."

Reference to McDonald's operating manual, in *Behind the Arches*

Corporate Life Cycle	Strategic Thrusts	Challenges and Demands	Strategic Hazards
• period of business security • company has mastered its primary market, built up substantial assets and is making a sizeable profit • perception that the company and its markets are "mature"	• maximising the financial success of the company by perfecting management systems and practices • gaining competitive advantage through high quality and low cost operations	• installing formal policies and standard operating procedures which save time and ensure consistency • putting in systems which regulate organisational activities so that the right things are done at the right time • establishing professional management through the clear definition of specific roles and responsibilities, and the development of proper planning and control	• overly focused on holding ground and maintaining order over existing systems rather than seeking out new opportunities in the marketplace • attending to cost and quality restricts creativity and radical thinking • beginning to manage the "numbers" and ceasing to serve the needs of those engaged in producing and selling • assuming all problems can be solved through the introduction of more policies and procedures and discourages risk-taking and innovation

"We try to create an atmosphere in which employees can enjoy themselves and make significant contributions. We all share a genuine desire for the individual to lead a full and rewarding life."

Harold Edmondson, Hewlett Packard

Corporate Life Cycle	Strategic Thrusts	Challenges and Demands	Strategic Hazards
• company has grown to the point at which too many functions have emerged, and fragmentation has created problems of communication and coordination throughout the workforce • morale has fallen, and there is a feeling of alienation and disillusionment	• bringing the business back to its key resource – its employees • recognition that sustained competitive advantage comes from the development of organisational capability through to attention to staff	• building bridges throughout the organisation by breaking down functional barriers to allow staff to work together collectively towards overall corporate goals • identifying conflicts of interest and political disagreement and encouraging coordi-nation and communication throughout the organisation • introducing imaginative personnel policies and practices which reinforce and reward excellent performance • putting in place plans for the longer-term training and development of staff	• introducing too many initiatives and programmes which create greater confusion among staff • attending to internal organisational processes which fail to address trends and developments in the marketplace • putting faith in the long-term training and development of staff places demands upon the need for short-term efficiency and productivity

Figure 6.13   Business types framework

USING SUCCESSION TO SET UP A STRATEGIC DEBATE

This perspective provides the basis for setting a robust business-driven agenda and set of "thinking tools" to identify resourcing priorities to pinpoint the succession focus and facilitate a "what if" debate about the organisation's future and the required leadership and professional capability. It can also be utilised as a "quick hit" leadership audit. Working with the top team, put up eight flip charts around the room, each headed by one of the eight questions in Figure 6.14. Then ask the first round of questions: who are the key players in the immediate term who represent a source of each capability? Who are the current executives who could advance this particular agenda? Note names on each of the flip charts, then ask: who are the potential players who could lead on each of these strategic challenges; the individuals with the mix of credibility, capability, career management and character who, with proactive development, could move the organisation forward? Again, note names. Finally, who is coming through the organisational ranks and represent bets for the longer term?

Review the flip charts at the end of this exercise. Which business themes are well covered with successors identified for the immediate and medium term? Do any areas look light? Does this matter? Reviewing the eight themes, what is the overall balance? What might this indicate about the breadth of leadership capability and the organisation's future strategic options?

Identifying resourcing priorities

Which business themes are most important to your organisation? All eight themes are relevant challenges and need to be addressed to keep in the game and maintain a competitive position. But which business challenges will build and strengthen your position *vis-à-vis* your competitors and customers? Which specific themes, if pursued with full commitment, will help your organisation "run faster" and take the initiative? Imagine a casino with eight roulette tables, each table representing one of the business types. How should your organisation bet on its future? Spread its bets equally across all eight roulette tables? Or should it play the strategic game at one table in particular? What is the strategic focus for the organisation? Where is most top management time and effort being directed?

What *capability* do you possess across these eight business challenges? Thinking specifically about your leadership talent, in areas are you behind the industry norm, around the industry average; where are you excelling and way ahead of the sector? Plot out the themes for your organisation using the matrix in Figure 6.15, indicating Importance and Capability for each of the eight business types.

Facilitating this exercise to map out importance and capability for each of the eight themes won't provide a definitive strategic analysis but it should encourage a debate about the alignment of strategic ambitions with your leadership capability. What emerges as critical and the greatest corporate risk: the zone of strategic importance but low capability? Does this set of business activities represent too great a challenge for the organisation? Is your strategy fundamentally flawed and you need to rethink organisational priorities? Or will this trigger a more committed approach to succession management and a willingness to be more imaginative in the introduction of new or improved processes for external recruitment and internal progression?

Business Challenge	Business Imagination	Business Entrepreneurship	Business Commitment to the Customer	Business Influence	Business Renewal	Business Efficiency	Business Focus	Business Transformation
Who represents the organisation's source of...	Innovative thinking to generate new business concepts	Seizing commercial opportunities to expand the business	Improving market share through improved sales, service and support activity	Advancing corporate interests with key opinion-formers and decision-makers	Creating innovative people processes to raise capability and motivation	Establishing financial control & administrative discipline over work activity	Concentrating on fundamental corporate activity to improve productivity and profitability	Utilising IT and progressive organisational processes to create innovative operating systems
Key players in the immediate term								
Potential players in the medium term (1-3 years)								
Future "bets": up-and-coming managers (3-5 years)								

Figure 6.14   Quick hit audit

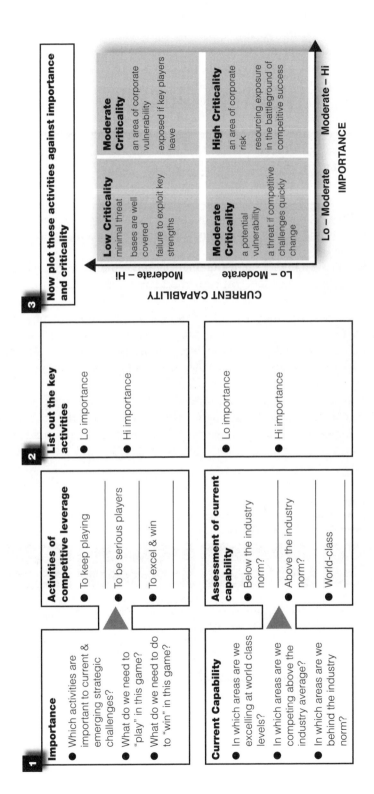

1

Importance

- Which activities are important to current & emerging strategic challenges?
- What do we need to do to "play" in this game?
- What do we need to do to "win" in this game?

Activities of competitive leverage

- To keep playing
- To be serious players
- To excel & win

Current Capability

- In which areas are we excelling at world class levels?
- In which areas are we competing above the industry average?
- In which areas are we behind the industry norm?

Assessment of current capability

- Below the industry norm?
- Above the industry norm?
- World-class

2

List out the key activities

- Lo importance
- Hi importance

- Lo importance
- Hi importance

3

Now plot these activities against importance and criticality

CURRENT CAPABILITY

Moderate – Hi

Lo – Moderate

Low Criticality
minimal threat
bases are well covered
failure to exploit key strengths

Moderate Criticality
an area of corporate vulnerability
exposed if key players leave

Moderate Criticality
a potential vulnerability
a threat if competitive challenges quickly change

High Criticality
an area of corporate risk
resourcing exposure in the battleground of competitive success

Lo – Moderate   Moderate – Hi

IMPORTANCE

Figure 6.15   Identifying resourcing priorities

"What if" succession management

The business types framework can also be used to ask "what if" questions (see Figure 6.16), generating scenarios to stimulate a debate about your organisation's succession priorities: to think about how the future may be different, the moves your competitors may be planning and how customer requirements may be shifting.

For example, you are an advertising agency finding it difficult to make the breakthrough from the middle ranks to become one of the industry's big players. Attempts to expand through poaching of creative staff from other agencies have failed. What could you do to out-manoeuvre your competitors? "What if", for example, you changed your business model to build exceptional capability in the "Regulator" theme? What would be the gains if you applied the same kind of financial controls and administrative disciplines as McDonalds has applied to fast-food retailing? "What if" you decided to strategically commit yourself to this theme? What would be the gains? What would be the impact on the organisation? What would be the implications for the kinds of professionals, managers and leaders you would need?

Alternatively, you are a highly successful financial services firm, utilising a combination of dominant market share and a low cost base to achieve impressive growth. "What if" you raised the competitive stakes even further by incorporating a "Visionary" theme? "What if" you decided to reinvent the industry rules through the development of phenomenally innovative products and services? "What if" you decided to become the Sony of financial services, developing imaginative products with "drum-beat rapidity"? Is this strategy realistic given the existing leadership capability? How would succession priorities need to shift?

Or, what if one of your major competitors decided to compete aggressively in the arena of "Lobbyist"? By raising their profile generally, with customers and the general public, and building greater influence with decision-makers in political and media circles, what would be the impact on your organisation's competitive position? How quickly would you be able

"What if" we wanted to become more?
Visionary; Explorer; Builder; Lobbyist; Integrator;
Regulator; Trouble-shooter or Architect?

Current roles	Obvious successors	External resourcing	Possible successors from emerging talent
● does our current structure reflect this theme? ● which specific roles are critical? ● how effective do we think we are now? ● which roles would we need to create in future?	● which individuals are capable of moving into current roles? ● which individuals are capable of moving into newly created roles?	● how easy or difficult would external recruitment be? ● can we identify any specific individuals we would want to bring in?	● which individuals with proactive development represent potential capability in this area?

Figure 6.16   "What if" succession

to respond to this challenge? How effectively would the current leadership respond in overcoming this threat?

Thinking through the implications of these "what if" scenarios generates another set of questions:

- Is this theme reflected in our current structure? Which specific roles are critical? How effective are the current role-holders? Which structural changes would we need to make to strengthen our effectiveness in these organisational activities?
- Which individuals would be capable of moving into these roles? Who are the obvious successors?
- How easy or difficult would external recruitment be? Are there are any specific individuals we would want to bring in?
- Which internal candidates with proactive development represent sources of capability?

BUSINESS CHALLENGE AND STRATEGIC REDEPLOYMENT

A major distribution company, its workforce one of the tenth largest in the UK, was planning a major reorganisation. The aim was to restructure what was at the time in the mid-1990s an immense corporate behemoth into discrete business units, decentralising power from a dominant centre to shift towards a more market-facing and entrepreneurial operating approach. The challenge was to redeploy the executive population across the new management structure, maximising existing succession data efficiently while implementing an open and defensible appointments process. At the outset, criteria were established to evaluate the success of this initiative:

- *Speed*, from initial conception to final appointments to get the new management in place quickly and build strategic focus to take on the challenges of the future while minimising organisational uncertainty.
- *Ensuring that internal talent had a "chance"* rather than hand over responsibility to an executive search firm for a complete corporate "wipe out" and mass replacement from outside. Although it was clear that the operating demands of the new structure would require external resourcing to bring in specific expertise, it was also important that the full range of available talent should be considered.
- *Avoiding short-term expediency* in managing the redeployment process which might jeopardise, not only executive commitment, but trust more widely throughout the organisation.

A steering group, involved in the strategic design of the blueprint structure, mapped out the key roles using structured check-lists and protocols to profile requirements against three elements: *Strategic orientation*: what would be the dominant business and organisational challenges of the role? *Management competency*: which specific managerial processes and practices would be critical in driving role effectiveness? *Technical know-how*: how important would professional expertise and know-how be; which specific aspects of functional and technical knowledge and application would be critical?

The 130 executive roles within the planned structure were analysed to identify similarities and differences in role requirements to group them into business leadership clusters. Four clusters were identified: Building the Business Future (Visionary/Lobbyist roles); Exploiting Immediate Opportunities (Explorer/Builder roles); Driving on Efficiency (Regulator/Trouble Shooter); and Planning Organisational Excellence (Integrator/Architect). At the same time the target population of around 400 managers undertook an assessment based on their track record and career accomplishments, the completion of a self-report questionnaire profiling breadth and depth of experience and effectiveness against the business types framework,[18] and structured interviews.

Database management ran an initial short-listing of the target executives based on suitability against the four clusters of roles. A first-round set of tough criteria based on experience and effectiveness formed the first short-listing of "obvious" executives, those credible candidates with the relevant profile of business experience, management capability and operating style. A second round of database matching loosened the criteria to be less demanding in the expectation of experience, focusing more on underlying skills and motivation. This second-round short-listing highlighted another group of executives, those without significant experience but with indicators of the talents and operating outlook which kept them in the frame for consideration. The aim at this stage was to keep searching through the database, interrogating the data not against formal job titles (these meant very little in the new organisational structure) but against business capability and outlook to identify an imaginative and far-reaching listing of candidates for final-round interviewing (see Figure 6.17).

This is the rationale of the business types model: to support a sustainable approach to strategic resourcing, by seeing leadership succession as more than identifying replacement candidates based on career resume for specific roles within fixed structures. Instead the aim is to be insightful in highlighting the capabilities that are critical to the organisation (capabilities that can be organised and structured in any number of different permutations) and to be imaginative in reviewing business leadership across the executive population.

Thinking about business risk assessment, from the perspective of critical roles, organisational structure or business capability, suggests there is no one succession plan! Instead there are a series of projections based on different scenarios, reflecting different assumptions about the future of the organisation and its leadership capability.

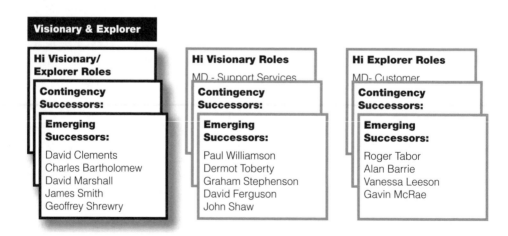

Figure 6.17 Succession by business challenge

Next steps

What metrics are in place to assess activity and progress in succession management?

- No measures are in place
- An ad-hoc evaluation
- Detailed tracking of succession coverage and exposure.

What process and format is currently in place to facilitate the discussion about resourcing risks and opportunities?

- Is this an annual chore to create a formal succession plan which disappears on compilation?
- Or an active dialogue between the strategic planning function, senior executives and human resources?

What are the expectations of different stake-holder groups?

- How should the outputs of business risk assessment be presented to respond to their requirements? High-level metrics; listings of roles and individuals; a detailed succession chart?
- What actions are made in response to this information? Compliance sign off, or a set of priorities to focus organisational decision-making?

What approach to business risk assessment will work best for your organisation?

- Conventional charting of coverage across the full management structure?
- Targeting succession only for critical roles?
- Mapping out succession coverage for role clusters or "strategic job families"?
- Identifying leadership capability against business challenge and capability?
- Utilising different perspectives for different audiences and applications?

What information flow is in place to inform the dialogue about business risk assessment?

- Between the corporate planning function and human resources?
- Between human resources and senior executives?
- Across the human resources function?

How are outputs of this dialogue informing the appointments process? What inputs are needed to facilitate a meaningful review of strategy, structures and individuals?

Notes

1. J. Collins, *Good to Great*, 2001.
2. Andy Grove, ex-CEO of Intel, "Business success contains the seeds of its own destruction", *Only the Paranoid Survive*, 1996.

3. Richard Koch, *The Power Laws*, 2000.
4. From William G. Flanagan, *Dirty Rotten CEOs*, 2003, and Robert Bryce, *Pipe Dreams*, 2002.
5. "It's top flight leaders who make a business great. The best measure of that quality may be the number of top executives who have been recruited to lead other organisations", Larry Bossidy, "The Job No CEO Should Delegate", *Harvard Business Review*, 2001.
6. Although why, for example, do female executives and professionals or those from minority backgrounds appear as ready in two to three years' time on the official plan, but are much less likely to advance to the "ready now" status?
7. Andy Grove, *Only the Paranoid Survive*, 1996.
8. Quoted from R. Kaplan and D. Norton, "Measuring the Strategic Readiness of Intangible Assets", *Harvard Business Review*, February 2004.
9. R. Giuliani, *Leadership* 2002.
10. There are at least 16 extreme caricatures and literally hundreds of variations accommodating these possible structural permutations.
11. G. Hamel and C.K. Prahalad, *Competing for the Future*, 1994.
12. To take a parallel highlighted in Chapter 4, the assessment of leadership should be less preoccupied with outcomes (what has been achieved in the past); instead, we should identify the attributes that will drive leadership success in the future. Attributes are the equivalent of the core competencies of leadership, fundamental assets which can be leveraged across a number of different situations.
13. Andrews Munro Ltd, "Measuring Organisational Resilience", 2001.
14. L. Eastman, *Succession Planning*, 1995.
15. Andy Grove, *Only the Paranoid Survive*, 1996.
16. See, for example, M. Gerstein and H. Reisman, "Strategic Selection: Matching Executives to Business Conditions", *Sloan Management Review*, vol. 24 (1983), pp. 118–207; R.E. Miles and C. Snow, *Organisational Strategy, Structure and Process*, McGraw Hill, 1978; T. Herbert and H. Deresky, "Should General Managers Match their Business Strategies?", *Organisational Dynamics*, vol. 15, Winter 1987.
17. There is a range of diagnostic tools for role profiling, self-assessment, interviewing and 360° feedback, as well as resource material to support this methodology (www.andrewsmunro.com).
18. An on-line assessment of business experience and effectiveness, Executive Audit, Andrews Munro Ltd.

7 *Creating a Talent Blueprint*

"How do you attract, retain and develop winning people? Those nine words represent the biggest single challenge facing many corporations." Barry J. Gibbons, former CEO of Burger King

"The leadership pipeline is dry." R. Charan, S. Drotter and J. Noel, *The Leadership Pipeline*

Although immediate business pressures encourage a series of short-term "resourcing fixes", this is not a sustainable position for the long term. Achieving and maintaining organisational success requires proactivity to strengthen the "leadership pipeline", maintaining a flow of talent at every level within the organisation. While senior management roles are important and the focus of much succession attention, the future success of the organisation hinges not simply on its current executives; it relies on another generation of professionals and managers.

"Talent" has become the new organisational buzz word, but confusion about its meaning is creating problems. Robust succession management requires a clear-headed analysis of talent and how it should be defined to create a meaningful blueprint to guide decisions about who should be developed and progressed.

THE PROBLEM OF POTENTIAL

The heads of the department have recently conducted a talent review exercise across the department. Each of the heads now has the responsibility for providing face-to-face feedback to their reports.

Individual: "So how did the talent review go?"

Head: "Pretty good I think...OK."

Individual: "As I said last week, you know, I feel really good about the initiatives this organisation is taking and I want to be part of its expansion. I feel I've got to grips with my role and I think I'm ready to move on to take on a bigger job. I've been looking through this prospectus...the MBA programme looks strong..."

Head: "Well, we reviewed...the problem is that, at this moment in time you weren't seen as being high potential..."

Individual: "What...but I'm performing well...you said so in our last appraisal. You know I'm keen, I'm motivated, I'm really keen to learn...so why am I not seen as high potential?"

Head: "It's quite difficult to explain. Potential well...it's more than how well you're doing now...it's...you're not seen as ready to move on."

Individual: "Why? What am I doing wrong? What am I not doing? Tell me."

Head: "Look. This wasn't my decision. There is a feeling with the other guys that you're not...you don't quite...you're not a team player."

Individual: "What does that mean?"

Head: "I don't know...you just...can we discuss this later? I've got another meeting scheduled in five minutes."

Challenges and dilemmas

Across the battle-grounds of succession management, the identification and development of talent is the force which is being assembled now to fight future business wars. The harsh reality is that the current organisational leadership will not live on to fight another day. Future corporate success will depend on another leadership generation, the leadership that can "preserve the core", build on the past, but which has the capability to stimulate progress and move the organisation forward to take on future challenges. Rather than simply rely on good luck or a Darwinian survival of the fittest, talent management is the organisational proactivity to identify emerging talent and accelerate its development. Talent management is a summary of the actions the organisation takes to strengthen its "pipeline" to ensure the stock of leadership and professional capability is progressing quickly, developing greater skill and maturity of outlook and increasingly ready to take on greater responsibility.

"Talent" is an easy word to throw around; it is the new organisational buzz word. But what does it really mean? What underpins it? Why and when is it important to the organisation? Key challenges in designing and implementing a robust game plan for talent management include:

- *Identifying priorities for talent management in the face of organisational change and uncertainty* about the organisation's future leadership requirements. Why does it make sense to invest in developing a generation of leadership and professional talent when competitors may poach your best talent, or business circumstances change and you have to shift strategy, refocus or downsize and lose this talent?
- *Targeting organisational investment around some individuals, not all* and avoiding the alienation of many. The option of playing "succession roulette" to bet on a few individuals rather than spread bets equally across the employee population can represent a smart talent management strategy, maximising the organisational impact of targeted investment on key individuals. But badly managed, this approach has the potential to be divisive and undermine a corporate culture based on collective "team spirit".
- *Avoiding the "self-fulfilling prophecy"*, fast-tracking those individuals with the "badge of high potential" leaves the "badgeless" colleagues behind. The challenge is to identify talent quickly. But what if this triggers a set of management expectations, which make it much easier for some individuals to advance, not through achievement or contribution, but through possession of the "high potential badge"? And what if this early assessment is wrong? What about those individuals without the badge who are denied such opportunities for career development? This is a fundamental dilemma: is leadership development the "strengthening and polishing of what already exists" or is it more about the acquisition of abilities, of "bringing new things into being?"[1]
- Reinforcing a performance culture in which individuals are continually accountable for their contribution while accepting that proactive development, placing talent in unfamiliar roles outside current experience to take on new challenges, runs the risk of failure. How do we *reconcile a track record of consistent achievement, often used as an indicator of "potential", with the experience of failure?* If failure is an important element in leadership development (after all, a career without failure is probably a career which hasn't taken any risks), how do you avoid the "black mark" phenomenon? This is a common hazard of fast-track high-potential programmes and probably the major reason why many previously well-regarded individuals fall off the succession plan.

Tracking the impact of talent management

Most organisations these days would claim to have a talent management strategy of some kind in place. So how is its impact tracked and evaluated? (See Figure 7.1 for metrics of talent management.) The first overall theme is *Protection*: how well is current talent being safeguarded? What percentage of your existing talent, for example, is being retained? To calculate the *Retention* index, you need to track overall turnover levels, and, more importantly, to break down overall figures by level, business area and, above all, by talent, that is, *those you want to retain*. An effective talent management programme, first and foremost, must hold on to current talent. Going out to recruit and develop new talent at the same time as the highly capable and talented are walking out of the door is a sign of an organisation in trouble. This is an organisation attempting to spend its way out of a pending debt, and a business in the advanced stage of corporate bankruptcy. Overall turnover or retention statistics miss the point. The focus should be on those individuals who are valuable to your organisation and you can ill afford to lose.

At risk metrics provide an insight into the potential loss of talent in the future. At risk identifies the percentage of individuals seen as ready to advance but blocked in their progression. This is an early warning sign of the future loss of talent, talent which is stuck and can't see where it can progress within the existing structure. This is a problem we saw, for example, in one professional services firm which had expanded quickly around the talents of a core group involved in its start-up, a close-knit set of individuals who had provided the original momentum for business growth. Additional talent had been quickly recruited to support further expansion. Reluctant to accommodate the rising aspirations of the "outsiders", the senior professional circle held on tightly to its power. After a period of rising frustration the "outsiders" left. Therefore the firm saw a mass defection of talent, a talent which proved difficult to replace; worse still, in some instances, talent which went on to competitors or set up rival firms.

Protection	Pipeline	Proactivity
Retention % of "key individuals" in post after 12 months ● retaining key talent	**Progression** % of target population seen as ready to progress to next level within X time scale ● strength of leadership in pipeline	**Development** % of target population with a personal development plan ● developing talent in readiness to progress
At Risk % of "key individuals" blocked in progression ● identifying blockages to the leadership pipeline		**Spend** average spend on training and development ● financial commitment to accelerate development

Figure 7.1   Metrics of talent management

A TALENT MISMANAGEMENT SCENARIO

A major FMCG business invested in the development of a sales manager. She has benefited from a range of business education and management development programmes and has been promoted to Sales Director. She is regarded as the best people manager throughout the business. There is a reorganisation at Group level, an external recruit is brought in to refocus the sales force and there is duplication of roles.

The Sales Director loses out. The organisational compromise: a generous outplacement and redundancy package and a six-month consultancy contract to manage the change process of moving to a new sales structure. After the six-month period she sets up as a high-performance coach, going on to share her expertise and knowledge with the firm's competitors.

Pipeline measures are a summary of the strength of the talent pool at different organisational points. What percentage of individuals of the target population are seen as ready to progress to the next level? It is this index that summarises the long-term resourcing health of the organisation. This index needs careful analysis. For those organisations who undertake performance-potential mapping exercises, the evaluation of potential can easily become wrapped up in a statement of who line managers regard as their best performers, performers they do not want to lose. Their identification as high potential is a kind of line management shorthand to reinforce a positive view of their contribution, ensuring they receive full organisational recognition. Current performance should be highlighted, praised and rewarded, but it shouldn't be confused with readiness to progress to the next level.

Proactivity is an index of "talent in development", an indicator that the promise of future contribution is being translated into effectiveness for the longer term. This is a more difficult measure to pin down, but nonetheless an important one in highlighting your organisation's commitment to "do something" with the talent it has identified. Without the momentum of challenging and stimulating development, experiences which stretch and test, and coaching and mentoring to support and encourage, talent stagnates. The typical measure of proactivity is the *percentage of individuals with a personal development plan*; not a hastily scribbled note to placate the human resources function, but a robust plan with specific goals and detailed actions.[2] Some organisations utilise financial measures as a bottom-line index of their commitment to the development of talented professionals and executives (for example, average training and development spend per individual). It is a troublesome statistic. While it may signal a shift in organisational attitude, indicating the willingness to invest in proactive succession, it may be no more than an input measure, saying nothing about the outcomes of development.

Talent management manoeuvres

Once organisational rhetoric, "people are our greatest asset", organisations are now moving to the reality of "the *right* people are our greatest asset". The succession management challenge is to identity, develop and deploy these individuals to maximise their contribution. For most organisations, most of the time, talent management is the ongoing relationship between line management and staff to provide employees with support, guidance and coaching. At best, enlightened managers are alert to spot and recruit individuals with that "spark" which indicates something special, are insightful in nurturing this talent, and imaginative in opening up opportunities to develop this talent further. At worst, incompetent, lazy or neurotic management recruits in its own image, filtering out talent that might challenge its status, and ignoring or bullying any talent that does manage to progress and might threaten its position.

The "free market" model, relying on a mix of external recruitment, day-to-day work activity guided by line management to grow talent, and open advertising to create opportunities for progression, has the virtue of simplicity. The drawback is its dependence on individual line managers to develop their staff, particularly if proactive development is needed which is outside the scope of day-to-day work. Organisations therefore embark on a number of additional manoeuvres in order to be more proactive as regards the talent which they bring in, develop and promote.

"BUY IN THE BRIGHT, BEAUTIFUL AND BEST"

To raise our business game and provide the calibre of leadership which will push ahead of our competitors, outstanding talent should be brought in from outside to shake up the organisation. This is the recruitment of the exceptionally gifted individuals, as evidenced by the universities and business schools they attended, the grades they have achieved, and their scores on standardised psychometric tests.

This strategy comes at a price and a risk. The price is the high resourcing costs and salaries demanded by the "bright, beautiful and the best"; the risk is that they aren't right for your business. Badly implemented, this strategy results in the over-promotion of intelligent and technically competent individuals, but who haven't mastered management fundamentals and whose actions begin to undermine the efforts of their colleagues. Alternatively, this strategy results in the loss of a cohort of high-potential recruits who, after 18–24 months of intensive induction and training, become disillusioned and leave in droves to join rival companies. This is a double whammy: not only has investment in recruiting talent been lost but you have also paid for part of the development of your competitors' future professionals and executives.[3]

This strategy works best when the organisation's management, if not "corrupt",[4] has reached the point of such complacency or incompetency that corporate survival can only be attained through the whole-scale removal of large numbers of the executive population and replacement with a group of leaders and professionals from outside, uncontaminated by the prevailing culture.

In the film *The Untouchables*, the account of the FBI's attempt in the 1930s to tackle Chicago gangsterism and associated police corruption, there is a scene where the investigating team is being assembled — "the untouchables". The worldly-wise cop remarks to Elliot Ness, the FBI prosecutor, "if the barrel is full of rotten apples, then go to the orchard to pick them". The "untouchable" team had to be selected from those outside the mainstream police culture, from independent individuals unconnected to the political system of corruption.

Occasionally you may need to start again. This is high risk, with a low probability of success, but for some organisations at some moments, it may be the only resourcing card left to play. Some years ago we worked with a leisure firm, planning a £100 million plus investment in its infrastructure, an infrastructure that had been sorely neglected for decades. Accompanying this investment in its physical fabric was a reorganisation of the management structure to centralise much activity back to head office. The driver here was the need for greater consistency around compliance to organisation-wide standards. It also wanted to establish an operating culture built around greater customer focus, based on highly trained employees, proud of their company and work. As part of the redeployment process, over 150 managers underwent a focused assessment programme. At this stage it became clear that a significant number of managers either couldn't or weren't prepared to make the required management shift in attitude or outlook. In addition, a management minority could be described as operating in that grey zone of ethical behaviour, of participating or colluding in dubious business practices. However, faced with the implications of a complete shake-up of the management population, and the associated redundancy, recruitment and training costs, the organisation decided to retain almost all of the existing management population. Within one year it became clear that the massive investment programme was not meeting its original financial forecasts. The organisation was sold in less than three years.

THE ACCELERATED DEVELOPMENT MODEL

In the accelerated development model, the organisation recognises that it probably employs considerable talent already but it hasn't been proactive enough in identifying, developing and deploying this latent capability. It recognises there is a range of talent throughout the organisation but it is talent which is stuck, lacking the power and influence to make a business difference. One CEO, frustrated by senior management's sluggish response to change initiatives, said to his HR Director, "What I want to see are those individuals who aren't afraid to put their heads above the parapet. Find these people and we'll work with them."

At this point the organisation implements a series of initiatives, typically involving:

- asking line management to conduct an exercise in mapping the potential of their staff
- coordinating a talent review session to review and agree a short-list of high-potential prospects
- formulating action plans to drive their development.

The worthy aim here is to tap into current organisational talent which is going unnoticed and unrecognised. The reality is that this approach also involves much deliberation over what potential is, and how it should be defined and evaluated, a series of extended discussions taking up considerable time and effort to plot individuals out on a matrix of performance-potential. But not much action. The end-point seems to be a listing of names but few meaningful recommendations and actions to make a resourcing difference. Alternatively, this is an exercise in advocacy in which managers push forward the career aims of their best people, those individuals who for their managers' own personal reasons they want to defend and protect.

As a variation of this approach and an acceptance that line managers may be either unwilling or unable to rate potential, the organisation introduces some more formal and objective evaluation process, sometimes utilising assessment centre methodology. At best this strategy genuinely throws up fresh sources of talent (and probably questions established players). At worst, if poorly integrated with other organisational initiatives, it can result in a set of mixed messages, confusing both individuals and their line managers. Line managers are annoyed that unexpected members of their team are seen as high potential. Individuals may be upset to discover that the organisation now doesn't think they are as good as their line manager had indicated.

The big challenge is the "what happens next" factor. Talent is identified but how is this talent then deployed? Well-designed fast-track programmes, incorporating intensive business education, coaching and mentoring, assignments and secondments, equip participants to take on greater responsibility. But they also raise participant expectations; expectations which if unfulfilled can be counter-productive. In our experience, accelerated development models work best when there is a clear focus, when the organisation needs to develop talent to move into specific roles within a defined time frame. They don't work when implemented in a vacuum, when there is no pressing business priority.

One of our most satisfying consulting assignments involved forming a group of eight executives to build a new support team for a home furnishing retailer. The objectives were clear: to have the new team up and running within a year, making an impact against defined measures of customer satisfaction. An initial internal search identified around 50 candidates who underwent an intensive assessment programme. Few of the selected managers were ready to get up to speed immediately, but all displayed the underlying skills, operating motivation and attitude that would be important in the new role. Over a 12-month period we worked with this group, supporting their line manager, the Customer Service Director, through a series of formal training events, assignments and projects, and coaching. This team became a highly capable unit, supporting their operational colleagues in driving improvements in customer service. This initiative was a success because the focus was clear (get this team up to speed within one year) and outcomes could be evaluated (improvements in the organisation's customer service).

Accelerated development can be a powerful tactic in talent management but only when grounded in specific goals, for the organisation and for individuals. Introduced as a manoeuvre to do something about your up-and-coming managers and professionals will do nothing.

THE "MOTIVATIONAL JAMBOREE"

Bringing in talent from outside can be problematic and attempting to fast-track talent from within also has its hazards. Perhaps the alternative, to treat every employee as "talented", might be the better approach. This strategy operates around the assumption that each employee has the potential to achieve greatness, but that each individual isn't exploiting or deploying the full array of his or her talents. Once the totality of individual energy and talent is released, every employee will be empowered to make a fuller contribution. After two or more decades of "big-tent-evangelical-zeal-motivational" events it is easy to dismiss this approach. The organisational conference, seminar or workshop, organised around the "call to arms" presentation from a senior figure, phoney awards, superficial employee incentives and the external speaker with inspirational anecdotes, is now the raw material of comedy sketches and close to the world of "David Brent's Office",[5] with the potential for employee cynicism.

However, this approach, if designed and launched with honesty and sincerity, designed around issues of substance which genuinely engage the aspirations and concerns of employees and, above all, takes place against a cultural backdrop of fairness and equity, signals to the entire workforce that everyone can and should make a difference. It is a statement that the organisation doesn't just revolve around the top team and a handful of the chosen few. Here again, the issue is one of alignment, of consistency between strategic message, cultural style, management behaviour, and personnel policies and practices and the way in which employee commitment initiatives are positioned.

Fighting "the war for talent": a message from the front line

THE START OF "THE WAR"

In 2001, a ground-breaking study was published based on the management consultancy McKinsey's analysis of the talent management practices of high-performing firms. The research aim was to determine how successful companies "build a strong pool of managerial talent, how they attract, develop and retain people and build a pipeline of younger talent to progress to more senior positions".[6] *The War for Talent* became a kind of bible to a generation of HR professionals who were beginning to recognise the constraints of the established competency movement but were still faced with the challenge of implementing something better.

The war had been sparked in the mid-1990s. The economy was expanding, and specifically the knowledge economy, not least in the fast-growing IT sector, was booming. Old economy firms were seeing the defection of some of their best people to the dotcom firms and other start-ups. Demand for smart and motivated employees was exceeding the available supply. In addition, the available pool of talent was made up of that generation of young professionals who had learned the tough lessons of corporate life from their parents. The mothers and fathers of "Generation X", who had been part of the 1980s downsizing experience, knew that loyalty counted for little and that job-hopping was the best personal strategy. Against this backdrop, the book *The War for Talent* outlined five imperatives for organisations (see Figure 7.2):

"Talent wars" reminded organisations that individuals make a big difference and some individuals make a bigger difference than others. This now seems obvious. But in the egalitarian culture of today, a culture in which everyone is equal,[7] "talent wars" made it clear that not only are we not equal, but we are more unequal than we might like to think. This is an echo of the Pareto principle, the 80-20 law, that 20 per cent of your employees probably account for 80 per cent of your organisation's profitable performance, and 20 per cent are responsible for 80 per cent of the organisation's problems. The message: to know who your best people are, to understand them, to ensure they are maximising their effectiveness, and to retain them, seems at one level pretty obvious, but it was a message that many firms had neglected.

The concept of the "War for Talent" also served as an acute reminder to organisations of the need for greater honesty in performance review and appraisal, to differentiate employee contribution, to confront under-performance and to recognise and reward superior performance. It focused attention on the obvious fact that failing to address under-performance represents a dangerous dynamic with the potential to threaten the future of the organisation. Apart from the obvious threat to competitiveness, under-performing employees undermine expectations and pull other employees down and they drive out the high-performing individuals.

The talent perspective also emphasised the need to look beyond a narrow pool of

Develop a talent mindset

make it an obsession to get the best people, because business performance is driven by exceptional contribution. The leadership focus should be about bringing in the best, empowering individuals to perform at their best, and coaching talent to maximise its impact. First and foremost it is people who make the business difference. Successful firms understand this and know how to maximise the performance of their employees.

Create an employee value proposition

build a culture and working environment which attracts the best people and encourages them to stay. Work out what it is your talented people want, why they would want to work for your organisation and provide it. Create an organisational culture and working environment which fosters the aptitude and creativity of your best people. Make your organisation a "compelling" place for talent, a challenging, exciting and fun environment in which talent can flourish.

Rebuild your recruitment strategy

specifically develop an aggressive stance and imaginative approach to locate and select talent. Don't wait to fill vacant positions. Instead keep scanning endlessly the market to seek out talent and bring it in at every level, not just for entry-level roles, but also for junior, middle and senior positions. Don't define your talent requirements around existing roles and vacancies. Be proactive in creating new opportunities for talent you uncover. Don't operate on the basis of resourcing for roles within the existing structure; search out those individuals who can make a difference and let them get on with it, unconstrained by formal job descriptions and reporting lines.

Accelerate the development of talent

identify ways to accelerate the development of talent and build these processes into the organisational fabric. Be imaginative in how you nurture and develop talent. Provide stretch assignments, utilise coaching and mentoring, tailor development to the individual. Don't be constrained by past patterns of career progression; focus on individuals, personalise their development, and be innovative in "flexing" career paths to accommodate employee aspirations.

"Differentiate and affirm" people

develop a greater candour to highlight the low and high performers and be more willing to reinforce and reward superior performance. Don't operate on the basis that everyone is OK. Recognise exceptional talent as exceptional and reward it in exceptional ways. Don't tolerate sub-standard performance; identify and manage under-performing individuals out of the organisation.

Figure 7.2   Talent wars: five imperatives

supposedly eligible and credible candidates to seek out more fundamental skills and attitudes. Companies constrain their resourcing options when they over-estimate the importance of credibility, of coming from the "right company with the right career resume". The search for talent means looking beyond the obvious to identify those underlying attributes which will have value to the organisation.

The talent perspective also reinforced the need for organisational flexibility. Structures and roles have value only in so far as they allow individuals to deploy their energies and talents productively. And an organisation committed to talent management needs to shift and flex in how work is organised to accommodate the range and diversity of its talent.

But within a year the backlash had begun and *The War for Talent* became the target of blistering attacks in the business press.[8] Fuelling much of the criticism was undoubtedly the identification of Enron as an exemplar of excellent talent management practice. It wasn't simply the incongruity between Enron as a first-mover in innovative talent management and the fireworks of its business failure. It was that its talent management philosophy and adoption of best practice prescription was seen as an important factor in explaining Enron's downfall. So why could this apparent common sense and cutting-edge innovation in talent management backfire so spectacularly?

THE ASSUMPTION THAT THERE IS ONE WAR WHICH BUSINESSES NEED TO FIGHT IN THE SAME WAY

Different wars require different strategies and different tactics. Not every business war is being fought on the battle-ground of talent. At the obvious and superficial level, employees are an organisation's greatest asset. But competitive success isn't simply about "talented" individuals. Most of the time it is about the organisational infrastructure to coordinate the efforts, skills and know-how of a group of individuals working collectively as part of a unified team effort. Concentrating organisational effort on a few individuals may be for some organisations the force that undermines a culture of team cooperation. Paradoxically an emphasis on talent management, far from providing a robust business model, can become reliant on a handful of talented individuals. This is not a strategy; this is a "hope and a prayer" based on individual brilliance.

"Talent wars" also ignore the fact that competitive advantage can be gained on a number of fronts: innovative products, brand position, marketing and distribution presence, supplier and customer relationships, smart knowledge systems and responsive information technology. People are one factor in this mix; smart companies understand this mix, knowing where talent has most leverage.

TALENT STRATEGIES AND FORMULA 1[9]

Formula 1, the world's premier motor racing sport, is an intensely competitive business. Eddie Jordan, entering the Formula 1 paddock for the first time as team principal, was greeted with the words, "Welcome to the piranha club". This is a sector in which the battle for the best aerodynamicists, best race engineers and best drivers is fought at a ferocious level. This is a competitive world: the margin between success and failure on the racetrack, measured in tenths of a second, translates into hundreds of millions of dollars in annual accounts.

Each racing team has a budget, the money raised partly by prize money from previous racing success, by TV revenues and, above all, by sponsorship funds. Sponsors of course want to see success, and racing success creates more sponsorship money to fund future competition. Every year, each racing team is faced with a series of complex decisions in the allocation of its budget. How should it spend its money to maximise its ability to win the championship?

- A *"driver package"*: buying in an established world champion, a proven contender, or a "rookie" new to Formula 1.

- *Race-car design and engineering*: building the most competitive car on the track and achieving the optimal combination of speed and reliability.
- *Team infrastructure and support*: the capacity to sustain a testing programme, to plan and coordinate logistical back up to mount a competitive challenge throughout the eight-month season.

Funds allocated to the recruitment of a world champion driver leave less money for race-car design and engineering or investment in the support infrastructure. Equipping the team with leading-edge design facilities and top-notch aerodynamic and engineering personnel to build a fast car reduces the available money for a proven race-winning driver, and so on. Different teams and their principals have a different outlook on the mix of success factors and implement different strategies, with different outcomes. For some, the focus has been on the car and directing maximum investment on building the

fastest one, preferring to spend money on research and development rather than pay the high salaries of established drivers. Other teams and principals have bought in championship winners on premium salaries. A handful of other teams have attempted to excel through their organisation of a professional infrastructure and the ingenuity of their race tactics.

In organisational terms, "talent wars" assumes that success comes from hiring the fastest driver. But it doesn't, as several teams attempting to break into Formula 1 have discovered to their huge cost. It comes from the combination of driver, car and support infrastructure. (It took Ferrari more than two decades to learn this lesson; when it did it won three back-to-back constructors championships.) A sustainable talent management strategy depends on the integration of talent, strategy, culture, systems and processes. Spending money on the "brightest and best" driver, when the car (product/service proposition) or infrastructure (systems and processes) is flawed, is a poor investment.

Building a competitive car	Selecting a driver combination	Putting in place the infrastructure to win
● Integrating engineering with aerodynamics ● win this season ● next season ● in the long term	● proven champions ● competitive contenders ● up and coming talent	● testing capability ● racing strategy and tactics ● sponsorship management
Focus on the best "product package"	*Leadership capability makes a difference*	*Improving the efficiency of organisational systems and processes*

Figure 7.3   Formula 1 and battle-grounds of success

A VAGUE DEFINITION OF WHAT TALENT IS AND WHAT UNDERPINS IT

Talent is defined as "the sum of a person's abilities, intrinsic gifts, skills, knowledge, experience, intelligence, judgement, attitude, character and drive. It also includes the ability to learn and grow".[10] In summary, talent seems to be an aggregation of everything. But when a definition covers everything it is about nothing in particular. Undeterred by this loose definition, the authors of *The War for Talent* point out that "you simply know it when you see it". This seems to be the opposite of most people's everyday experience. It is true there are probably a handful of obviously exceptional gifted individuals performing at an extraordinary level of performance whom everyone considers to be outstanding talent. But you don't need a talent management process to identify them: they stand out in a prominent way. There are other individuals who obviously just aren't making it. With organisational honesty they can be identified and addressed. Most of the time, there are most people, who some of the time perform at extraordinary levels but some of the time struggle to make an impact. This seems to be the key challenge of a talent management programme — to be insightful in identifying the *"non obvious" individuals*:

- Those individuals in the wrong role at the wrong time, who have fallen between the "corporate cracks".
- Those whose careers have stalled and are stuck and are not making the contribution their skills and energies might indicate.
- Those who are setting out on their careers but have not had the opportunity to demonstrate their talent.

An effective talent management initiative will be astute in knowing how to identify talent, looking beneath the surface to spot underlying qualities, and be shrewd in recognising how to maximise these aptitudes. It will be insightful in acknowledging there are different talents, and skilled in nurturing and developing these talents. It will also be prepared to question the "obvious" talent to go beyond track record and past educational or professional achievement. You simply don't know talent when you see it.

THE TACTICS OF PERFORMANCE DIFFERENTIATION AND THE POLICY OF "RANK AND YANK"

Enron's approach is illustrative of the "rank and yank" prescription in its introduction of a review process to sort employees into performance categories. Officially called the Performance Review Committee (PRC), otherwise known as the "pit of vipers", the PRC was described by CEO Jeff Skilling as "the most important thing for forging a new strategy and culture — it is the glue that holds the company together".[11] A's were the superstars who needed to be retained, to be given greater responsibility and to be rewarded extraordinarily well. B's were the middle group to be encouraged and motivated. For C's, the message was clear: "shape up or ship out". To ensure a clear "sorting", evaluation followed a "forced choice distribution"; A's were the top 10–20 per cent, Bs the middle 60–70 per cent and Cs the bottom 10–20 per cent. But performance can only be evaluated in a fair and equitable way if performance is known. It is clear that in the "freewheeling" culture of Enron this was all but impossible. Those awarded A status, the superstar individuals, were continually pushed into new roles where consistent delivery of results was impossible to track and measure.[12]

"We are not discussing D players, the clearly incompetent or unethical managers since all companies take quick action on them."[13] In Enron it was quite clear they didn't. In the topsy-turvy world of Enron, band D managers were the band A managers. Various insider accounts indicate an operating culture in which the badge of band A allowed individuals to operate with complete impunity. One senior executive, despite a series of business bungles but with the mark of superstar, left the organisation with a massive pay-out. Another executive promoted a secretary with whom he was having an affair to a position paying in excess of $500 000.

MANAGING TALENT: RANK AND YANK STYLE

You are the manager of a business unit of 85 employees. As a result of a whole series of initiatives you and your colleagues have undertaken — improved recruitment, better training and workflow management — the unit has exceeded its targets and surpassed all expectations. Productivity is high and the mood is upbeat. You are asked to submit your annual performance reviews for the unit. Noting that your ratings are higher than those of your peers in other units, your manager asks you to rerun the exercise using a forced distribution. You must indicate your top 20 per cent performers, the middle 60 per cent, and the bottom 20 per cent. Your heart sinks; you know where this is heading.

"Rank and yank", made famous in large part from the positive experience of General Electric, is now becoming an established part of performance management in many firms. Having attempted to imitate the GE approach, many organisations are now regretting its introduction.

Firstly, there is the practical problem of the threat and cost of legal action. An increasing spate of lawsuits (for example, Ford, Microsoft, Conoco) has prompted organisations to rethink their "rank and yank" strategy. Apart from flagrant abuse by some organisations (to remove "unwanted" personnel such as older employees or minority groups), it is intrinsically unjustifiable and unfair. Secondly, it breaks down line management accountability for the management of performance. "Rank and yank" and the hidden complexities of statistical recalibration across units and departments break the open and explicit link between business objectives and goals, employee contribution and reward.

As one of our clients, a global player in the IT sector, said, "I don't get 'rank and yank'. We recruit the best we can, we train them pretty well and we attempt to encourage a team culture which values everyone's contribution. Then we say, 10 per cent of you haven't made the grade. And it's not that your performance is poor; if your performance is poor that's a different issue. No it's because you're not quite as good as your exceptional colleagues. Forced distribution rankings assume a normal distribution, but our entire effort has been skewing the performance distribution upwards."

Designing a talent management blueprint

UNDERSTAND THE ROLE OF TALENT WITHIN YOUR BUSINESS

The importance of talent within your organisation will depend on:

- *Your business strategy and how it is choosing to compete.* Fighting on established territory, where incremental improvement based on investment in streamlined processes produces profitable dominance, has one set of implications for talent management. Embarking on a strategy to break new ground through the design of innovative product-service concepts will have a different set of priorities. As a generalisation, *the greater the ambiguity, unfamiliarity and complexity of the strategic challenge, then the greater the talent requirement.*

- *The way in which you decide to organise work activity, the number of levels and the size and scope of roles.* A highly structured organisation, based on a multi-levelled hierarchy and tightly defined roles, will require "less" talent than one operating around a loose organisational template, with few levels and broad-based roles.
- *The dominant culture.* Is the operating ethos one of freedom, flexibility, discretion and the encouragement of initiative and innovation or is it largely about compliance with well-established disciplines? Is the working climate about "safety first" or about, "it's better to apologise than to ask for permission"?

Three years ago we conducted a research programme to analyse the range of indicators which organisations utilise to help identify emerging talent. It was no surprise that the most frequently mentioned was "proactivity": proactivity of intellectual outlook and interpersonal impact. Talent wants to make a difference; it wants to see ideas accepted, to persuade and influence others to get these ideas implemented.

DON'T START WITH AN ATTEMPT TO EVALUATE POTENTIAL

If succession management is about the anticipation, planning and preparation for the organisational future to ensure that key roles can be filled easily and quickly, then "potential" is the "promise" to achieve that future. If the ebb and flow of business strategy establishes organisational demand, then it is "potential" that should help us predict supply. At one level, we can all agree with the basic definition that potential is "the work that one can do in the future". The problem with this definition is that it doesn't help answer the questions: which types of work? Is this all types or just some specific kinds of work? And it's a bit woolly about time frames. What do we mean by future? Is this next week, next month, next year?

WARREN BUFFETT'S "HIDDEN SECRET" AND THE CIRCLE OF COMPETENCY

"Buffett does not know when, where or how opportunity will present itself. But he does know that it will, how to identify it when it does, which requires an ability to evaluate opportunity, and how to capitalise on it."[14] Buffett focuses only on investment opportunities within his "circle of competency", the circle that lies in *what is important and what is "knowable"*, reviewing the range of business options to make shrewd judgements on only the industries and companies he understands. "There are important things that are not knowable…and there things that are knowable but not important, and we don't clutter up our minds with those."

Good investment decisions are made in the zone of importance and knowability, decisions that allow consistency and accuracy of forecasting. Bad decisions are made when investors extend themselves into "unknowability", making financial predictions under the illusion that they can generalise from patterns of the known to what is fundamentally unknowable. (Staying within the "circle of competency" is not a bad strategy when it delivers compound growth of 25 per cent per year over a 37-year period.)

The identification and development of talent represents a series of investment decisions across the organisational portfolio of professionals and executives. Decisions need to be made to back some individuals rather than others, to identify those individuals who will provide a better return for the organisation than those which represent poor investments. How do you make these decisions? By keeping within Buffett's "circle of competency", of staying within what is important and knowable. *The concept of potential represents an attempt to move into the zone of "unknowability".*

"Potential" is a woolly concept, difficult to pin down. It is a loose concept with many different meanings. For some organisations, potential is a kind of organisational shorthand description for "valuable", but value perceived in a hazy way. Each company builds up its own terminology (for example, "good egg", "top banana", "rising star") to convey this theme. In essence "potential" is a way of highlighting those individuals who display a vague set of qualities which somehow are important to us as an organisation.

Defining potential is trying to "hit a moving target"; in making an evaluation of potential we are making a prediction of future performance. But if our view of the future changes and the kinds of leadership we need shift, then what are we predicting? We are "shooting arrows at a target which keeps moving". One retailer implemented a high-potential programme at no insignificant cost. The first phase involved a sophisticated assessment centre to highlight those senior executives who would be key players in providing future leadership capability. After a few months a new CEO was recruited and the executive team changed. At the next scheduled succession review forum the CEO went through the short-listed names from the assessment centre. Two of the original 12 were agreed; the other ten dismissed as no good. Why? It may be that the CEO was eliminating talent that might challenge his position, or that the assessment centre had got it wrong. More likely, organisational life had moved on to reshape structures and roles and the leadership requirement had changed. But if business circumstances keep shifting and the requirement for talent changes then why do we keep attempting to make long-term forecasts of potential?

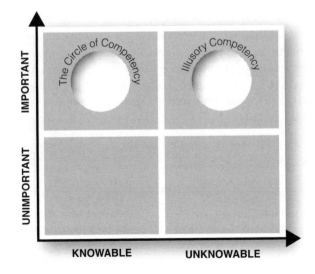

Figure 7.4   Warren Buffett's circle of competency

Of course it isn't just that the organisational requirement keeps shifting; individuals change too. Attempts at long-range forecasts of potential seem to assume a fixed, unchanging set of attributes and qualities. But if an important factor in "potential" is motivation, that complex mix of values, aspirations and energies; and motivation changes, which it does over the life span of a career, then what is the point of long-term predictions?

Attempts at precision are unrealistic; other organisations have accepted that this kind of loose definition isn't helping it manage the succession process and have attempted greater precision, defining potential either as readiness to progress within a certain time period (for example, ready to progress to next level within the next two years), or even more ambitiously, to determine the eventual organisational level individual potential might indicate it is destined to achieve (for example, potential to attain level 5). This quasi-scientific approach is seen in the type of complex graphs which, based on the combination of a "black box assessment" with an expert and the individual's age, plots out a career trajectory to pinpoint the organisational level the individual can be expected to attain. As an aside, this activity must be one of the most pointless exercises that an organisation could undertake. First, there is an absence of research evidence; the validation of this kind of assessment seems nigh on impossible.[15] Second, this approach is unrealistic. What is the point of predicting an individual's career trajectory 20 years' time from now? What organisational purpose is being served to say to one individual in his or her early thirties that they have the "potential" to master the challenges of a CEO of a global business enterprise, or to another that the assessment indicates they have reached their "natural level", whatever this might mean? What possible kind of practical business difference can this kind of assessment make?

"Potential" doesn't drive development. Of all the objections to potential as a concept or as an overall index of individual "futurability", the greatest difficulty is that it says nothing to inform the specific development activities which will translate "current potential" into "future performance". Too often talent review sessions agonise over rankings and ratings, plotting individuals onto matrices of potential and performance. At the end of the meeting, the job is done: a listing of agreed high-potential individuals. But what changes in the organisation as a result? The aim of these exercises is not to produce a piece of paper with a set of names, but to decide organisationally where additional development needs to be directed. For those key individuals the organisation is deciding to "back", how should this development investment be made? What specific career development recommendations need to be actioned to translate potential into performance? Either an individual is ready to assume greater responsibility and progress to the next level or they aren't. If they are rated as high potential what, practically, is holding them back? What is it they're doing or not doing which makes the difference?

WHERE ARE THEY NOW?

Think back three years ago within your organisation to the specific individuals highlighted as high potential. Where are they now? We have conducted this exercise with a number of organisations and the consistent findings are:

- A modest number of "shots on target": individuals seen at the time as high potential who are now progressing in line with organisational plans and in key roles. Invariably these are the obviously exceptional individuals.
- A sizeable number of "false hits":

individuals who although seen at the time as high potential are now stuck, sidelined, demoted or fired.

- *Lost talent*: individuals who despite/because of their talent have left

the organisation.

- *New faces*: individuals who weren't highlighted by the succession or talent management initiative but are now occupying key roles.

One of our clients, after a period of becoming bogged down in unproductive debates about potential, the criteria needed to define it, and fruitless discussions about which individuals were or weren't displaying it, reached the point when it dawned on him and his colleagues that they were attempting something which was impossible. "In our industry we're doing well if we can anticipate and plan business goals over a 12-month time scale. So we shifted our talent review process to concentrate on a practical discussion of what we should be doing in the next six months. We abandoned overall evaluations of potential; they were leading us nowhere. Instead we said to our line managers: "Tell us about the experience base of your people; where are the gaps? Talk through their strengths and limitations; let us know about their aspirations and what they want to do and where they're heading." So we now spend high-quality time on the specifics of our people. And that was a lot more helpful than debating who to place in which quadrant. We repeat the exercise after another six months. For us, lots of short-term stuff which we keep tracking is taking us further ahead than attempts at long-range predictions of potential."

The view that potential is "something" that some of us have more of than others, and that the more we have of this thing then the further we can progress up the organisational hierarchy is a simplistic analysis, and one that has hindered rather than helped organisations in managing succession. There are some fundamental traits and qualities,[16] which, all other things being equal, do predict future leadership effectiveness. But to put in place a framework which informs judgements of where proactive development needs to be directed requires more than an assessment of managers' cognitive power, work energy and interpersonal impact; the three most predictive components of leadership effectiveness. There is an irony in that organisations systematically collect different strands of data — informative data about the individual, where they've been and what they've done, what they're good at, what they're not so good at, what they want to do and not do in their future career, what motivates them and what demotivates them, and so on. This is rich information which is then condensed down into some kind of overall index of potential, readiness or promotability. Faced with this index, managers don't know what to do to put in place the specific actions which would provide a targeted development plan for the individual.

DESIGNING AN ORGANISATIONAL TALENT MAP

Figure 7.5 outlines one model of the talent pipeline. Careers progress through a series of transitions, reflecting the different challenges and demands of leadership capability within the organisational hierarchy.[17] Each transition demands a *new way of thinking* about the problems to be tackled, a *new way of operating* and a willingness to abandon previous styles which have been successful but will constrain effectiveness at the next level. Each transition requires a *shift in motivation* to take on a different set of organisational priorities, putting to one side previous tasks which had provided satisfaction and enjoyment but are no longer

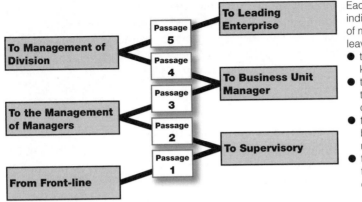

Figure 7.5   The talent pipeline

relevant. Attempting to boil this complexity down into a listing of 10 to 15 competency dimensions misses the point. Progression isn't about the gradual building of current competency or the acquisition of new competencies. It is a complex dynamic in which individuals need to shake off established ways of operating and be willing to redefine themselves, to assume a different career identity.

Different organisations define these transition points in different ways depending on their organisational structure (see Figure 7.6). Broadly, however, each passage through the organisational hierarchy can be summarised as a set of challenges, which require:

- building greater *credibility* to reassure stake-holders, typically peers and line management of leadership authority and legitimacy
- displaying the *capability* to take on the new challenges which emerge at each level and putting to one side the "old problems" of the previous level
- increasing maturity about *career management*, shifting career goals to reflect new operating demands, developing self-management skills and acquiring career tactics to adapt to the increasing number of hazards within the corporate hierarchy
- developing *character*, shifting horizons progressively from short-term personal interests to assume greater responsibility for long-term stewardship.

Front line to supervisory/junior management

On the front line, work is pretty much clear-cut. There is a job to be done and if there are any problems there is a supervisor to call on to resolve unfamiliar or difficult issues. The immediate challenge is to look and sound the part of an effective employee, building positive relationships with co-workers and line management, mastering the operating processes and procedures within the role, gaining an insight into the responsibilities of co-workers, and demonstrating the interpersonal skills to contribute fully to the team. It is also important to develop those self-management disciplines of time management and personal organisation. Front-line workers need to display high personal standards of work excellence, integrity and honesty in the management of work transactions and personal relationships.

Progression to the next level, advancing from a front-line role to a supervisory position, requires a shift:

	Credibility What needs to be done to build and maintain reputation?	Capability What skills are critical to operate effectively?	Career Management What tactics will optimise personal aspirations?	Character What leadership outlook and ethos is needed?
Top Management	Providing reassurance to external constituents of the organisation's strategic purpose Operating as a figurehead in communicating aims and goals	Strategic insight and "story telling" Culture management through communication Team leadership to assemble a balanced and business decision-making team	Managing personal life style within a demanding work schedule Shifting focus from personal advancement to organisational stewardship	Operating as a custodian of the organisation's fundamental principles Leading senior executives in rediscovering and reapplying the organisation's ethics and values
Senior Management	Taking an active role in building relationships with different stake-holder groups Conveying "gravitas" to establish authority within peer group	Translating strategic direction into business priorities Problem-solving and decision-making under uncertainty Negotiational impact	Rethinking life goals to direct effort towards realistic career ambitions Resolving emerging political tensions and interpersonal conflict to advance personal agenda	Taking a high profile in articulating the organisation's purpose and values Educating managers in exercising judgement to balance commercial reality and ethical principle
Middle/Professional Executive	Publicising the outcomes of personal accomplishments Drawing on business experience to establish personal influence	Resourcing and deployment skills Work flow analysis and productivity management Forward planning and financial management	Gaining organisational support and sponsorship for new initiatives Conflict resolution to optimise own position	Reinforcing clear ground rules for professional and business behaviour Being an exemplar role model of the organisation's ethics and principles
Junior/Supervisory	Supporting organisational initiatives to indicate commitment and loyalty Building a reputation for reliability and consistency	Prioritisation and scheduling of others' time Skills in review, feedback and coaching Relationship building with other business units	Discovering personal strengths to focus career aims and strategies Coming to terms with political realities to manage the "art of the possible"	Directing resources in a responsible way to avoid waste and inefficiency Communicating the organisation's views of what is and isn't acceptable in the workplace
Entry level	Building positive relationships with line manager and peers "Looking and sounding the part" of an effective employee	Mastery of operating processes and procedures Interpersonal skills as an effective team member	Self-management to prioritise effort around conflicting goals Impression management to convey enthusiasm and confidence	Setting high personal standards of work excellence Displaying integrity and honesty in all work transactions and relationships

Figure 7.6 Four Cs and leadership progression

- *Building credibility*: enhancing personal levels of credibility through the willingness to support organisational initiatives and displaying a personal commitment to the corporate cause. For those front-line employees who are unwilling or unable to make this commitment, credibility will be constrained.
- *Displaying capability*: the capability requirement increases at this point. It is not enough to be a highly effective front-line worker, although personal proficiency continues to be important. More significant is competency in the management of others and their work; skills in prioritisation, scheduling and performance management; reviewing employee contribution; giving insightful feedback and providing practical coaching in skills. This is a massive shift in operating approach for some, seeing results as achieved not simply through personal effort but through the coordination of the contribution of others.
- *Maturity of career management*: this transition requires a shift in personal identity, from being the "best front-line worker" to accepting responsibility for others; a change in career focus which some find too difficult an adjustment. It also involves the beginnings of an insight into organisational life, recognising that the organisation operates in an imperfect manner, and that as a supervisor they are now part of the problem as well as the solution.
- *Developing character*: this too grows in importance, representing a career shift which some are reluctant to make. At this point, character is expressed in the growing sense of ownership and responsibility to manage the organisation's resources efficiently, being prepared to tackle waste and low productivity. It is also the willingness to stand up and be counted, to express to others what is and isn't acceptable, to deal, perhaps for the first time, with unpopularity and resentment from work colleagues.

Supervisory to middle management

A new set of challenges emerges at this point. Whereas supervisory/junior management involves working with a close-knit group engaged in a specific organisational task, the move to middle management typically widens the horizon to span a range of different issues. Personal expertise to operate as the problem-solver for the team counts for less at this point than the willingness to coordinate diverse activities, many of which may be outside the individual's zone of familiarity.

- *Building credibility*: manoeuvring through this transition requires a growing awareness of organisational competition, recognising that those wanting to advance to this level are almost by definition a set of individuals skilful in gaining organisational attention. A key theme at this stage therefore is maximising authority with team members and peers, and raising personal profile more widely with other work units to build a reputation as an important player in the wider organisational game. At this stage internal candidates can be at a disadvantage *vis-à-vis* external candidates, who can draw on a broader base of experience to establish their authority. Internal candidates need to have established their own identity, being seen as a reliable worker who can be trusted to do the right organisational thing.
- *Displaying capability*: managing others throws up its own challenges. Managing those who have their own management responsibility provides a new and distinctive set of challenges. The dynamics of power and authority shift in a subtle but important way. Managing those with their own management responsibility requires greater subtlety of interpersonal and communication skills. Additional competencies include effectiveness

in work-flow analysis and productivity management, and skills in assessing resourcing requirements to deploy staff across a number of different work areas. Planning capability to see beyond next month's activities to identify priorities for the year, and financial analysis, using management information to go beyond budgetary control to identify opportunities to make a business difference, are key differentiators. Above all, the ability to see new problems, rather than tackle existing and well-defined issues, is a critical theme.

- *Maturity of career management*: to progress through this organisational transition, individuals must appreciate and engage fully with the realities of corporate conflict. Previously protected by their manager from this aspect of organisational life, individuals, if they are serious about their career progression, need to come to terms with the fact that their exciting proposals and initiatives will meet opposition from their peers. Advancement depends on skill to win broader organisational support, overcome opposition and win the backing of key sponsors. At a personal level, career goals need to change, shifting personal identity from being the best in a specific area of professional and technical expertise to now coordinating different strands of organisational activity, some of which are unfamiliar challenges.
- *Developing character*: advancement to this level requires a greater willingness to reinforce clear ground rules for professional and business behaviour throughout the work area. This can't be done through the simple communication of the organisation's mission and values. To be meaningful, this requires the kind of personal growth which has gained direct experience of the fundamentals of business ethics and integrity and has had real-life personal exposure to the harsh realities of working life. Importantly, progression to this level also requires the willingness to grapple with important life choices. On the one hand there is the drive to achieve peer recognition and status and financial recognition; on the other, there is also the need to stand out as a distinctive individual, staying true to personal values and beliefs and maintaining integrity.

Middle management/professional executive to senior management

Operating at middle management is difficult. Mid-ranking professionals and executives have to reconcile two sets of pressures: the upward pressures of employees, channelled through junior management, who may lack the authority to make decisions versus the downward demands of senior management, driven by the dictates of top management to see quick results. At one level the progression to senior executive roles should therefore be relatively straightforward with a gain in organisational power and influence. But new demands emerge. For one thing political pressures grow. Doing a good job increasingly isn't enough. It is about being seen to do a much better job than ambitious peers. In addition, working life becomes more complex and uncertain. At senior management levels there are few, if any, defined problems with obvious solutions. Instead there is a fuzzy set of issues where the challenge is defining what the problem might be, never mind generating a solution. Short-term commercial advantage needs to be traded against long-term organisational gain and the competing and contradictory demands of stake-holders need to be reconciled.

- *Building credibility*: in some organisations the quantum leap of interpersonal style known as the "gravitas jump" is triggered at this point. Some individuals have that certain bearing, that combination of dress sense, voice projection and overall demeanour; the facility to project self-assurance that encapsulates credibility. (For other organisations, of course, "gravitas" is insufferable pomposity.) But at this transition point, more often than not, credibility emerges as a critical theme. Advancing through this passage involves more than establishing authority throughout the peer group. It requires the acceptance and the approval of the top management group, a sense that you are "one of us" and can be trusted. But it is also probably for the first time that credibility needs to be established outside the organisation with other stake-holders, with key customers, suppliers, consultants and contractors, not simply within the organisation. In a "small corporate world" of tittle-tattle, gossip and hearsay, reputations can be built and destroyed overnight.

- *Displaying capability*: here the transition from being an effective middle manager to progressing to a senior executive position requires a significant step change. Two themes are critical. The first is the kind of problem-solving and decision-making skills which can accommodate and deal with ambiguity and uncertainty to make sense of unfamiliar and complex data to spot the fundamental issues. The second is negotiational effectiveness, the influencing skills to manage the subtleties of interpersonal encounters, overcome opposition and resistance and win support. "How to" management manuals increasingly lose their usefulness at this point; the challenge is drawing on advanced problem-solving and interpersonal skills to set the agenda rather than allow the agenda to be imposed by others.

- *Maturity of career management*: navigating this passage requires high levels of self-management skills to balance a range of competing working and life demands. Pressures on time become increasingly intense. There is a greater need to discriminate across the range of issues clamouring for attention, those that will advance personal goals from those that might distract effort and result in a career dead-end. Career ambitions, organisational priorities and longer-term life goals need to be balanced and traded. Operating at a senior level is likely to intensify political conflict. The challenge is to manage it positively and constructively with colleagues who may be negative and destructive.

- *Developing character*: at this stage in progression, character is required to take a higher profile in articulating the organisation's purpose and values, being prepared to stand up and be counted in business decision-making. In the hurly burly of corporate life, at this level there is pressure to take the easy way out, to go for short-term expediency. Character is required to battle for longer-term consistency of purpose. A key theme at this level is the need to become more actively involved in educating younger managers and professionals in business judgement, engaging them in the complexities of decision-making, balancing commercial pragmatism and ethical principle. This is a role that needs a maturity of outlook, authentic values and ethics, grounded in real-life experience to establish a credible role model.

Senior management to top management

The most significant theme for this transition is the time-scale and scope of the leadership imperative. Genuine leadership, that is, leadership that is motivated to secure and protect the interests of the organisation, must look beyond the current year's operational priorities to advance a long-term agenda. It also needs to broaden its horizons to see the organisation as part of a complex matrix of stake-holder relationships. Financial expectations need to be met in the short term at the same time as making decisions, the long-term consequences of which may be not yet known.

- *Building credibility*: credibility has to be established across an increasingly wider and demanding set of stake-holders. Relationships need to be forged with a variety of external constituents to communicate the organisation's aims and goals in a believable way. Credibility also needs to be reinforced internally, operating as figurehead, to find imaginative and inspirational ways of engaging the management population and workforce. In a world of sceptical stake-holders, internal and external, credibility is needed to restore, establish and maintain trust.
- *Displaying capability*: the big challenge in moving onto this level is the need to assemble a team, a balanced and diverse group which can provide a forum for business decision-making. This requires outstanding levels of team leadership to recruit those individuals with the right mix of capability and character (and remove those who don't) in order to "get the right people on the bus". At this level, high levels of strategic insight and "story telling" are critical. The challenge isn't simply to work with the top team to craft a business game plan that is sustainable, but to articulate it to others in a coherent way, a simple strategic story which clarifies priorities and focuses effort.
- *Maturity of career management*: at this stage the focus needs to shift from personal advancement to an outlook of organisational stewardship. Financial reward remains an important motivator but, if it is the dominant career driver, will represent a constraint to operating effectively at this level. Self-identity and work satisfaction must come from the desire to make a positive difference on others' lives, to achieve something long-lasting and worthwhile.
- *Developing character*: by this point character should have evolved and developed to produce a leadership outlook that is balanced and mature, with the wisdom to recognise what is and isn't important. Character possesses the insight to translate ethical principle into practical business judgement, and the commitment to instil a sense of stewardship within the senior executive team.

This approach is illustrative only. The point is to construct a blueprint for your organisation to highlight the shift in leadership requirements at different points in the organisational hierarchy. The challenge is to go beyond the mapping of competency on its own to incorporate those elements of credibility, career management and character which need to be reviewed in the consideration of emerging talent. This blueprint should summarise the key factors that guide progression within your leadership hierarchy, providing a framework to guide the identification and development of emerging talent as well as provide an explicit framework of the "rules of the career game" for your employees. For employees this should be condensed into a one-page summary; for line managers, no more than a three-page digest.

Once a talent map has been drawn up, the challenge then is how should talent be identified and assessed?

Next steps

What metrics are you using to track the impact of your talent management initiatives?

- None
- Minimal use of measures
- Sophisticated metrics linked to business and financial outcomes.

What is your overall approach to talent management?

- The concept of talent is not on the corporate agenda
- A reliance on "survival of the fittest"
- Bringing in the "bright, beautiful and best" from outside
- Fast-tracking the development of internal employees
- Maximising the contribution of all through the implementation of a variety of employee commitment activities.
- What are the current advantages and disadvantages of this strategy?

What assumptions does your organisation hold about talent?

- Talent is about having the "right stuff" and the focus is on spotting it
- Everyone is talented and development should be for all
- Talent is evident in different ways for different individuals and requires an imaginative and flexible strategy to identify and develop it.

How well does your organisational infrastructure and operating culture encourage talent?

- Talent is being "squeezed" out of the organisation
- Talent is encouraged and developed if it "plays by the rules" and fits in
- Talent has significant freedom and discretion to express itself and make a difference.

What framework is in place to help guide resourcing decisions?

- There is no framework; rather a reliance on inconsistent and subjective "guestimates"
- Use of overall indices of potential
- An organisation-wide model outlining a listing of standard competency dimensions
- A map of the key factors that drive progression at different organisational levels.

Notes

1. This is what Morgan McCall has called the "agricultural" and "Darwinian" model", leadership effectiveness as growing or selecting talent, and a variation of the broader nature–nurture debate. Is talent more to do with what you're born with and development the release of this latent potential, or is talent the outcome of experience; what you become over time through exposure to life's challenges? Clearly it is both, but some talent management strategies put more emphasis on the *identification of the few*, those with the "right stuff"; others on the *development of the many*.
2. The importance of a personal development plan emerges in a number of surveys of executive development (for example, Council For Leadership, 2001).
3. Take the scenario in which an organisation has evaluated its middle management as operating around the 25 percentile of management effectiveness in comparison to an industry norm. In response the organisation brings in a cohort of high-potential recruits, say at the 85 percentile. What is the outcome of this scenario? If the high-potential recruits are going to be managed by the current middle managers it is pretty much inevitable that a substantial number of these high-potential individuals will either leave, or become caught up in the prevailing management culture of under-performance.
4. There are different types of corruption. Fraudulent management will clearly destroy an

organisation and do so very quickly. There is also a growing moral bankruptcy which occurs from a loss of ethical bearings. It may take longer but it will still destroy the firm.

5. David Brent: "What upsets me about the job? Wasted talent. People could come to me and they could go, 'Excuse me, David, but you've been in the business 12 years. Can you just spare us a moment to tell us how to run a team, how to keep them task-orientated, as well as happy?' But they don't. That's the tragedy." BBC Worldwide, 2002, "The Office, *The Scripts: Series 1.*

6. Ed Michaels, Helen Handfield-Jones and Beth Axelrod, *The War for Talent*, 2001.

7. Here it should be emphasised that we don't mean equality in law or in the eyes of God, but equal in aptitude, skill and motivation.

8. Malcolm Gladwell, "The Talent Myth", *The New Yorker*, 22 July 2002.

9. Russell Hotten, *Formula 1: The Business of Winning*, Orion Business, 1998.

10. *The War for Talent*, 2001.

11. Quoted from Robert Bryce, *Pipe Dreams: Greed, Ego and the Death of Enron*, PublicAffairs, 2002. This book is an excellent analysis of the factors contributing to Enron's demise.

12. Malcolm Gladwell, "The Talent Myth", *The New Yorker*, 22 July 2002.

13. *The War for Talent*, 2001.

14. James O'Loughlin, *The Real Warren Buffett*, 2003.

15. Despite the extravagant claims of proponents of this kind of methodology it has proved difficult to find peer-reviewed research in the academic literature to support this approach.

16. The trait approach is not only "alive and well" but is flourishing. After a period in the academic doldrums, the power of cognitive and personality attributes to predict a range of important life and work outcomes is now well established and accepted. See, for example, Deary and Matthews, *The Psychologist*, vol. 6, (1993), pp. 299–311; F. L. Schmidt and J. E. Hunter, *Psychological Bulletin*, vol. 124, (1998), pp. 262–74.

17. Ram Charan, Stephen Drotter and James Noel, *The Leadership Pipeline*, 2001.

8 Strengthening the Leadership Pipeline: Identifying and Developing Talent

"I have yet to see any method that can predict a person's development more than a short time ahead." Peter Drucker

"Look inside for some part of the organisation where extraordinary results have been produced but there is no person standing forth to take excessive credit for these results." Jim Collins, The Conference Board

---

A well-constructed talent blueprint should summarise the organisation's resourcing requirements, outlining leadership demands at different levels and set the "rules of the career game" to clarify what individuals need to do to develop and advance their careers.

The talent blueprint should also provide a workable set of criteria to guide assessment and development activity. Credibility and career management can easily overshadow genuine capability and character. An effective talent programme needs to be insightful in identifying those individuals with the fundamental skills, attitudes, beliefs and motivation which will provide sustainable leadership for the long haul. We cannot complain about the breadth and depth of current and leadership talent while retaining those methods that have selected it in the first place. The challenge is to utilise those methods most predictive of long-term performance while still reinforcing line management responsibility for the management of talent.

Talent management must be more than the identification of a high-potential elite. It needs to be proactive in the imaginative implementation of ways to accelerate the development of emerging leaders.

Assessing talent

In 2000 we conducted a review of the methods that organisations utilise in the assessment and development of talent.[1] By far the most common method was line management evaluation; indeed for the majority of organisations this is the foundation of their talent management programmes (69 per cent of surveyed firms indicating they make extensive use of line management assessment in talent identification). Psychometric testing, assessment centres and 360° feedback processes were employed to a much less significant extent, by around 20 per cent of organisations.

Contrast this pattern of usage with the validity of different assessment methods in Figure 8.1. Those methods with the strongest predictive power are less likely to be deployed and the methods with the weakest track record, more often utilised. But the impact of an assessment method depends not simply on its potential to predict leadership effectiveness but on how its outcomes are used to influence resourcing decisions. And for most organisations the integration of assessment information is a major constraint in talent management. Only 16 per cent of organisations reported that this was well addressed and over half acknowledged it was a weakness in their talent programmes. It is difficult to avoid the conclusion from this survey research that a significant number of firms that have taken the time and trouble to introduce more objective talent assessment aren't in fact using the results to improve decision-making. More assessment data is being used but little change is evident in the talent identification process.

The challenge then is not only selecting those methods that "work best"[2]; it is how to utilise assessment information to optimise decisions about the organisation's investment in talent. We need to rethink not only which assessment methods we use but, above all, how we implement them to improve the success rate of our resourcing and development decisions.

LINE MANAGEMENT EVALUATION

While some line managers may know talent when they see it, most line managers are understandably uncomfortable about making evaluations they cannot justify either to themselves or to the individuals they manage. Candid feedback about *current* contribution, effectiveness and impact is difficult enough. Line management recognise that extrapolating from day-to-day activity and contribution to make projections about *future* effectiveness is even more problematic. When line managers are asked to make open evaluations of potential, evaluations which will be disclosed to the individual, the results are overwhelmingly skewed towards highly positive ratings. Although there is less, but still

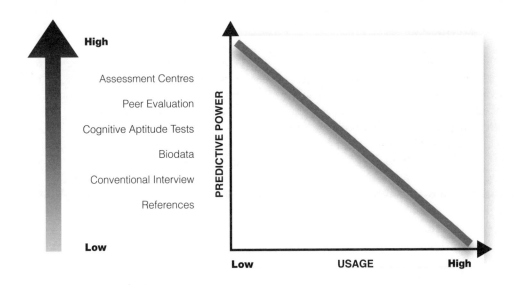

Figure 8.1   Methods of identifying talent

substantial, skew in closed exercises (those processes in which management ratings are not made available to the individual), this approach suffers from problems in action planning. How do you translate judgements of future contribution into a practical action plan for development if individuals are not aware of how the organisation has made its evaluation?

Line managers may be either unwilling or unable to provide accurate assessments of potential but clearly their perceptions cannot and should not be ignored. The issue is what specifically we want line managers to evaluate. What line managers can comment on is *credibility*, the credibility the individual has within the managers' peer group as well as with their own peers. Credibility can be a highly fickle component of leadership, prone to a variety of social biases, but without it individuals will find it difficult to progress. No doubt in some instances this is an unfair and harsh reality but nonetheless still a reality which we can't ignore. Leaders need followers, and if staff and peers question legitimacy and authority it is difficult to see how leadership can be sustained. Line management should be well placed to judge an individual's standing within the cut and thrust of the power dynamics of the organisational hierarchy.

A line manager, at least one with good interpersonal judgement and an insight into organisational realities, should also be able to evaluate the *outcomes* an individual has achieved and those tasks and activities where they display proficiency. A shrewd manager should be able to differentiate between those individuals who may have met their objectives easily because of highly favourable business conditions and those who have failed to meet targets, but in fact have performed extraordinarily well given adverse circumstances.

Effective line managers generally discern sensibly the range of performance contribution within their team, and poor line management either avoids tackling under-performing team members or encourages and advances the wrong kinds of individuals. But even the most insightful manager will find it difficult to make projections of individual effectiveness to tackle future challenges that may be very different from current work priorities. We should therefore remove the burden of judgement from line managers in the identification of talent. We should continue to encourage their role as spotters of talent, but build in checks and balances from alternative assessment methods.

360° FEEDBACK

If the line manager is not always the most accurate judge of employee effectiveness or of future progression, then one strategy would be to widen the sources of feedback to incorporate others' views: the individual's peers and team members, and potentially other stake-holder groups such as internal customers. Could it be that work colleagues have a better insight into the individual than the line manager detached from day-to-day organisational realities? Largely applied as a tool to support personal development planning, 360° feedback methodology is becoming a powerful perspective in talent management programmes. As organisations move toward more flexible structures, with broadening spans of control and employees working on a variety of projects and assignments outside of hierarchical command-and-control, a reliance on the line manager as exclusive arbiter of individual contribution and impact is frankly unsustainable. The line manager may be able to assess overall outcomes but is less insightful about how these outcomes have been achieved (through personal effort or as a result of coasting on others' talents or good fortune) or the attributes and qualities which underpin these outcomes and are relevant to effectiveness in other roles or at more senior levels. Peers and team members, those working directly alongside the individual, may be better placed to evaluate the direct impact of the individual's behaviour and identify the individual's skills. And there is the indication that 360° feedback may be not only more cost effective than assessment centres, the "Rolls Royce" of talent identification, but provide better long-term prediction of managerial performance.[3]

So is 360° feedback a solution to the identification of talent? Not according to Watson Wyatt, the human resource consulting firm, in reporting their Human Capital Index survey. Their headline-grabbing news was that 360° feedback programmes may "hurt rather than help", based on the analysis of the links between specific human resources practices and shareholder value at 750 organisations. 360° feedback programmes were associated with a 10.6 per cent decrease in shareholder value. "That's what we know. What we don't know is why."[4] So is 360° feedback another fad in danger of destroying organisational effectiveness? In fact the "why" is simple and straightforward to explain. Badly conceived feedback programmes, implemented for the wrong reasons in the wrong way at the wrong time, involving excessively long content and attempting to rate every specific aspect of leadership, are consuming vast amounts of corporate time and undermining organisational productivity. And a lack of follow-through with no consequences for poor evaluations or minimal recognition of good performance will not drive organisational improvement.

THE TIMING OF 360° FEEDBACK

In scenario 1, in an operating environment of gross incompetency and bad management practice, 360° feedback will provide a wake-up call to top management that "all is not well" further down the organisation. Here, the mechanism incorporating upward feedback allows employees to highlight any emerging or current problems which otherwise might not be identified.

Scenario 2 represents that situation in which 360° feedback, far from driving performance improvement, reinforces the existing set of problems, often occasioned by a combination of arrogance and complacency. The prevailing view is that we're doing the best we can in difficult circumstances, and that this is "as good as it gets". Within this organisational climate, where expectations of excellence are low, the results of 360° feedback will be highly favourable, but also illusory.[5] Here 360° feedback acts to reinforce the current problem. It is this group of organisations which is responsible in part for Watson Wyatt's finding of a decline in shareholder value.

Scenario 3 is where the potential gains of 360° feedback are greatest. Here the cultural mood is one of stretch goals and continual improvement. Staff and peers have ambitious expectations of leadership effectiveness and high standards of excellence which are reflected in the evaluations they make. The feedback therefore is robust and challenging, identifying those individuals who are making a significant organisational impact and setting an agenda for future development, as well as highlighting those who are constraining work activity and are blockages to organisational improvement.

This creates a paradox of 360° feedback. Effective managers in a climate of stretch and business ambition receive "worse" feedback than mediocre managers operating in a culture of lethargy, complacency or arrogance. If your managers are receiving glowing feedback evaluations, ask why? Is this a genuine reflection of leadership impact or a statement about your organisational culture?

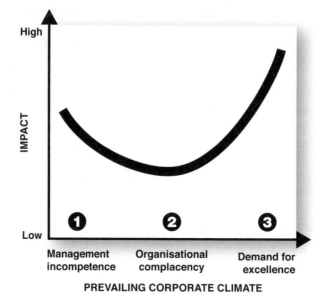

Figure 8.2   The timing of 360° feedback

The following are ways to maximise the impact of 360° feedback

- Keep your 360° feedback system short and simple. Don't attempt to evaluate every specific aspect of leadership behaviour; prioritise and focus on only a few themes to keep completion times to less than 10–15 minutes. Don't ask respondents questions they can't comment on. Apply the "who knows what" principle, recognising that different stake-holder groups can comment on some issues but not on others. Peers, for example, can evaluate levels of support and cooperation, but will find it difficult to rate team motivation skills. Don't ask questions that can't be answered meaningfully.
- Use on-line technology to speed and streamline the process and eliminate the "paper shuffle" which bogs organisations down in tedious form filling. On-line technology also allows the efficient delivery of different systems for different levels and roles to tailor content to individuals and maximise the relevance of the feedback.
- Build in consequences. The outputs of 360° feedback represent potentially powerful organisational intelligence, data to inform key resourcing decisions. Although it is tempting in the initial stages of implementation to build a feedback programme around the principle of personal confidentiality (where results are only available to the individual participant), build in individual, line management and organisational accountability to respond to the results.[6]
- Encourage and reinforce a culture of honest, mature and meaningful feedback. Communicate clear views of what great leadership is, in order to establish challenging response expectations and give feedback to those providing feedback. Are your managers being sufficiently aspirational in their evaluations, or are they over-estimating the impact of your leaders? Track trends to provide feedback on the quality of evaluations reflected in the 360° feedback process.
- Don't use 360° feedback to raise an agenda for development if there is no organisational commitment or infrastructure to follow through. Well-designed feedback systems ask

incisive and challenging questions to highlight personal strengths and limitations for everyone. *Put in place the support and resources to respond to the development issues that emerge.*

PSYCHOMETRIC TESTS

There are two categories of psychometric tests, assessments of *power* — what the individual can do — and of *preference* — what the individual is predisposed to do. Power assessments, notably in measures of cognitive aptitude, have an impressive track record, providing massive "bang for buck", the ratio of predictive power to cost. Relatively inexpensive to use, well-designed and implemented tests of cognitive aptitude have proved themselves across a range of different roles, sectors and organisations,[7] despite inherent management scepticism that a 50-minute standardised test can provide substantial predictive power of leadership effectiveness. In a leadership world of information overload, the cognitive skills to make sense of complexity and uncertainty are likely to become increasingly critical and our prediction is that aptitude tests are likely to become an even stronger indicator of future capability. It is worth emphasising here that cognitive aptitude is only one, albeit a strong, predictor of future leadership outcomes. Just as a card game can be won with a modest hand, individuals can operate successfully as leaders with relatively limited cognitive ability. But cognitive aptitude provides a stronger hand, making the chances of winning more likely.

Tests of power are not without their potential problems. The dominance of a small number of test publishers has created over-use of specific tests and associated test practice effects, as well as a real risk of unethical "leakage" of results from the expanding number of trained practitioners. In addition there is a reluctance by some to introduce a testing programme which may be subject to (usually ill-founded) criticisms of unfair discrimination across different ethnic groups.[8] Customised adaptive tests providing content tailored to individual capability are likely to become the model of future testing programmes but have yet to establish the same research base as conventional standardised tests.

If the assessment of cognitive power represents a major advance in the identification of a key component of leadership talent, then the application of psychometric tests of *preference* has had a more chequered history. Despite their growing popularity (there are now several hundred self-assessment questionnaires, from comprehensive evaluations of personality and temperament to specific measures of motivational, emotional, interpersonal qualities, work interests and values), this area still remains highly controversial. On the one hand, critics point to the problems of self-assessment, notably self-deception (unconscious bias) or impression management (intentional "faking good") and the minimal evidence of predictive validity in real-life selection applications.[9] Advocates of personality testing highlight the impact of personal qualities in determining effective and ineffective work performance and the consensus around the "big five" building-blocks of personality. They also point to the body of validation research which has accumulated in more recent years, suggesting that although personality doesn't have the pervasive impact of cognitive aptitude, for specific roles and organisations assessments of temperament and character can make a substantial improvement to decision-making.[10]

In planning the introduction and implementation of psychometric tests to support talent assessment:

• Don't fall back on the handful of well-marketed tests from the major publishing houses.

There are now a growing number of reputable firms offering a spectrum of well-researched instruments. There are also an alarming number of charlatans who are easily recognisable by the extravagance of their claims.

- Establish a mechanism to track test data against measures of ongoing leadership performance and impact. Validation methodology and analysis is complex, often needing specialist support, but the cost is justified in establishing the utility and credibility of the test as well as refining its application to decision-making.

- Know what to do with the results. Introducing tests without thinking through their integration with other assessment data and organisational processes is a wasteful enterprise. Take time to educate managers in what tests can and can't do. Some managers over-interpret test data, seeing the information as a simple solution to their selection problems; others under-interpret tests, dismissing the results as of no consequence. The objective is to create a mature and balanced view of how test data form one part of the jigsaw in building an overall picture of individual talent and progression.

ASSESSMENT CENTRES

From their origins in officer selection in World War Two, and their industrial applications in the 1960s via the famous AT & T studies, assessment centres have become an established aspect of "high potential" evaluation. Assessment centre methodology, appearing in a variety of manifestations, is now part of the "tool-kit" of the talent management expert. Based on a range of exercises simulating different work challenges and tasks, typically over a two- to three-day programme, assessment centres have a reasonably impressive research base in providing an objective evaluation of individual skills to predict future leadership effectiveness.[11]

But one UK bank, with an extensive historical commitment to the application of objective assessment, is now dispensing with this approach entirely. Its rationale: that assessments outside of direct work activity allow line managers to duck questions they need to answer: just how good is this individual, and how far can they progress? Line managers need to look each individual "eyeball to eyeball" to provide open and candid feedback about their likely impact and contribution in future. Commendable in its motivation to encourage greater honesty of feedback, this response doesn't address the problem that we are asking line managers to move out of their "circle of competency" into a zone of "unknowability". Well-designed and professionally implemented assessment centres, despite their initial set-up cost, have the potential to help organisations rethink their leadership supply, identify neglected and forgotten talent, validate recognised talent, and question and challenge those currently well-regarded individuals higher on credibility and career management than capability or character.

Ways to maximise the impact of assessment centres:

- *Set specific goals with well-defined organisational outcomes.* Assessment centres can be implemented for a variety of reasons, several of which have little to do with any business priority: as a corporate status symbol, a statement of organisational size and a public signal of commitment to talent management; as a smoke screen to conceal expedient management judgements and justify difficult resourcing decisions that line managers have avoided; or as a job creation programme for human resource consultants. The introduction of assessment centres needs to be grounded in a specific organisational imperative, arising out of the evaluation of business risks and resourcing pressure points with tangible outcomes clarified. For example, an initiative prompted by the need to have 50 store managers in place within the next 12 months is likely to have much more impact than a programme introduced with the vague objective of catalysing personal development planning.

- *Determine in advance how the results will be utilised*. Specify how the outputs from the assessment centre will be integrated with other information about individuals, and how this data will inform talent management processes. Ensure the outputs from the assessment centre can genuinely shape a full dialogue about individuals and their progression and development. Personal reports produced from an assessment centre, facilitated by an internal consultant or external coach, will prompt development planning for the individual participant. But to support the organisation's talent management priorities, assessment centre outcomes need to be aligned with wider organisational priorities. Build in tight linkages across assessment centre delivery, talent review and the evaluation of your organisation's succession pressure points.

- *Design the event around "challenge not competency"*. The classic assessment centre is based around a matrix of criteria, typically competency dimensions and exercises, the rationale being that different exercises measure different aspects of the competency dimensions. The review, often known as the "wash up", collates competency ratings from different exercises to finalise an overall competency profile. The problem with this approach is that it doesn't work![12] Assessment centres don't provide discrete measures of competency; rather they identify summary measures of exercise performance. Or, put another way, assessment centre performance is determined not by the display of competency inputs but by effectiveness in delivering exercise outputs. This doesn't imply that assessment centres don't work, they do; but they work not because of their design around competency but because they tap into those situations individuals have to face and resolve in their managerial lives.[13] Design your event around four or five challenges facing participating managers. Typically these exercise challenges are: *how to analyse a problem* (a written exercise to master a brief quickly, identify the key issues and formulate robust conclusions); *how to present a position* (a presentational exercise to translate a set of ideas into a compelling communication which engages and influences others); *how to manage a difficult interpersonal situation* (often a role-play, a one-on-one exercise to apply a combination of empathy and assertiveness in negotiating and resolving a complex employee problem); *how to establish presence* (a group exercise involving working with peers and requiring interpersonal influence); *how to resolve conflict* (a role-play or group activity requiring the willingness to surface disagreement and resolve different points of view). These five themes represent a bottom line test for any aspiring manager. The specific competencies the manager utilises to meet these challenges is almost irrelevant. Different individuals have different attributes and behavioural strengths to draw upon, and the focus should be on successful outcomes not competency inputs. The assessment issue is: can these talents be deployed effectively to tackle the typical problems of leadership life? Design exercises that mirror the challenges facing your organisation and ensure the exercises are based on issues which reveal not only capability but provide an insight into individual character.

- *Maintain an "adult–adult" approach*. Don't build a "them and us" assessment process. Treat your participants as mature adults. Consistency and objectivity of evaluation doesn't have to rely on humourless, silent, clipboard-wielding assessors, monitoring every participant's every move. Create a process that allows informed interaction between facilitators and participants. Indeed one of the key trends emerging from our consulting assignments is the move away from classic assessment centre design (a model that has remained unchanged for around 40 years) and the emergence of an event, positioned somewhere between a business conference and a development centre. Badly managed it runs the risk of becoming a glorified "business cocktail party", a forum in which emerging leaders higher on credibility and career management out-manoeuvre their peers higher on capability and character. But well positioned it provides a two-way dialogue, an exchange of views between the senior team and the organisation's emerging leaders. Senior leadership discuss openly the business challenges facing the organisation, listening to the views of potential next-generation leaders, and there is an engagement of business minds. This event focuses on issues of business substance, a platform for senior leaders to articulate the organisation's future and provide a realistic job preview of what it would be like to take on leadership responsibility. Ambitious managers can evaluate the match between their own aspirations and what is required to operate as a leader. It is also an opportunity for emerging leaders to raise their profile with key stake-holders through the quality of their thinking and ideas. This approach no doubt compromises the measurement purity of conventional assessment centre design, but it is a price worth paying if it engages the senior team more proactively in the management of the organisation's emerging talent.

The challenge of data integration

Although many organisations do need to rethink their assessment practice, to jettison those with little predictive value and introduce those with the potential to improve decision-making, the key issue is not simply selecting an assessment method. Despite the over-hyped claims of "silver bullet" consultants, selling "high-potential products", typically an expensive repackaging of standard assessment methodology, the real challenge is how to use assessment information and integrate different streams of data into a meaningful summary which is more than the description of personal attributes, competency and experience but generates robust conclusions and recommendations for resourcing and development. Organisations have files and folders, a miscellany of personnel records, career resumés, appraisal data, and for some, results from 360° feedback, assessment centres and psychometric tests. Perhaps the greatest problem facing many organisations in their talent management programmes is not what additional data they need to collect, but how to create meaning from the information that is already available.

Figure 8.3 outlines a number of different scenarios in the flow of information to inform organisational decision-making in its talent investment. Scenario 1, in which individual self-assessment drives talent management, is unrealistic. Nonetheless, individuals have direct access to information unavailable to anyone else: their own personal hopes, aspirations and career aims, a key element in shaping progression and therefore informing organisational decisions. But this strand of information is likely to be biased. Individuals want to make a strong organisational impression, expressing their commitment and flexibility to progress, or at least to protect their position in the next organisational restructure. But the motivation and skills to make a positive career statement to the organisation are not necessarily those needed to operate effectively over the longer term.

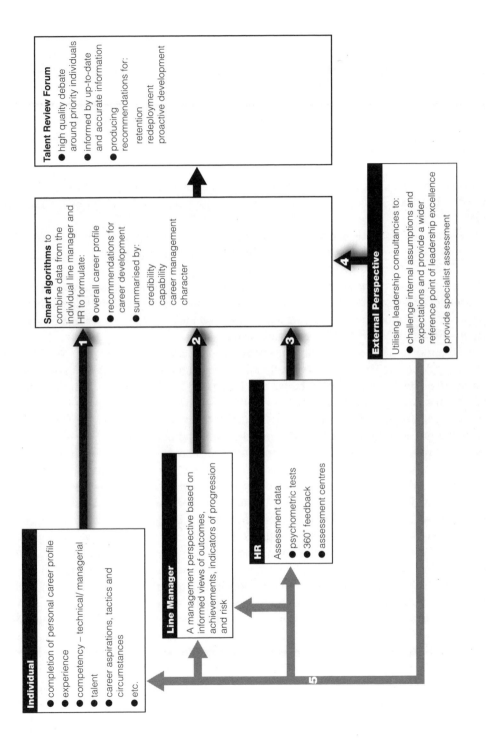

Individual
- completion of personal career profile
- experience
- competency – technical/ managerial
- talent
- career aspirations, tactics and circumstances
- etc.

Line Manager
A management perspective based on informed views of outcomes, achievements, indicators of progression and risk

HR
Assessment data
- psychometric tests
- 360° feedback
- assessment centres

Smart algorithms to combine data from the individual line manager and HR to formulate:
- overall career profile
- recommendations for career development
- summarised by:
  credibility
  capability
  career management
  character

Talent Review Forum
- high quality debate around priority individuals
- informed by up-to-date and accurate information
- producing recommendations for:
  retention
  redeployment
  proactive development

External Perspective
Utilising leadership consultancies to:
- challenge internal assumptions and expectations and provide a wider reference point of leadership excellence
- provide specialist assessment

Figure 8.3   Information flows in talent management

Indeed the encouragement of those qualities of self-advancement and impression management may threaten the modesty and humility indicative of genuine leadership character. If an effective tactic in talent management is "look inside for some part of the organisation where extraordinary results have been produced but there is no person standing forth to take excessive credit for these results" then talent management driven by self-promotion may be hazardous.

Scenario 2 is the typical organisational approach. Line management dominates the talent management process. Line managers provide evaluations of their reports for wider organisational review. While this approach reinforces line accountability for talent management, drawing on relevant information from work contribution and impact, it can also generate subjective, inconsistent, parochial and politically charged judgements. Highly effective for those organisations where the current management population combines exceptional insight and business aspiration with personal maturity, a reliance on line management evaluation is likely to problematic for those organisations looking to "raise its game".

The Human Resource function, through its access to appraisal information and assessment data, takes responsibility for moving talent identification forward in scenario 3. Here, Human Resources personnel, recognising the problems of inconsistency and subjectivity in the talent database, look to improve the quality of information being presented for organisational decision-making. At best this introduces greater rigour into the process. It can also run the risk of being a talent management initiative in an organisational vacuum, disconnected from real-life resourcing decisions.

In scenario 4, the organisation outsources the assessment of its professional and leadership talent to a third party, typically a HR consultancy specialising in management assessment or an outplacement firm with a leadership consulting arm. This is a fairly common manoeuvre during times of organisational change, when a business is in trouble and it is being decided who it should and shouldn't retain as part of a downsizing exercise or during a phase of merger and acquisition. Here, an external consultancy should be able to provide a broader perspective, introducing a reference point to help the organisation take a dispassionate view of its capability and ask itself just how good is its current and emerging leaders. This approach can, however, be simplistic, lacking sensitivity to the interactions between individual talent, organisational culture and business strategy. A battery of tests and a three-hour interview — a fairly typical format — no matter how skilfully managed by an external consultant, can't do justice to the complex dynamics of the individual and their leadership impact in a specific organisation. As one of our clients observed, "the parts of the assessment process which were most insightful we could have conducted in house at much less cost. The part of the assessment from the consultant interviews was a kind of managerial horoscope of generalised comment and vague recommendation."

For some organisations, external assessment is unnecessary. For others it may be the only objective way of identifying genuine talent within political gamesmanship across the senior executive population. Line management evaluations may produce consistent assessments of leadership talent, or may be so limited through prejudice and bias that their reviews of talent will be counter-productive. The aim should be to create an information flow — scenario 5 — which incorporates different strands of information, recognising the strengths and constraints of each source of data to provide balanced and insightful assessment of individuals and generate practical career recommendations to inform organisational dialogue. From our perspective we would advocate the Four C framework as a powerful vocabulary to summarise individual data and highlight practical career recommendations based on the different permutations of credibility, capability, career management and character. Figure 8.4 summarises the information flow.

Individuals can and should provide the kind of detail about their career experience to gain an insight into their perceptions of credibility and capability and indicate the focus of their career aims. Management evaluation should provide another yardstick to assess credibility and also appraise current capability across the range of leadership activities and tasks. 360° feedback provides another measure of credibility with peers and team members as well as identifying those key behavioural qualities of initiative, proactivity and perseverance, which are predictive of effectiveness.[14] Psychometric tests offer an objective insight into the cognitive components of capability as well as an evaluation of character, the underlying traits, qualities and values which shape leadership outlook and operating style. And assessment centres, comprising a range of exercises and activities, have the potential to provide a methodology exploring all four components of leadership in depth.

This is not to imply that all of these methods should be utilised at all times. A mix of budgetary, cultural and political factors will determine your organisation's assessment strategy more than any appeal to research findings. But your assessment strategy needs to address how different strands of data will be integrated to improve resourcing decision-making.[15] Above all, the integration process needs to generate "what now?" questions. From the balance of available information about each individual and the assessment of their current credibility, capability, career management and character, how as an organisation do you need to respond? Is this an exceptional individual, who despite relatively limited experience possesses the deep-seated character and capability to make a career jump and take on significantly greater responsibility? Or is this a professional whose interests and those of the organisation are best served through career specialisation and allowing the individual to develop greater technical proficiency rather than agree a promotion to a managerial role? Should this individual, despite high levels of current credibility, career management and capability but lacking those qualities of integrity and moral purpose, be encouraged to advance their career elsewhere?

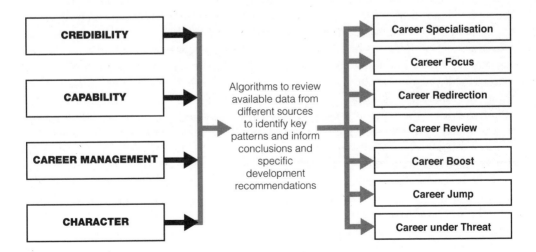

Figure 8.4   Data integration for career recommendations

Managing a talent review

"BEAUTY PARADE" OR "PIT OF VIPERS"

Officially described as a variation of an organisation and management review, but sometimes known to managers as the "beauty parade" or "show ground", or in Enron's case, the "pit of vipers", this is the exercise in which managers meet to review the management and professional population, agree which individuals form the high potential group, and decide actions. Jack Welch saw General Electric's reviews as a critical driver of organisational improvement: "That set of reviews is where it's at! Imagine what we could gain if we doubled the time spent on them." Whirlpool Corp used what it called "the bunker", a room dedicated to tracking the progress of its top 500 managers. In the bunker the four walls were divided by regions of the world, containing the names, titles and photographs of the top talent: an effective way of signalling the organisation's commitment to proactive talent management. For the company Honeywell, the "talent review was the main social operating mechanism of the people process".[16] But for other organisations, the talent review is a:

- "talking shop"; lots of discussion but not much practical action
- "politically charged forum"; participating managers using the exercise to protect or advance the agenda of their specific function
- "smoke screen"; an organisationally endorsed activity to hide behind indefensible resourcing decisions
- "dumping ground" for managers to pass on their problem employees to the organisation for resolution.

A talent management programme should not replace the ongoing coaching, direction and support that is part of mainstream line management responsibility. Indeed it is important that well-intentioned organisational initiatives to identify and develop talent do not weaken the relationship between line managers and their staff. In one financial services organisation, we saw how a well-intentioned solution, the introduction of assessment centres to address poor management judgement in the identification of talent, reinforced the original problem. Line managers began to look to the assessment centre as the organisational mechanism for talent management to deal with their staff problems and make their promotion decisions. And over time they detached themselves further from their responsibility; an example of the "law of unintended consequences". An effective talent management programme should bolster line managers' role in identifying, nurturing and deploying talented individuals. But it should also recognise the limitations of exclusive reliance on line management evaluation and tackle those issues that are outside the scope of line managers to resolve. Figure 8.5 indicates how the filtering process can operate.

Line managers should have responsibility for the recruitment, induction and development of their staff, preferably supported by specialist input from the human resource function. Talent identification and development is a fundamental management accountability which shouldn't be undermined by other organisational initiatives. But far-thinking and progressive managers do need the support of the organisation to address those issues outside of their sphere of influence. The talent review mechanism provides the forum in which these issues can be debated and resolved. The "work backwards" rule again applies: what do we want this forum to achieve; what can this forum do that can't be done elsewhere

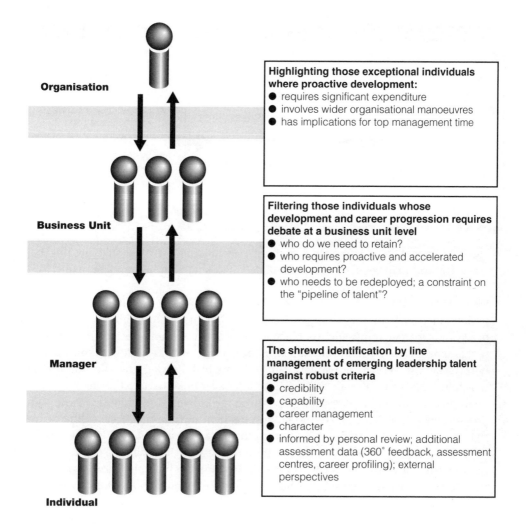

Organisation

Highlighting those exceptional individuals where proactive development:
● requires significant expenditure
● involves wider organisational manoeuvres
● has implications for top management time

Business Unit

Filtering those individuals whose development and career progression requires debate at a business unit level
● who do we need to retain?
● who requires proactive and accelerated development?
● who needs to be redeployed; a constraint on the "pipeline of talent"?

Manager

The shrewd identification by line management of emerging leadership talent against robust criteria
● credibility
● capability
● career management
● character
● informed by personal review; additional assessment data (360° feedback, assessment centres, career profiling); external perspectives

Individual

Figure 8.5   Talent management filters

in the organisation? This drives the agenda: what needs to be discussed and agreed to achieve these outcomes? What does a typical agenda need to include? And this in turn determines: what needs to happen in advance of this forum to work productively through the agreed agenda? What preparation will focus minds around the issues where participants will make a difference?

WORK BACKWARDS: BUSINESS PRIORITIES DRIVE TALENT MANAGEMENT

The kind of exercise which assesses potential and then works out what to do with these evaluations rarely succeeds in directing organisational investment around the practical actions which will drive development. A more sensible approach may be to ask line managers about the specific resourcing pressures and priorities they are facing:

● Who are we at risk of losing: who are the key individuals in organisationally critical roles whose loss would have a significant business impact? What factors underpin this risk:

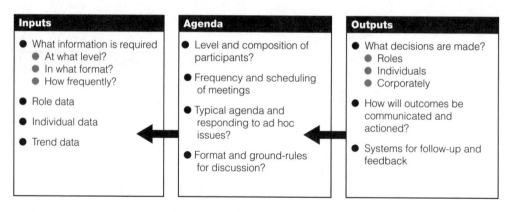

Figure 8.6   Setting a talent review agenda: working backwards

specific personal reasons or deep-seated organisational flaws? What steps are now being taken by line management to retain talent? What actions need to be made by the business unit, by the organisation?

- Who represents blockages to the "leadership pipeline": those individuals whose current performance may or may not be acceptable, but are threatening to constrain the progression of emerging talent? What are the options (move to an alternative role; reorganisation to deploy the blocking individual within a less significant role; outplacement)? Which individuals can and should be tackled by the line manager; which individuals need to be identified for a broader organisational review?
- Who needs proactive development: those promising individuals whose future progression will depend on additional development outside the scope of their current role, or where significant investment needs to be made to accelerate their development? What is the specific focus of development? Which aspect of credibility, capability, career management or character needs to be addressed for the individual to progress? What investment is needed, within the business unit or as an organisation, to make this development practical?

Figure 8.7 outlines the kind of material which line managers should review in advance of the meeting. Rather than prepare a detailed listing of all their reports, the management focus should be on prioritising those high-potential individuals and highlighting them for the attention of the business unit and wider organisation.

TALENT REVIEWS: SOME DOS AND DON'TS

- Be organised and disciplined in the preparation and follow through but don't overplay the formality of the meeting. Informality encourages a greater willingness for participants to open up and talk freely and honestly. Don't run the agenda around a series of highly structured PowerPoint presentations which stifle debate. Be creative in organising the physical aspects of the meeting room. Move furniture around to shift the meeting dynamic. Create images of "what if" scenarios. Put up the business plans of your competitors, stick up press cuttings on the wall, have photographs of priority individuals displayed prominently. Be imaginative in challenging expectations of the conventional talent review to ask new questions in a fresh way to create purpose, energy and focus.

Talent Review Preparation

Risk of losing

Who within your structure represents a possible loss and will have an adverse business impact? For each individual you list, analyse the possible reasons. Is it:
- boredom through a lack of stretch and challenge?
- dissatisfaction with work colleagues/the organisation?
- frustration with slow career progression?
- perceptions of under-compensation?
- the target of head hunters?

Given this analysis and the likelihood of losing this individual, within the next 6 months, what are your preliminary recommendations?
- plan for their departure; assess coverage
- restructure role
- move to another function
- agree additional compensation

Individual	Recommendation

Pipeline Blockages

In any structure there are those individuals who, although they may be performing at a tolerable level, are either not driving the business forward in the way you feel represents what is required in future; or are showing signs of blocking the development and progression of emerging talent within their work area.

For each individual assess the implications. What is the likely impact of doing nothing? If this individual represents a major constraint to the development of future talent, what are the options?

- encourage a move to an alternative role
- reorganise structure to redeploy the individual
- "pay off"
- others

Individual	Recommendation

Talent Review Preparation

Proactive Development

Who are your most promising managers and professionals? While it is tempting to "hold on to your best people" and resist a move that might challenge your work area, in the long run, a "free trade area of talent" will create win–win outcomes for everyone within your business area and the organisation.

List out those individuals who:

- are exceeding current role requirements
- display indicators to take on greater responsibility
- have credibility with their peers
- are motivated to grow and develop and test themselves by taking on new and unfamiliar challenges.

Review each individual in detail to analyse:

- what are the specific challenges they need to address to progress their development?
- what is it which right now is stopping them from moving into a larger role with more responsibility?

Credibility:	Capability:	Career Management:	Character:
lack of experience in key areas? which? poor relationships with important stake-holders? why? limited social impact? why?	lack of know-how in specific areas? which? specific gaps in management competency? where? contra-indicators of effectiveness; signs of derailment? which?	poor self-management skills? which? lack of tactical awareness in managing organisational realities? why? misguided/unrealistic career aims?	uncertainty about the fundamentals of leadership outlook and ethics ■ integrity ■ resilience ■ distinctiveness why? a lack of life experience or indicative of a more fundamental question mark?

Then provide your preliminary **recommendations** to help inform the talent review debate.

Recommendations could include:

- specific assignments/projects to tackle new challenges
- a cross-functional move/secondment to take on increased responsibility and test their effectiveness
- support from in-company mentors and coaches
- specific training/educational activity
- external development.

Talent Review Preparation

Individual	Constraints to Progression				Recommendation
	Credibility	Capability	Career Management	Character	

© Azure Consulting International Ltd 2003

Figure 8.7 Preparing for a talent review

- Emphasise the importance of candour in reviewing individuals. The aim is to maximise the organisation's pool of talent, not protect favoured friends or dismiss former adversaries. Ensure the chair creates the right kind of tone, facilitating an honest discussion to provide frank feedback to participating managers who may be holding back or are being subjective in their evaluations. In one food manufacturer, the CEO, with little experience of succession management, found it difficult to manage the agenda of talent review meetings. An external coach was brought in with the single objective of improving the CEO's skills in chairing meetings. It worked and future sessions became much more open and productive. Be prepared to direct the resource and support to make the talent review process work. It has the potential to have a massive business impact. Invest the time and energy to maximise its organisational contribution.
- Create action orientation to formulate recommendations and decisions. Avoid a "talking shop" to exchange organisational tittle-tattle; keep the agenda focused around business problems and talent solutions. Challenge any attempts to divert the meeting with subjective "throw-away" comments based on long-gone history. But if an individual being reviewed is arousing strong negative emotions, ask why? Is this more about the individual or a reflection of the collection of individuals who are part of the talent review?
- Keep meetings short and frequent. A one-day annual event, the "succession jamboree", will not establish or maintain the momentum to keep talent management an ongoing priority. Don't overload the agenda by attempting to review the entire management and professional population. Put in place filters to focus on a handful of individuals and agree specific actions.
- Follow up meetings quickly with a summary of action points and accountabilities. Don't hand over responsibility to the human resource function. HR can and should coordinate and facilitate follow-up actions, but it is the chair's role to manage activity subsequent to the review meeting. Ensure that agreed actions are reviewed at the next meeting. Success in developing talent should be communicated back and reinforced and learning lessons highlighted. Failures to action next steps should be highlighted and analysed.

Figure 8.8 summarises the move to a new approach to talent reviews.

The "prisoner's dilemma of succession"

Imagine this scenario: "Two members of a criminal gang are arrested and imprisoned. Each prisoner is in solitary confinement with no means of speaking to or exchanging messages with the other. The police admit they don't have enough evidence to convict the pair on the principal charge. They plan to sentence both to one year in prison on a lesser charge. Simultaneously the police offer each prisoner a Faustian bargain. If he testifies against his partner, he will go free while the partner will get three years in prison on the main charge. But there is a catch... if both prisoners testify against each other, both will be sentenced to two years in jail.[17]

Figure 8.9 shows the "prisoner's dilemma", a scenario from game theory, exploring the dynamics of cooperation and competition. You are A, one of the prisoners; what do you do? What are the possible outcomes: the "pay offs"? By defecting (turning state's evidence) while prisoner B cooperates with the other prisoner (refusing the deal), you have the best

Conventional approach	Business-driven approach
● HR led to remind reviewing managers "it's that time of the year"	● Head of business unit communicates priorities and directs attention to business imperatives
● Extensive documentation including: detailed summaries of each target individual; performance-potential mapping	● A two page overview: emerging business challenges which have resourcing implications for other work areas; listing of names: talent at risk and targets for retention; talent requiring business unit/organisational attention
● Co-chaired by business leader and HR partner 　○ Focus on achieving consistency and consensus of high potential names 　○ Working through a large population	● Chaired by business leader; emphasis on agreeing specific actions for a small number of key individuals
● Extended minutes circulated for comment 　○ HR tasked with follow up of actions	● Line manager debrief and feedback of practical outcomes 　○ HR coordination of cross functional development activity and database update

Figure 8.8　The move to a new approach

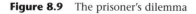

B turns state's evidence	**3** **years**	0 years	**2** **years**	2 years
B refuses deal	**1** **year**	1 year	**0** **years**	3 years
	A **refuses deal**		**A** **turns state's** **evidence**	

Figure 8.9　The prisoner's dilemma

outcome; this is the Temptation pay-off. However, if you reason like this, there is no reason why your opponent shouldn't come to the same conclusion: to defect. In which case when you both defect, you both suffer the "Punishment pay-off". In which case perhaps you should cooperate (refuse the deal), knowing that if your opponent also refuses the deal (cooperates); you both achieve the "Reward pay-off". However, if you refuse the deal (cooperate) and your opponent turns state evidence (defects), you achieve the worst outcome: the "Sucker pay-off". And so the dilemma continues.

The "prisoner's dilemma" is a theme played out in many organisations in the management of talent. Imagine you are a Divisional Head in an organisation, responsible for running a significant business activity. The Group HR Director approaches you to discuss the organisation's plans for succession management over the forthcoming year and is looking for your support. She wants you to cooperate in the planned corporate talent management initiative. Specifically, she is looking to you to accept high-potential managers from other business units into your division to give them broader organisational experience. And in order to develop further your best talent you will be asked to release some of your people to other business areas, providing them with new challenges to prepare them for future roles. Furthermore, the launch of a corporate-wide business education programme for senior executives is planned, and you are asked to contribute £150 000 from your budget.

In the language of "game theory" you have to decide to cooperate or defect. This is succession dilemma, as demonstrated by Figure 8.10. Cooperate means signing up to the implications of the proposed initiative. In defection you hold on to your best people and refuse to accept any managers from other divisions. Where you have vacancies you cannot fill from within your division you recruit from outside. Defection also means holding back from contributing funding to the corporate business education programme. Of course in deciding your course of action you are doing so in the context that the other Divisional Heads are also deliberating whether to cooperate or defect. This is game theory in organisational action.

In any event you decide to cooperate, but the other Divisional Heads defect. The outcome for you is "Sucker". You end up as a net loser. You lose some of your best people and find that you have accepted the "problem children" from other divisions. You also find yourself having to make up the funding shortfall in the business education programme since your Divisional colleagues refused to contribute to its cost. The following year the Group HR Director agrees that things have not gone well but is still looking for your support for the second year of this initiative. Not amused, you decide to defect. The organisational pay-off if your Divisional colleagues continue to defect is "Punishment". The organisational outcome is a smaller pool of talent which constrains everyone's resourcing options for the future and everyone loses. Of course the desired organisational outcome is "Reward". If all Divisional Heads cooperate, everyone wins through the creation of a bigger pool of corporate talent. So why don't organisations achieve the Reward outcome more often? This is the succession equivalent of the "prisoner's dilemma". Despite the gains of the Reward pay-off, cooperation for an individual executive is an unattractive option if he or she thinks others will defect. The Punishment pay-off is the outcome.

Is this a dilemma that can be resolved? Firstly, does the dilemma matter? What is the organisational impact of executive cooperation or defection? What difference does cooperation across the divisions make? What are the consequences of defection?

In a corporate scenario in which business units are run as autonomous, stand-alone

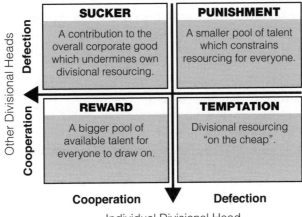

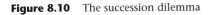

Figure 8.10 The succession dilemma

activities, and where the skill sets and technical know-how create very different resourcing requirements, there is no dilemma. Those business units that are successful in attracting talent, from within or outside, continue to flourish. Those units unable to recruit, retain or optimise talent will struggle to survive. Here the organisation allows a "free trade area of talent" to operate. Profitable activities are backed and invested in further; those that don't perform are allowed to "wither on the vine". This is an unforgiving business scenario, an operating culture of "survival of the fittest". Here the "prisoner's dilemma" doesn't figure. For other organisations — although different businesses and functional units need to stand on their own two feet, demonstrating their ongoing contribution to overall corporate performance — there is a recognition of the gains to be made from organisational cooperation. After all if there isn't a financial benefit from the sharing and pooling of technology, knowledge and expertise it is difficult to identify the rationale for the organisation. Where there is a need for coordinated resourcing and development effort across different work areas, departments and divisions, what might constrain cooperation and what might encourage defection? What is clear is that the organisational pay-offs need to be changed to encourage more cooperation and discourage defection. What specific "sticks" can be used to deter defection? What specific "carrots" can be used to encourage cooperation?

Two approaches seem to work: the tactics of interpersonal trust and a shift in measurement and recognition. Firstly, interpersonal trust and influence need to be established between the CEO and his or her team and their reports. One CEO outlined his vision of succession, saying to each of his Divisional Directors, "My personal commitment is that if you have to lose one of your key people to another business, I'll ensure you get an equally capable replacement." Here succession management operates within an operating culture of mutual respect and support across the management team. One Divisional Director's gain is not another's loss. Without this culture being established and maintained the "prisoner's dilemma" will continue, as senior executives look to protect their immediate interests, suspicious of the intentions of their colleagues.

"What gets measured gets managed." The second successful response to the resolution of the "prisoner's dilemma" has involved establishing metrics to link organisational resourcing targets for talent management and cross-functional movement to executive performance and reward. If senior executives responsible for running major business units are recognised and rewarded exclusively for their unit's annual financial performance, then it is easy to see why they would focus on maximising their own unit's short-term interests and ignore everything else. The personal Reward pay-off, however, becomes the organisational Punishment outcome in the longer term. But if the executive role also incorporates contribution to corporate stewardship then performance should be evaluated against broader measures of commitment to the organisation's overall and longer-term well-being. The strategy is to balance the short-term interests of each Divisional Director ("I want the best people now") with the overall needs of the organisation ("Are we developing the breadth and depth of leadership capability and character to build resilience for the long term?").

The days of the "succession chess master", except in a handful of organisations we encounter, have largely disappeared. There was a time in corporate history when an influential individual, armed with a "black book" of names, reviewed the pieces and determined those moves to plan proactively the careers of key individuals. This was the approach taken by one pharmaceutical firm which applied a "two-plus-two-plus-two" formula for its senior positions to summarise that potential successors should gain experience in two business units, two functional areas and two countries. Useful as a road-map of career progression to indicate the development required to operate effectively at senior levels when the destination is known, in a world of business uncertainty and change, when the rules of corporate chess keep shifting, and professionals and executives see themselves as more than pawns, the model of centralised talent control and coordination to resolve the "prisoner's dilemma" looks increasingly unrealistic.

Perhaps the first step is to do the "obvious", to remove those blockages that are constraining a "free trade area of talent". Sometimes an organisation needs to stop doing things before it introduces new practices. In talent management the aim should be to identify the "stops" before the "starts", in particular to eliminate those artificial barriers often created by inflexible job evaluation and remuneration practices, which impede the movement of talent within the organisation.

A REALITY CHECK

If you are unsure about the impact of your talent review process, stop it and see what happens. One of our clients, in re-aligning his organisation's fundamental approach to succession, cancelled the next scheduled meeting. In his view, if he started getting calls from managers to ask what was happening, the process was probably having a positive impact. If no one complained about its absence, he figured it wasn't making any difference, and therefore shouldn't be continued.

Developing talent

The talent review is designed to highlight key resourcing risks and opportunities which the business unit and organisation need to address: to identify the talent the organisation might otherwise overlook or question those apparently successful individuals whose future progression might undermine the organisation's future. A robust talent review forum, one that contributes to sustainable succession, also needs to be proactive in shaping talent development. The question becomes: what is the quickest and most cost-effective way to translate leadership promise into leadership impact? Relevant to all organisations, it is a critical necessity for those firms who cannot afford the price of credible individuals imported from outside with an impressive track record of previous experience and an established portfolio of leadership capabilities. For them, ingenuity and speed in talent development becomes a competitive imperative.

The last 20 or 30 years have seen a massive expansion in the business education and management development industry. In the UK there are now scores of business schools providing a range of programmes, literally thousands of training providers, and an array of specialist firms, all providing solutions to "transform your business through people". In addition, this same period has seen the huge growth of what was once known as "self-help" literature, now described as the personal development movement. The spectrum of choices for those planning a strategy for talent development is vast, running the gamut from the faddish — for example, "horse whispering", "fire walking" and "whirling dervish dancing" — to the more down-to-earth "finance for the non-financial manager" or "business negotiation". In the midst of this set of programmes, initiatives, workshops and coaching —

activity that has now had several decades to establish its business value — it is extraordinary that so little has been published to establish what does and doesn't work. There is no "consumer's guide of talent development" to evaluate what has been tried and tested to separate the wheat from the chaff.[18]

The identification of talent is essentially an ongoing series of investment decisions to direct organisational time and resources towards those individuals the organisation sees as key to its future. The development of talent is the implementation mechanism to maximise the return on this investment. The difficulty is that we know remarkably little about the impact of different development options: which activities work, with which individuals, under which circumstances?

THE DEVELOPMENT AGENDA: WHAT IS THE FOCUS OF DEVELOPMENT?

Development, the kind of development that shapes genuine leadership to sustain a positive organisational impact over the long term, needs to grapple with four themes: credibility, capability, career management and character. A development programme based only on the acquisition of additional competency may be relevant to building greater technical and managerial proficiency but will miss the point in growing the kind of leaders who will build trust in the face of challenge and adversity. Leadership isn't simply a bundle of skills to be bolted on as part of ongoing career development. An informed development agenda needs to explore:

- How *credible* is this individual? What is the breadth and depth of their experience base? What gaps might undermine their credibility to take on greater responsibility? How do significant stake-holders perceive this individual? What interpersonal impact is the individual making to establish leadership legitimacy? What is holding the individual back from maximising their authority? Is it a lack of experience or low social confidence which may be sabotaging others' estimates of their capability?
- What balance of individual strengths and constraints is driving *capability*? Which outstanding strengths are evident? How can these be deployed further to maximise effectiveness? Which limitations will hold this individual back? How deep-seated are these limitations; will these fundamental traits and qualities be difficult to change, or issues that can be overcome relatively easily?
- What is the maturity of the individual's *career* goals and tactics? How determined and focused is the individual in pursuit of their career aims? What life circumstances are helping or hindering the individual from maximising their career energies? How realistic is the individual about their aspirations and what is required to progress? How effective is the individual in managing themselves, their time and energies, in coping with the organisational realities of power and politics?
- Does the individual possess and display genuine *character*? What life and organisational experiences have provided the kind of tests and challenges to create a maturity of leadership outlook? Where do they need greater exposure in grappling with complex ethical issues, in coming to terms with adversity, in standing out as an individual in their own right?

DEVELOPMENT OPTIONS: HOW DO LEADERS DEVELOP?

There is no shortage of development options, reflecting a range of philosophical views based on deep-seated assumptions about human nature, the impact of heritable and environmental factors, as well as theories about the mechanisms in which individuals develop and how personal change operates.[19] The current views, dominant in talent development, can be summarised as in the section below.

Development as a shift in mind-set

The starting-point for this perspective is that we are all talented, capable of greatness, but are constrained by our negative thoughts and feelings. It is our beliefs about the past, our expectations of the present, and our fears about the future which hold us back. Our growth, as individuals and the fulfilment of the life and career possibilities that our talents provide, is held back by our negative patterns of thinking. The more strident advocates of this approach would insist on a full reprogramming of our psychological systems. But because this sounds too much like the mental auditing associated with brainwashing cults, it makes most of us nervous. A more organisationally acceptable and toned-down version involves attendance at some kind of "pep talk seminar" facilitated by an energetic communicator who combines positive pop psychology with anecdotes of life transformation and success achieved through a fundamental shift in thinking, for example, the evangelical fervour of Anthony Robbins and his message to "awaken the giant within", or Mindstore's Jack Black's exhortation to "build a house on the right bank". A cottage industry of "positive thinking" has grown around the central message that: "anything is possible if we think big thoughts and eliminate the negative".

Although the positive thinking school seems more preoccupied with questions of credibility and career management (how to achieve personal success now) rather than building capability and character (how to do what is right and how best to make a contribution on behalf of others), it does provide a powerful insight beyond the obvious point that we "could all do better". There is no shortage of talented professionals and executives who are being held back through negative patterns of thought and behaviour, making it difficult for their full talents to be released. Confidence is a key component of leadership, and self-belief is needed to make a positive impact and establish credibility. For some individuals identified in the talent review this perspective will challenge their attitudes and assumptions, those limiting beliefs that are constraining their impact, and provide them with the tools to increase their personal power and influence.

Development as the acquisition of knowledge

This development strategy starts from the premise that effectiveness depends in large part on what we know and how we utilise this knowledge to tackle the organisational challenges that face us. It is this perspective that underpins much business education and management training, the focus being to equip our future leaders with the tools, techniques and expertise to operate as problem solvers. The priority here then is to find the most efficient way to impart knowledge quickly through well-designed training events or smart e-learning. But with the sheer pace of knowledge accumulation and the increasing sophistication of knowledge management systems, the emphasis is less on what we know, but more about how we learn, knowing how to ask the right questions, how to master new information quickly and, above all, how to exercise judgement in the face of complexity and uncertainty.

Progressive organisations have recognised for some time that a priority for their talent development initiatives is building learning agility, equipping not only professionals and executives but employees at all levels with the tools of problem analysis, creative thinking and decision-making. While business fundamentals still need to be mastered, increasingly we will see development less concerned with "knowing more" and more about helping managers "think how to think". We anticipate that executive development programmes will see the greater involvement of disciplines as diverse as philosophy, history, law and economics, drawing upon their analytical skills and sense of perspective about the "big questions". This input will be positioned not as interesting "slots before dinner", but fully integrated in the fundamental design and implementation of development programmes.

Development as the deployment of our fundamental talents

If positive thinking preaches the message that we can reinvent ourselves to be what we truly want to be, only held back by our lack of imagination about our life possibilities, then another perspective, popularised in the Gallup publication, *First Break All the Rules*, rejects its assumptions to point to the constraints of personal change. The view here is that:

> "people don't change that much; don't waste time trying to put in what was left out; try to draw out what was left in; this is hard enough."[20]

From their research database, based on profiles of "what the world's greatest managers do differently", the authors highlight that the greatest gain comes from playing to our strengths (not trying to fix our limitations); that our strengths emerge out of our "talents" ("naturally recurring patterns of thought, feeling or behaviour"); and that these talents are fundamental and enduring qualities (probably established early on in life) which don't lend themselves readily to change.

The development strategy therefore becomes less about attempting to work on limitations to create fully rounded leaders and more about recognising existing strengths and finding ways to enhance and maximise their impact. For a generation of training and development professionals, frustrated by their lack of success in developing the "all singing, all dancing leader", despite a massive investment, this was a refreshing insight. Talent development programmes shifted gear to focus more on the identification of strengths and encouraging promising managers to sculpt their leadership roles around their natural talents. The development aim is simple: know what you're good at, operate in roles that allow you to do it more and develop it further to become outstandingly better.

Development as grappling with "inner demons"

Nothing is simple or straightforward in the world of leadership development. At the same time as the "natural-born strengths" approach was gaining acceptance, the directors of the Career Development Programme at Harvard Business School outlined a very different view, one with very different implications for talent development.[21] As executive coaches they asked: "Why do good people fail or fall short of their potential?" Their conclusion: while individuals can be successful for many very different reasons, the ways in which they fail are quite limited. Their analysis highlighted 12 patterns, recurring themes that result in failure or block progress and advancement, the "Achilles heels" of corporate life which constrain individuals from operating at their full potential.

THE TWELVE PATTERNS WHICH HOLD BACK EFFECTIVENESS

Never feeling good enough: the "career acrophobia" which is afraid of "heights" and lacks self-belief and conviction in taking on greater responsibility.

Seeing the world in black and white: reliance on strict rationality and a difficulty in accommodating ambiguity and "messiness".

Doing too much, pushing too hard: the compulsive perfectionism to the heroic that strives for the impossible.

Avoiding conflict at any cost: the need for affiliation and to be liked which is reluctant to resolve disagreement and conflict.

Running roughshod over the opposition: the adversarial style which operates around "win–lose" and bulldozes through interpersonal relationships.

Rebel looking for a cause: the need to challenge authority and provide ongoing confrontation.

Always swinging for the fence: the desire for the quick and spectacular achievement.

When fear is the driver's seat: the pessimism that highlights the problems and is fearful of change.

Emotionally tone deaf: impaired in the facility to tune into others' feelings and emotions.

When no job is good enough: the expectation of great accomplishment and recognition which procrastinates in getting started.

Lacking a sense of boundaries: a difficulty maintaining appropriate professional and social conventions.

Losing the path: the misalignment of deep-seated life interests and career direction.

"Development proceeds, not from building on known strengths, but from an honest recognition and response to our shadow",[22] those psychological themes which we have neglected, ignored and denied. The development emphasis then is on recognising and facing up to the weaknesses that hold us back.

Faced with these very different views, play to your strengths (and manage around weaknesses) or address the limiting factors that are constraining effectiveness, it is not surprising that managers become confused. The reality of course is that both approaches are correct and both are simplistic.

Effectiveness comes from a realistic insight into our personal assets and liabilities, our strengths as well as our limitations. Playing to our strengths is a good general principle but one that needs intelligent application. After all, a major finding in executive derailment[23] is that strengths, when over-deployed, flip over to become career limitations. Development therefore needs to encourage the tactics of self-management and the recognition that strength in one situation may be irrelevant or counter-productive in another situation, and a potential limitation to be addressed. Some limitations can be managed and their impact minimised through anticipation, delegation or other compensatory manoeuvres but others can't be ignored and need to be the focus of development.

Development through exposure to critical experiences

There is no short cut to leadership effectiveness. Various development interventions — classroom education and training, mentoring and coaching — might accelerate the process. But the reality is that leadership emerges out of experience, of personal and direct exposure to the challenges of organisational life. It is only through experience that aspiring leaders can:

- *establish their credibility*: "I've done it. I know what it's like and have the legitimacy to lead others."
- *generate capability*: "I can do it again. I have the skills to tackle future leadership challenges."
- *focus career management*: "I know how doing it advances my personal aims and can progress my career by becoming smarter at doing it."
- *build character*: "I have the maturity to know what to do, to do what is right and best even when it's tough and there are no easy answers. I have the moral authority to lead."

The development agenda then lies in pinpointing the specific kinds of experience that make most impact and then being proactive in managing leadership careers around these experiences. "The lessons of experience" perspective[24] acknowledges that fundamental talents are significant, but emphasises the greater role of specific challenges at different points in leadership progression. Key themes in their analysis of successful executives include: the importance of early job challenge and responsibility for managing others; having to manage without formal authority; dealing with ambiguity when lacking technical expertise; in start-up and turnaround assignments; working for a variety of bosses, "good, bad and ugly"; the traumas of setbacks, adversity and mistakes, and so on. But is not simply an impressive array of experience that makes the leadership difference — "there is a fine line between successful and derailed executives"[25] — the difference is that some executives are more ready to grasp or create opportunities, to put themselves in situations that might expose their shortcomings and, above all, to extract as much learning from the experience, no matter how scary and difficult it might have been at the time.

The impact of proactive and guided experience, for the right individual at the right time, to accelerate development explains why talent and succession reviews should look beyond listings of high-potential names or the casual perusal of career resumes. Meaningful dialogue about individuals to generate imaginative developmental recommendations needs to "dig deep". The breadth and depth of succession candidates' previous experience should be profiled to highlight any gaps and pinpoint the specific experience factors that will make a difference in translating promise into leadership performance.

BUILDING A TALENT DEVELOPMENT PROGRAMME: PRINCIPLES

- *Recognise that "development" happens; the issue is development into what?*
  Whatever your stated organisational policy and investment in planned or formal development, your managers and professionals are continuing to develop. This is the nature of personal change. The question is: "developing into what"? Leaders with the right mix of talents, skills and ethics to move your organisation ahead quicker than your competitors? Or into a generation of executives who lack the authority, capability, experience, savvy and moral compass to lead your organisation forward?
- *Link your development agenda to the succession review process*
  Why, despite the expansion in business education, executive development and personal development over the last two or three decades, do we now have a leadership crisis? No doubt what Dave Ulrich and Bob Eichinger have described as "frou frou",[26] that mix of largely irrelevant (but occasionally entertaining and enjoyable) nonsense, is in part responsible. But it is also an outcome of the lack of connection between the organisation's dialogue about its future and leadership requirements and the design of

management development programmes. The strategy and tactics for accelerated and proactive development need to arise out of the assessment of business risks and the need to pinpoint specific actions for key individuals to equip them for targeted roles. It should also emerge from the analysis of talent review exercises and the identification of the challenges facing significant numbers of professionals and executives.

- *Acknowledge that some individuals are more "developable" than others and build in "developability" as a key theme in talent management*
Playing "succession roulette" to bet equally on all professionals and executives is an expensive resourcing strategy. The reality is that some individuals, despite their early promise or impressive results at the start of their careers, have a "short runway".[27] Build in an assessment of "runway" to differentiate the individuals who may have achieved quick success but whose growth potential is limited, from those individuals who represent a better investment for the long term. A "runway assessment" should incorporate an evaluation of individuals' curiosity about the world and openness to new experience; the emotional maturity to accept that past assumptions might be incorrect and need to be revisited; self-confidence to admit mistakes and ignorance and the readiness to take a risk to try something new and different.
  We don't know exactly what the future will hold or which specific skills and knowledge will be relevant in five years' time. But we do know that speed and flexibility will be required to shift priorities and acquire new expertise and the character to face new challenges with confidence. It may then make more sense to direct investment towards those individuals with high "developability".

- *Don't select targets to fit a tool*
Not every development issue is a nail for your development hammer. A particular development intervention may have worked outstandingly well elsewhere, in another organisation, or with other groups. But don't see this as the standard solution to the development priorities you're facing. The charismatic business school professor who catalysed management thinking with one group may well bomb with your executive population. Action learning can be powerful in driving development, but may prove highly resource-intensive and organisationally disruptive. An executive coach may have glowing references from other organisations but may struggle with your executives who view coaching as an admission of failure to do the job.

- *Target development on the individual, make it relevant to them and understand their "career focus"*
Company-wide initiatives organised around standard training and educational activity for a professional/management group have huge value in reinforcing organisational values and cultural norms and creating a shared understanding of leadership requirements. The downside is that participants have different pasts, face different challenges in the present and have different aspirations and ambitions for the future. This represents a genuine dilemma in planning a strategy for talent development. An exclusive focus on each individual and their personal development makes it difficult to create collective purpose across the leadership population. But standard programmes can easily become "sheep-dip" exercises, where delegates are herded through a series of modules, few of any relevance.

- *Development needs real-life experience of the "tough stuff"*
Formal training and educational events have the capacity to accelerate learning around specific issues, and coaching and mentoring can do much to guide and support personal

development. But the development of leadership comes from exposure to the trials and tribulations, the uncertainties and adversities of organisational life. There is no easy "how to" of leadership. To paraphrase Goethe, "If talent develops in tranquillity, then character only emerges in the full current of organisational life." This is not an argument for "trial-by-fire", but an appeal for development to be grounded in challenge not concepts, in action not contemplation. Development to drive change and build leadership capability and character needs to be based on:

- *Accountability*: putting individuals in those demanding roles where there are clear expectations of outcomes and criteria to evaluate contribution, and where there is pressure to deliver "big results". This isn't "sink or swim". It is the recognition that genuine talent needs to be tested and proved by taking on new responsibilities and making an organisational difference.

- *Adversity*: giving emerging leaders the challenges which require them to dig deep and discover new qualities in themselves. The "natural-born strengths" perspective seems to operate around the assumption of an orderly organisational world, of clearly defined roles in which individuals pick and choose which talents they deploy. But leadership in the real world is messy. When a member of staff has lost a loved one, do you delegate the task to a colleague because "counselling" isn't one of your strengths? Or when you take over an under-performing team do you avoid the issue because "confrontation" isn't one of your talents? No, faced with these challenges you deal with them, and in dealing with them you develop greater effectiveness.

- *Autonomy*: giving individuals the scope to do things their way. If leadership is largely about managing uncertainty and challenge, then its development cannot be summarised in a "how-to" check-list. Development assignments should have clear outcomes but allow individuals the freedom and discretion to achieve those outcomes their way, through utilising their strengths and exercising their initiative.

- *Ensure your development strategy has a major external perspective*
  Succession from within brings many advantages. The belief that we're good enough to "grow our own" also contains the real risk of management arrogance and complacency. Building a generation of leadership that can do more than "preserve the core" but also stimulate progress requires that talented professionals and executives are challenged and stretched from outside. If "good is the enemy of great", encourage your emerging leaders to keep looking for signs of "greatness". Don't assume it resides in your own organisation. Organise benchmarking trips for your emerging leaders — not "tourist trips" to conventional "best-in-class" firms, but to other sectors and organisations pioneering new business approaches. Ensure your most promising people are spending time outside the organisation, meeting key customers, suppliers, regulators and other agencies. Bring in external speakers to stimulate your professionals and managers with fresh ideas and research. Rethink how you utilise external consultants. Use them highly selectively to help coordinate and facilitate project activity not to conduct fact-finding exercises. These should be development assignments for your most promising and talented managers.

THE "FROU FROU" TEST

Spotting the popular and faddish practices which don't add value:

- it is simple and easy and solves complex problems
- it applies to and helps everyone
- it isn't based on any established theory
- there are no references to its impact in respected academic research

- proponents find it difficult to explain how it works
- its appeal lies in the personal experiences of proponents
- it is too good to be true.

Adapted from D. Ulrich and Bob Eichinger, *Human Resource Champions*

Next steps

Which methods do you draw upon in talent assessment?

- None; future leadership somehow "emerges" without any formal evaluation or review.
- A reliance on line management appraisal.
- The deployment of additional assessment methods (which).

What systems are in place to track the impact of these methods? What criterion of leadership is used to validate the effectiveness of your organisation's assessment methods?

How is data from different sources integrated to produce overall recommendations for resourcing and development?

- Disparate information residing in different locations.
- Ad-hoc attempts to provide career summaries and conclusions.
- Reliance on "paper shuffling" rather than any electronic data capture or database management.
- Systematic review of the assessment data which generates insightful recommendations to inform resourcing options.

How well is your talent review process operating?

- There is no mechanism for agreeing key individuals who require broader organisational attention, support and investment.
- An "official" forum but little more than an organisational ritual which goes through the motions and makes little impact.
- A commitment to planning and coordinating talent investment across different work areas or business units but a forum lacking organisational influence.
- A well-functioning mechanism which identifies those key individuals requiring organisational attention and establishes robust actions.

What is hindering progress? Inadequate information; insufficient planning and coordination; poor preparation by participants; interpersonal tensions and political rivalries; lack of accountability in the follow through; no integration with other resourcing and development processes?

How effectively is "leadership promise" being translated into leadership effectiveness?

- What is the focus of your organisation's development strategy? Minimal; essentially "sink or swim" and "survival of the fittest"? Targeted development on a handful of individuals being prepared for senior roles? Extended development across the technical, professional and management population?
- What methods are drawn on in the proactive development of talent? Skilful coaching from line management? Mentoring from senior executives and/or external coaches? Reliance on formal training events, business education programmes and skills workshops? The use of projects, assignments?
- Have you applied the "frou frou" test to review current development activity? How well is your investment evaluated to track its impact? What metrics of resourcing success are used to indicate how well development is preparing individuals for future roles?

Notes

1.   "Current Potential, Future Performance", Andrews Munro Ltd, 2000. Another survey, "Executive Knowledge Works", found that approximately only a third of surveyed firms use formal assessment tools to identify high-potential candidates.

2.   What is meant by "work best" is a difficult question. Systematic validation procedures depend upon an objective and meaningful criterion against which to evaluate the predictive power of different assessment methods. Obtaining reliable measures of long-term leadership impact and success is problematic and the majority of validation studies appear to rely on short-term indicators of leadership performance. Unsustainable conclusions have been drawn from studies essentially examining leadership emergence to claim an insight into those leadership traits and qualities predictive of leadership success over the long haul.

3.   G. M. McEvoy and R. W. Beatty, "Assessment Centres and Subordinate Appraisals of Managers: A Seven Year Examination of Predictive Validity", *Personnel Psychology* vol. 42 (1989), pp. 68–74.

4.   Watson Wyatt, Human Capital Index Survey, 2001.

5.   This is one reason why we are dubious of those "off-the-shelf" 360° products providing industry-wide benchmarking. Since feedback data is very much bound up in response sets that are a reflection of organisational culture, comparisons of 360° feedback data across very different firms are likely to be highly misleading.

6.   M. London, J. W. Smither and D. J. Adsit, "Accountability: The Achilles Heel of Multi-Source Feedback", *Group & Organisation Management*, 22 (2), (1977), pp. 162–84, found that feedback had little impact when individuals were not accountable for using the results.

7.   I. Deary, *Looking Down on Human Intelligence: From Psychometrics to the Brain*, Oxford University Press, 2001; U. Neisser *et al.*, "Intelligence: Knowns and Unknowns", *American Psychologist*, 51, (1996), pp. 77–101; L. Gottfredson, "Why g Matters: The Complexity of Everyday Life", *Intelligence*, vol. 24, (1977), pp. 79–132.

8.   Keen to avoid the US experience where any organisation planning to use psychometric tests appears to need a full-time occupational psychologist and lawyer, this criticism has resulted in the withdrawal of cognitive tests by some organisations. The irony is that psychometric tests, where the data can be tracked systematically for any adverse impact, are being replaced by ad-hoc interview processes where trend analysis is rarely conducted or selection outcomes evaluated.

9.   For example, S. Blinkhorn and C. Johnson, "The Insignificance of Personality Testing", *Nature*, vol. 348, (1990), pp. 671–72.

10. M. Barrick and M. Mount, "The Big Five Personality Dimensions and Job Performance: A Meta Analysis", *Personnel Psychology*, vol. 44, (1991), pp. 1–26; J. F. Salgado, "The Five Factor Model of Personality and Job Performance in the European Community", *Journal of Applied Psychology*, vol. 82, (1997), pp. 30–43.

11. B. Gaugler, D. Rosental, G. Thornton and C. Bentson, "Meta Analysis of Assessment Centre Validity", *Journal of Applied Psychology*, vol. 72, (1987), pp. 493–511.

12. The correlations across different competency criteria within one exercise are higher than the same competency criterion across different exercises. See I. Robertson, L. Gratton and D. Sharpley, "The Psychometric Properties and Design of Managerial Assessment Centres: Dimensions into Exercises Won't Go", *Journal of Occupational Psychology*, vol. 60, (1987), pp. 171–83. Since its publication over 15 years ago this set of findings has unfortunately had little impact on assessment centre design.

13. Most assessment centre data, irrespective of the number of competency dimensions or exercises, when subject to factor analysis, seem to "boil down" to three recurring themes: intellectual ability, interpersonal impact and work energy.

14. S. Siebert, J. Grant and M. Kraimer, "Proactive Personality and Career Success", *Journal of Applied Psychology*, vol. 84, (1999), pp. 416–27.

15. There are now a number of software products to help guide data integration. See, for example, www.azureconsulting.com

16. L. Bossidy and R. Charan, *Execution*, 2002.

17. William Poundstone, *The Prisoner's Dilemma*, 1993.

18. The standards that have been established for the validation of assessment methods have not yet been applied to the evaluation of development interventions with the same rigour. As a result, charlatanism, a problem in the field of assessment, is rampant in the training, development and education sector. See W. Cascio, *Costing Human Resources: The Financial Impact of Behavior in*

Organisations for an excellent overview of the methodologies which can be utilised to evaluate the impact of different "HR solutions".

19. See an overview in Stephen Pinker's *The Blank Slate*, Penguin Group, 2002.
20. M. Buckingham and C. Coffman, *First Break All the Rules: What the World's Greatest Managers Do Differently*, 1999.
21. J. Waldroop and T. Butler, *Maximum Success*, 2000.
22. J. Waldroop and T. Butler *Maximum Success*, 2000.
23. M. McCall *High Flyers*, 1998.
24. M. McCall, M. Lombardo and A. Morrison, *The Lessons of Experience*, 1988.
25. M. McCall, M. Lombardo and A. Morrison *The Lessons of Experience*, 1988.
26. D. Ulrich and B. Eichlinger, *"Human Resource Champions"* 1997.
27. L. Bossidy, "The Job No CEO Should Delegate", *Harvard Business Review*, 2001.

▌▌▌ *Implementing Sustainable Succession Management*

This final section addresses the realities of implementing a positive programme of succession management in the face of the priorities and pressures of organisational reality. Sustainable succession needs to be based on a clear analysis of the relevant business problem and a coherent view of how its supporting activities are linked. It also depends on a shrewd game plan and practical measures to establish and maintain momentum.

What is the starting-point in implementation? How do we go from A to Z? Which stakeholders need to be managed and influenced? What role does information technology play in improving succession intelligence? What tactics will ensure that succession becomes part of the organisation's way of thinking about resourcing and development rather than a one-off initiative?

9 The "Nuts and Bolts" of Succession Management

"It is not necessary to do extraordinary things to get extraordinary results." Warren Buffett

"Planning is bringing into the present the future so that you can do something about it now." Alan Lakein

---

If Z is the end-point of your succession efforts and A is your starting-point, implementation is the game plan to advance from A to Z. This is obvious. This game plan is unlikely to be a standardised sequence of activities programmed into project-planning software. The complexities and uncertainties of business strategy and corporate politics and the vagaries of human nature make implementation more the "art of the possible" than the application of an established change management formula.

A clear understanding of organisational priorities is critical if implementation is to be more than the drafting of formal policies and procedures. Successful implementation will also require the support and backing of competing stake-holder groups and coordinated activity across the range of end users. The "law of the few" applies; identifying the few who can make an organisational difference will be critical to focus time and effort in planning the optimal tactics of implementation. Clarifying roles and responsibilities and recognising the impact that human resources should and shouldn't have will build a robust infrastructure, lasting beyond changes in personnel. Essential to implementation will be improvements in the speed and quality of the information flow to highlight options and shape resourcing decisions.

TECHNOLOGY FAILINGS

The new HR Director is late for the weekly review meeting with her team. She has come out of a difficult meeting with the Operations Director.

HR Director: "Before we get to the agenda at hand, can I ask a quick question: why aren't we able to pull down key data about our executives? I'm not talking about fancy stuff; I'm talking about the basics. The Ops Director has just asked me some pretty standard questions about his people and I've had to stall him."

Executive Development Manager: "Well, the new HR system is still in development. We're way behind schedule, but I think Procurement and IT are getting on top of things with the supplier."

HR Director: "This is the 'all singing, all dancing' system which was scheduled for implementation two years ago?"

HR Manager: "Yes, I think the problem was that we kept changing the spec. In all honesty the project was all over the place. But I do know that a module to support succession management is part of the new package."

HR Director: "When I go home I see my children playing idiotic computer games, but games with the most extraordinary functions and graphics. Games you pick up for £30. And then I come into work for an organisation with an annual IT spend of over £150 million, and we can't access even the most basic stuff about our execs. Doesn't that strike anyone as odd?"
Head of Executive Development: "Last year we did buy in a stand-alone succession software package. The trouble is no one could use it and we kept getting hit with big consultancy fees every time we wanted to adapt it."
HR Director: "So how much did we spend on this?"

Challenges and dilemmas

"Among the companies that actually commit to a succession plan, few follow through with the rigorous implementation required. In fact, 70 per cent of succession plans fail due to execution errors."[1] This is the challenge. Most attempts at succession management fail because they either lack sufficient aspiration or are excessively ambitious. Organisations struggle to make succession a key business driver by restricting its scope to closed discussions about top-level appointments. On the other hand, over-engineered systems, which impose a corporate straitjacket of detailed procedural form filling, quickly meet management resistance.

In our experience, most implementation problems flow from the lack of connection between stake-holder expectations of the solutions which succession should provide and HR's priorities in moving the people agenda forward. Either the HR function runs ahead of the intentions of the top team, putting in place progressive processes for proactive resourcing and development out of synch with business realities; or, alternatively HR lags behind the strategic agenda, finding it difficult to provide senior executives with practical support to help tackle the specific business problems that they are facing. A core theme in mapping out a game plan for implementation must therefore be tightening the linkages between the debate about the organisation's future and the levers of recruitment, induction, performance management and career development which shape resourcing priorities.

Is a "top-down" approach, a game plan led and coordinated from the centre, the better strategy or should implementation emerge from a series of "bottom-up" initiatives in which different business areas are encouraged to improvise and innovate? Or is it possible to combine the advantages of speed and consistency that a top-down approach brings with the gains of relevance and ownership from bottom-up change?

Does "big bang" implementation, the strategy of coordinated change at the same moment across a range of resourcing and development activities, work? Should the full set of resourcing and development practices be integrated into a succession solution, a coherent set of activities fully aligned around an overall vision? This is the "architecture" school of change management and its belief that a solid organisational "building" needs to be based on the simultaneous construction of the "pillars" of implementation. Exclusive focus on one building-block will create a lopsided infrastructure. Or is working to an architect's blueprint unrealistic in the face of today's organisational pressures? Perhaps implementation is best carried out by incremental change through the "back door"? Should succession then be broken down into separate activities, targeted at discrete populations? If so, what are the specific "triggers" to successful implementation? Which changes in organisational policies or practices will build momentum to create the "succession tipping point",[2] that moment of sudden and dramatic change?

"Big bang" succession has the virtue of coherence, of mapping out a rationale to connect organisational goals with HR priorities and plans and creating consistency of practice against a strategic template. This strategy may, however, suffer from the same problem as many other change initiatives, attempting to do too much and achieving little. Is then a piece-meal approach, despite the appearance of fragmentation, the smarter move? Or will it simply create management confusion about the organisation's fundamental priorities?

What level of detail should be specified in putting in place the supporting infrastructure to facilitate implementation? Prescriptive processes, accompanied by detailed procedures, extensive guidelines and documentation, aim for consistency. But they may lack flexibility in accommodating the distinctive issues facing different business areas and be unresponsive to changes in organisational requirements. Should your game plan therefore be based on a loose high-level approach, addressing the "what", the outcomes of succession activity, but providing little detail about the "how", the specific practices to achieve these outcomes? Or will this level of flexibility result in a vague implementation process confusing executives about what is involved and expected?

Figure 9.1 highlights four overall approaches to implementation. Historically a number of organisations have driven implementation from the centre, a top-down approach accompanied by the succession manual and the corporate policies and processes to prescribe not only what succession involves but the detail of how its supporting processes should operate. Effective perhaps for highly integrated businesses where the culture is receptive to consistency, this is a model which our research and consulting indicates is becoming less sustainable. Top-down prescription works in times of organisational stability, when the strategic emphasis is to "Play the Same Game" but lacks the speed to respond to fast-moving events or flexibility to adapt to the distinctive requirements of different business areas. Conversely, bottom-up approaches may be effective if "Wait and See" is the strategic game. But there comes a decision point: when to take business action to back an emerging idea or continue business procrastination with the risk of allowing promising innovation to die. Attempts at "bottom-up change" without prescription, while encouraging experimentation

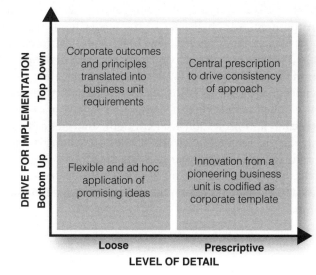

Figure 9.1   Implementation options

and innovation from different business areas, may fail to achieve the momentum to make a wider organisational impact.

Planning an implementation game plan then is a series of trade-offs, a set of judgements reflecting: your organisation's history of managing succession and the success or otherwise it has achieved with different approaches; the current resourcing pressures and priorities you face and how similar or different these are across the organisation; and your organisation's aspirations for the future and the role that proactive succession management needs to play in supporting this strategic ambition. Succession driven from the centre may be counter-productive for "Wait and See" organisations but might be essential if the intention is to "Bet Big on the Future". The trick in implementation of course is to adopt the game plan which is right for your organisation, *not now, but the one that will help it reach its future*. Formulating a succession approach that feels right for your organisation now is relatively straightforward but may miss the point. Your implementation plan is not about reinforcing the present but about preparing for the future. And this is the challenge of implementation: to accept that what is working today may not be sufficient for tomorrow and the willingness to change those existing practices which currently appear successful.

Z and A thinking

WHAT IS "Z"?

What represents the definition of succession success? What is the end-point of your efforts to introduce succession? Is Z an ambitious goal to transform your organisation through a major change in the profile of its leadership and workforce in support of a radical shift in business strategy? Or is Z a more modest aspiration to formulate a succession plan to prepare for the anticipated loss of several of your key senior executives in the next two years? Z hinges on the scale of your business aspiration. As we have seen, "Bet Big on the Future" requires a serious commitment to building the kind of leadership continuity and capability that can provide immediate strategic focus to outgun your competitors while developing sufficient diversity to respond to the unknown challenges of the longer term. Here the agenda is less about succession by replacement strategy and more about the proactive management of leadership talent and the use of "what if" scenarios to inform development priorities. If the strategy is "Focus on the Short Term" or "Play the Same Game" then Z may be a straightforward series of manoeuvres, either accessing leadership capability from the external market as and when it is required or cranking the current resourcing machine to maintain the same supply of leadership and professional talent. Both strategies of course have massive business risks but if they represent the agenda of the top team and senior executives this is the reality in formulating succession priorities and practice.

Z needs to be more than a collection of performance metrics, important as these are in establishing rigour to track activity and evaluate progress. Z needs to be presented in a way that engages management attention.

DRAW A SUCCESSION PICTURE

Working with a key management group, ask:

- What are we trying to achieve in improving the way we manage succession?
- How will life be different; what will we be doing, what won't we be doing?
- What will this mean personally for us as managers; what will it mean for up-and-coming talent?
- What are the business gains; how will this affect our customers; what impact will it have on our competitors; how will this look to our stake-holders?

Now take a piece of paper and draw a picture of how this might look if used in a presentation to your staff. What images will you use to create a sense of what you're setting out to achieve? Think imaginatively of the analogies you might incorporate in your succession picture (sport, transport, entertainment, arts, history).

Review the images to pull out the key themes and the practical implications of moving forward in implementation.

Z also needs to incorporate a sense of time-scale and urgency. Are you embarking on a programme of action to support a five-year strategy or is Z driven by pressing competitor threats requiring a much more rapid response? (See Figure 9.2.)

WHAT IS "A"?

Working through the metrics outlined for the appointments process, business risk assessment and talent management will highlight the scale of the challenge. If the answer is you don't know the answer, then the starting-point is to agree which measures are needed to provide a preliminary analysis. At this stage, don't conduct a detailed evaluation. Embarking on an exercise to review every metric will take you down a route of implementation before you have established a game plan. But you do, however, need to begin the process with a sense of the scale and scope of the current situation. Some fundamental questions need to be asked to evaluate your current resourcing and development activity and its consequences for the organisation. Have key roles been

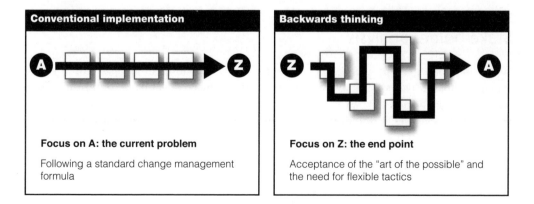

Conventional implementation

Focus on A: the current problem

Following a standard change management formula

Backwards thinking

Focus on Z: the end point

Acceptance of the "art of the possible" and the need for flexible tactics

Figure 9.2   Z and A thinking

identified and succession coverage reviewed? How effective — cost, speed and impact — is the appointments process? Do you have the breadth and depth of talent within your leadership pipeline to move you forward as an organisation?

How do different organisational groups perceive these issues? Is there dissatisfaction with the quality of key leadership and professional groups, their current contribution and future progression? A sense that business opportunities are being missed? A growing frustration about the organisation's speed of change and the lack of talent to support planned business expansion? Or is the mood more one of "we're doing as well as we can in the circumstances"?

"A" also needs to include an analysis of the resourcing and development infrastructure in order for a dispassionate assessment to be made of the impact of those people policies and practices that are the key levers in shifting succession priorities. First ask:

- Is your recruitment and induction process working well to bring in the right kinds of people you need for the future?
- How effectively is your training and development activity being directed?
- Is your HR system and supporting technology an enabler or constraint to succession decision-making?
- Are your career management systems identifying and progressing those individuals who will safeguard the future business?
- Do your structures for recognition and rewards encourage proactivity in managing succession?

Reviewing your preliminary evaluation of Z and A, what is the scale of the challenge that lies ahead? A modest gap which can be overcome relatively easily through straightforward changes in specific HR practice? Or a massive gulf between where you want to be and where you are right now?

Conventional implementation programmes begin at *A* and embark on a step-by-step sequence of manoeuvres to reach Z. And of course it is important to plot out the chain of activities that go from A to Z. Where Z is clearly defined, parallel to this thought process, also work backwards. Once Z is defined as the set of outcomes that succession management will deliver, what is Y? In order to achieve Y, what is X? And keep tracking backwards to A. This is a powerful discipline in ensuring that activity — the things which need to be done to advance the agenda — isn't confused with outcomes.

Stake-holder analysis

Succession management means very different things to different people. For the non-executive Board, succession may be little more than a piece of A3 paper outlining options for the passing of the CEO baton to demonstrate its commitment to corporate governance. For a progressive CEO, ambitious for the future of the organisation and determined to future-proof it from the adversities it will undoubtedly face, succession management may be the prompt to over-haul organisational systems and processes. Here, proactive resourcing and development may be the focus of initiatives to restructure organisational activity and shape a new operating approach, remove those managers whose complacency is drifting into mediocrity, and a trigger to shift the fundamental basis on which leadership is identified, promoted and rewarded.

A key step in mapping out implementation options therefore is to gain an insight into how different stake-holders define succession and the solutions it can provide. In any organisational implementation scenario there are three categories of player (see Figure 9.3):

- Those who *"care"*: individuals who are concerned to do what is right and is best, and who want to take pride in working for an organisation which isn't only successful now but has the momentum to keep succeeding in future. Those who care have the commitment to raise the difficult issues and highlight the need for change.
- Those who *"know"*: insightful individuals who see through the superficial issues to identify the complex dynamics underpinning problems and can contribute intelligently to the formulation of solutions. It is those who know who provide a realistic appraisal of the options and will help you navigate through the complexities of implementation.
- Those who *"can"*: powerful individuals who, by virtue of their status within the hierarchy, their reputation or the sheer force of their personality, command the loyalty and backing of key groups. These are the influential players in a position to make things happen, or indeed, stop a new initiative immediately in its tracks. There is an important sub category of "those who can" — those who are *"connected"*[3] — those individuals with the network of connections throughout the organisation to build or block support. They may not have formal status or power but their extended relationships, not simply to many others but to many *different* people, give the "connected" important organisational influence. This is an under-looked organisational grouping, comprising at times an unlikely set of individuals but one whose attitude to proposals for change is vital to make progress.

Successful implementation does not require a communication campaign to win the hearts and minds of all employees. Rather, the kind of change to drive improvement is shaped initially by a small number of individuals, whose response to new initiatives and positioning

Figure 9.3   Stake-holder analysis

within the network of organisational politics and network of relationships will trigger dramatic change. This is the "law of the few" and your implementation efforts need to identify and focus on this key group of individuals, those who "care", "know" and, above all, those who "can".

Implementation would be a relatively straightforward business if those who "care" were those who "know" and "can". The challenge for implementation is that rarely do these three types of player coincide. Instead those who "care" may lack the power to deliver and those who "know", with the insight to penetrate the issues, may be disengaged from the process.

Work through the exercise in Figure 9.3 to indicate the extent to which each group "cares", "knows" or "can do" something about succession and the implementation of improved practice within your organisation. You may want to highlight the names of specific individuals and your evaluation of why they care, know or can do. Review the worksheet. What does this pattern suggest about the ease or difficulty of future change? What does the balance indicate about the way in which implementation may unfold? Is it driven by powerful individuals motivated to set their own agenda without an informed insight into the real issues? Or in danger of stalling because well-intentioned individuals find it difficult to connect with the important power players? Or a brilliant game plan for innovative practice which lacks the energy and enthusiasm to see it through to delivery? Or is implementation going to be facilitated by the convergence of concern, intelligence and power to create the momentum for change which makes a long-lasting difference?

THE CEO AND TOP TEAM

The best indicator of an effective succession process can be stated easily: the sheer amount of time the CEO and top team direct towards its activities.[4] Implementation therefore requires a CEO and top team who believe succession is an important organisational function, one with substantial business leverage, and who recognise their role in making it happen and allocate the required time to its execution. This is an executive team who take a personal lead in shaping the scope and direction of resourcing and development, undertaking succession reviews at senior levels to role model good practice and provide high-impact coaching to their own reports. But what if your CEO and top team doesn't match this description? Is succession destined to stay an unfulfilled aspiration of well-intentioned human resource professionals?

If your top team is currently making a limited contribution to the management of succession, it may be due to a *lack of awareness* of the role that succession can play. Perhaps the top team has had little previous involvement in proactive resourcing and development. Team members may be sophisticated in the analysis of market research data, in their assessment of the organisation's numbers, or skilled in operations management to identify priorities for productivity improvement. But for them succession management remains a closed book. Here the response may need to be educational, to present a clear business logic and outline the practical implications for their role in the introduction and implementation of a programme of proactive succession management. Or do the CEO and top team frankly lack the *personal commitment* to make succession happen? If the business strategy is "Focus on the Short Term" then succession will never be a priority. If "good is good enough" and there is little ambition to "future-proof" the organisation towards greatness, then succession management will be little more than another corporate formality. Accept the reality rather than push ahead on initiatives which can only harm the careers of those senior executives who do attempt to support a more progressive agenda.

THREE COMPELLING ARGUMENTS

The financial case

What are the financial consequences of your current resourcing and development activities? What do the financial projections look like given your human resource plan over the next three years? What, for example, are the relative costs and benefits of internal versus external recruitment? One FMCG organisation embarked on a detailed analysis of all its resourcing costs for its top 150 executives, factoring in full recruitment spend, the cost of pay-offs for those appointments that didn't work out, and so on. Presenting the results back to the Board, the directors were horrified; they had no idea how much the organisation was spending on executive resourcing. From then on succession was very much on the agenda and this organisation adopted an innovative approach to succession management. If the numbers drive your top team, then present succession as an objective business proposition supported by a financial appraisal of the options.

The competitive proposition

What is at the heart of your organisation's competitive position? Not every business needs to attract, develop and retain world-class talent to execute its business strategy. But there are few organisations that do not need a coherent view of their leadership requirement now and for the future. In one facilities management firm, at the end of a two-day conference for the global HR community to shape a fresh approach to succession, the Group Marketing Director outlined its expansion plans. The reality he presented, a challenge to the HR leaders, was that current resourcing and development practice could not support the firm's ambitious growth strategy. Quoting Packard's Law, "no company can grow revenues consistently faster than its ability to get enough of the right people to implement that growth and still become a great company. If your growth rate in revenues consistently outpaces your growth rate in people you simply will not — cannot — build a great company",[5] he asked the group to rethink the organisation's resourcing priorities. What do we need to do to generate imaginative ways to speed up the recruitment and induction of new talent, accelerate the development of promising managers and professionals and manage those under-performing individuals? His plea: give line managers the practical tools to help them meet their business plans.

Present the competitive argument persuasively using "what if" scenarios. Figure 9.4 illustrates the trajectories of three different organisations. Trajectory 1 is the path of those select organisations who will make the transition from "good to great", organisations who are building the business momentum to make the breakthrough to deliver superior results. Trajectory 2 is the "downfall" graph, the future decline of currently admired and respected companies but heading towards failure. Trajectory 3 is the "roller-coaster curve" of those organisations who will achieve fleeting success but find it difficult to sustain superior performance, go into decline, but then manage to reinvent themselves, and so on. Nerve-wracking for their investors! There are many other permutations of business trajectory. The point is to ask: "Where as an organisation are we now?" How would you summarise your current position as a balance of your competitive strengths and opportunities, risks and

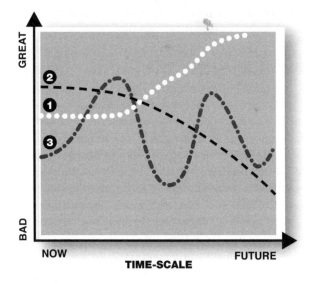

Figure 9.4   Business trajectories

threats? Today, how would you place it on a continuum of "bad to great"? If you were to do nothing at all to improve your approach to succession, the way in which you manage the appointments process, evaluate succession coverage and exposure, or identify and develop emerging talent, what is your likely trajectory over the next three to four years? If you do nothing, will you achieve "greatness"? Preserve and maintain your current position? Go into decline? Find yourself in a cycle of "boom and bust" and an exhausting process of organisational trauma and transformation?

For most top teams, the competitive argument is the most compelling, but articulate it not as a vague sentiment that we need the best people, but as a robust evaluation of the gap between your organisation's strategy and its current capability.

The "stewardship" argument

What is the career history of your CEO and top team? Which firms have they previously worked in and what has been their commitment to succession: external hire and fire or the encouragement of "home-grown" talent and progression from within? How has each member of the top team personally progressed; as a result of proactive development and coordinated succession, or by good fortune and being the "fittest to survive" in a free-for-all operating environment? How has this career experience influenced their views about succession for your organisation?

What business pressures is the top team currently under? Is it losing market position, being squeezed by aggressive competitors and needing to demonstrate respectable numbers to meet next quarter's expectations? Or is it reviewing strategic options to decide how best to position the organisation for a long-term future? Specifically, how does your CEO personally want to be remembered? As leaving a legacy of a sustainable organisation in sparkling business health and admired for its vision and progressive people practices? Or is their agenda largely one of working out how to exit quickly, preserving face within their peer group while maximising their personal remuneration?

The CEO and top team can have different motivations for addressing or ignoring succession management. For some it is the simple business logic of managing resourcing efficiently from within to reduce costs. For others, a determination to build a talented workforce and leadership cadre to compete more aggressively in the marketplace. And for others, it is the pressure to conform to stake-holder expectations of good corporate governance. Ultimately the drive for succession must arise out of leadership character, that desire to make a real difference and take pride from achieving something worthwhile and lasting. Without leadership character and its integrity of purpose, succession management is likely to yo-yo, at times a priority on the corporate agenda, and at others, a distraction from current commercial pressures.

Will the top team take the lead in moving towards a more proactive approach to the management of talent and succession? Ask them:

- Does a policy of internal development and progression from within make business sense? Can and should the majority of key positions be filled from inside the organisation?
- Should we address as a priority any artificial barriers to the flow of talent within the organisation? Should we remove the barriers of cumbersome structures, budgetary mandates, idiosyncratic reporting relationships and Byzantine terms and conditions to encourage greater career movement?
- Are we willing to recognise and reward those managers who demonstrate effectiveness in talent management in practical and financial terms?
- Do we accept that future successors to leadership positions may (and should have) different backgrounds and management approaches?

The "Achilles heel" of succession: information flows and technology

Good decisions require good data. If succession reviews are to become more than informal, ad-hoc discussions, based on the swapping of corporate yarns and throwaway comments, they need access to high quality and timely information about individuals. In our survey of Best Practice in Strategic Resourcing and Succession[6] we were astounded to discover that only 3 per cent of organisations see themselves as making good use of information technology in support of succession activity, while 80 per cent report that IT makes little or no impact on their succession efforts. Astounded because, firstly, the survey findings were not based on badly managed firms with little commitment to progressive human resource practice. Quite the opposite, the sample included a substantial proportion of FTSE 100 organisations. Secondly, many of these companies had made a significant investment in succession technology, from buying in dedicated succession software products to installing fully integrated human resource management systems. So what was going wrong? If talent is a key organisational asset why is it that so many organisations know so little about this asset? Why, for example, does an executive search firm know more than most organisations about the organisations' own professionals and managers? The immediate answer: that an executive search firm's entire business hinges on its capacity to access accurate and up-to-date people information is telling. If your organisational strategy depends on the quality of your people, then you need to develop the same kind of capability as the executive search firms in the management of your people database.

There is a gulf between the possibility of technology to revolutionise the way in which resourcing and development activity, talent management and succession planning operates and the reality of what currently happens. Why?

WHY THE HUMAN RESOURCE AND IT FUNCTIONS FIND IT DIFFICULT TO TALK

Why have systems for human resource management lagged behind innovations in information technology? Why are functions such as finance, marketing and operations so far ahead of human resources in developing IT solutions to support their organisational contribution? No doubt there are political tensions between these two support functions as they lobby for funds for different solutions to similar problems, concerning how best to improve organisational effectiveness. The IT Director looks to the automation of business processes; the HR Director to better people capability. But perhaps the real reason for the divide between HR and IT lies in a *different outlook and operating style* across the two functions. Human resources personnel argue that their IT colleagues are blinkered by their need for technical perfection and state-of-the-art innovative design and less concerned with the swift delivery of practical solutions. They might even suggest that their IT colleagues use complex technical jargon to bamboozle and confuse as a smoke screen to conceal their own mistakes and shortcomings. On the other hand, IT staff complain that human resources doesn't take the time to appreciate the complexities and constraints of what is and isn't possible and this reluctance to understand IT processes and their implications creates a barrier to constructive dialogue. And rather than specify their detailed requirements, human resources generate a wish list on a flip chart and then keep changing their minds about what they do want, but with the expectation of original time-scales for delivery.

In fact the reality is that *business priorities determine the "pecking order"* of IT developments, and historically human resources has been the "poor cousin" in the scheduling of IT innovation. IT effort has been deployed towards the high-profile "business assignments" and requests for improvements in the management of people data have been pushed down the project list. HR functions have found themselves in the unhappy situation of making do with a variety of ad-hoc fixes which constrain its capability to give the organisation the information it needs to inform the cycle of planning and implementation. The alternative, buying in systems from external providers, has proven a difficult experience for many organisations. Stand-alone succession packages have been exactly that, standing isolated in one corner of the organisation. Attempts at integrated systems have produced over-engineered solutions above budget and behind deadline, the eventual complexity of which has bewildered end users.

OPTIONS FOR SUCCESSION INTELLIGENCE

Maintain a reliance on paper systems

Although not a viable option, except for the smallest of firms where any kind of formality of succession process is probably irrelevant in the first place, this is still the preferred option for a staggeringly high number of major organisations. Typically two systems operate, the computerised personnel records system utilised by personnel administration to track basic data and manage payroll, and a Dickensian system of different formats in folders in filing cabinets, potentially useful information but so scattered across different locations it lacks the coherence to inform succession management. In this scenario, preparation for a talent review is a monumental paper-shuffling and collation exercise. Hard copy career resumés are painstakingly retyped into Word documents; other data, appraisal forms or assessment reports, held somewhere else, are eventually accessed and summary ratings added. The result is a highly inefficient process, constraining speed of decision-making in planning and implementing resourcing manoeuvres.

Utilise standard office software

Standard office applications such as Excel or Access possess formidable facilities for the storage, manipulation and interrogation of data. And for some organisations this represents a perfect "fit-for-purpose" solution. It is inexpensive with high levels of flexibility to adapt and change to new requirements. As a Head of Strategy commented, looking at his organisation's project plan to introduce a new HR system, "We're trying to build a Rolls Royce when all we need right now is a Mini." Standard office software can be a reliable way to get you on the road to improving succession intelligence. The downside: typically data needs to be manually captured, collated and re-collated and processed, and a degree of PC proficiency is needed to optimise the full potential of these applications, proficiency which is lacking in many HR departments.

Buy in a dedicated software package

There is no shortage of commercial providers developing packages for the management of succession data. Although most in fact are based on standard database applications, their initial appeal lies in the "user-friendly" functionality for the analysis and presentation of succession data. The provider has made it "easy" for end users to utilise the database for the specific purpose of succession planning. But the phenomenal range of facilities, for example replacement charting and mapping out "what if" organisational scenarios, rests on the assumption of operating around a stable structure, an assumption which is unrealistic. In our experience this IT solution, after extensive set-up, struggles to keep pace with the rate of organisational change and quickly becomes redundant.

Go for integration

The three big providers — Oracle, PeopleSoft and SAP — are active in marketing fully integrated human resource management systems. A competitive convergence is emerging with each claiming to provide complete HR solutions — from recruitment and applicant tracking, training administration and payroll management through to workforce planning. Succession management represents another module in the impressive portfolio of offerings. The appeal lies in the seamlessness across different HR applications. The problem is that the task of integrating the full spectrum of HR activities and end-user requirements proves too much of a challenge. Too many organisations are still waiting for the "promised land" of integration while faced with today's pressures to speed up the information flow in talent management.

Outsource to an application service provider

This represents a major shift in the management of succession. The basic concept here is that while organisations need the outcomes of people data management, the processes for its capture and manipulation are not a core capability and can be outsourced to expert providers who provide functionality through the Internet. The gains: organisations eliminate the need for internal database set-up and installation, networking and software maintenance, and the associated convoluted "hoops and loops" of complex negotiation across HR, network support and procurement. On-line technology for data capture, analysis and reporting speeds up the information flow to provide more responsive decision-making.

INFORMATION FLOWS, CAREER PROFILING AND TALENT MANAGEMENT

It may be that the next few years will see a revolution in technology, the emergence of simple tools that transform the way in which organisations manage their people data to support flexible ways of linking strategy, structure, roles and people. Of course the IT function would argue that the revolution has happened; the problem is that the HR function has not been receptive to the opportunities IT capability provides. But the reality for most organisations is a tangle of historical activity, largely paper-based systems, current personnel software to access basic people records and planned developments for an "all singing, all dancing" system. Attempting to accommodate the constraints of the past, the complexities of present activity and the uncertainties of future IT solutions are likely to defeat anyone but the most determined. It is unsurprising then that three quarters of firms are dissatisfied with their management of succession intelligence.[7]

Plans for the future, particularly where they involve the promise of integration, seem to put on hold any immediate action to improve today's need to improve succession data. However, a growing number of HR functions, impatient with the lack of progress in achieving full-blown integration but under pressure from their senior executives to provide high-quality and timely data, are moving towards new approaches. The emphasis here is on using career management as a key driver of succession and exploiting the potential of on-line systems targeted at discrete populations rather than wait for the arrival of the seamless system that can be deployed throughout the full workforce.

Figure 9.5 outlines a realistic approach to succession data management. *Individuals* from the target population access an on-line career profiling system, either via the organisation's own intranet or through the Internet. Typically this allows individuals to record basic career history information, the conventional career resumé, work through different assessment modules, including an evaluation of technical know-how, management capability, business experience, leadership character, and highlight their career aspirations and priorities. The aim here is to capture individual perceptions of different facets of career past, present and future in a structured format which allows consistency and comparison across the target population. This approach also eliminates the need for the manual assembly of career and self-assessment details, an ongoing source of annoyance for individuals required to submit personal information annually in advance of a management audit or succession review exercise. Individuals can update and pull down their own results, an integrated summary of key themes and priorities to support their own personal development planning as well as for review with their line manager.

Line managers also have access to the results for each member of their team. The intention here is to engage managers fully in the management of their team's current and future performance, to encourage managers to know their people. Line managers need quality data about the experience base, skill sets and aspirations of their team members to identify how best to maximise current contribution and put in place resourcing plans for the future.

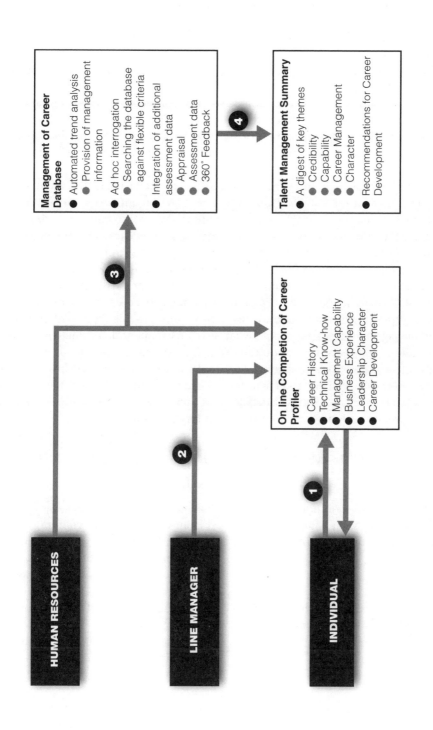

Figure 9.5   On-line career profiling and talent management

Individual completion of career profiles across the target population creates a management database for human resource personnel to access. As well as pulling down individual results, trend analysis can be run across the population to review key patterns. What is the breadth and depth of the management experience base? In which areas of technical know-how do we have outstanding levels of capability or where are we relatively light? This database is also available for ongoing and ad-hoc queries to interrogate the information against specific criteria. Who, for example, has extensive experience in managing R & D, with capability in trouble-shooting productivity problems, and is fully mobile if required to move to a different location?

Career profiling has the virtue of kick-starting the information flow, and opening up succession to incorporate individuals' own career priorities. Without this perspective, succession decisions will be taken in the dark. This approach also makes it easier to involve line managers more actively in talent management. The drawback is that the information at this point is based on self-evaluation and line management review only. Within this model, human resource personnel have the facility to review individual data, and draw on assessment data from other sources (for example, 360° feedback, assessment centres or psychometric testing) to produce *integrated talent management* summaries.

At a superficial level, integrated talent management is a simple "electronic bucket", capturing data from different locations and in a variety of formats to provide a consistent structure for database management. More importantly, it makes sense of the data to spot patterns, interpret consistencies and inconsistencies, and provide an overall evaluation to stimulate management thinking about "what next". Assessment data, whether it resides in folders or filing cabinets or is electronically stored, is still data. The value is in translating this data into organisational meaning. For us the Four Cs of leadership — credibility, capability, career management and character — are a powerful way to pull together strands of information to create not simply a detailed and comprehensive leadership evaluation but to pinpoint preliminary career recommendations for succession debate.

DOS AND DON'TS IN IMPLEMENTING SUCCESSION TECHNOLOGY

Dos	Don'ts
Accept that IT is a tool not a solution; however good your succession intelligence system, it is only one part of your game plan.	Assume that a new succession software system will transform your organisation's approach to how it manages resourcing and development. It will facilitate but it won't overcome more fundamental problems.
Keep it simple, loose and flexible; build in the capability to shift direction without extensive and expensive rework.	Over-prescribe the detail and complexity of the format of your information requirements; organisational needs change and highly engineered solutions become quickly redundant.
Build your database around people.	Create sophisticated systems based on organisational structures, reporting lines and relationships and detailed role profiles.

Work to a three-month time-scale; if the proposed system can't make an immediate impact after three months' design and implementation, don't start the project.	Go for "big bang" IT developments; keep the system focused on a discrete population and defined application. Believe that genuine integrated systems will be implemented easily and quickly.
Keep end users informed and utilise their feedback to shape the final design.	Consult every possible stake-holder and incorporate their distinctive requirements into the system specification.
Work only with external providers who understand the connections between IT systems and HR processes.	Commission design from a software house, promising low-cost development, with little experience of implementing people systems in the real world.

Tactics of implementation

"Strategy without tactics is the slowest route to victory. Tactics without strategy is the noise before defeat."[8]

START NOW; DON'T WAIT FOR A SUCCESSION CRISIS

Business history is the story of once-successful companies who took their eye off the ball while more nimble competitors moved into their strategic space. The odds are stacked against achieving and sustaining "greatness" but a constant focus on succession will maximise the chances of your organisation entering and staying within that exclusive "business club". Start talking about and acting on succession now. Leadership succession doesn't lend itself to quick-fix solutions. If you don't take action now it will almost certainly be too late to tackle it later. A former personnel manager of Shell attributes its current leadership crisis to over-cautious recruitment after the student revolts of 1968. "We didn't get the best graduates. We were too arrogant and we didn't understand the attitude shift."[9] Resourcing decisions made almost 40 years ago have caught up on a company once described as "in a class of its own: the model for multi-nationals".

In many of the organisations we have worked with, succession only became a priority when they noticed they had a problem on their hands: the unexpected departure of a high-profile executive, the loss of their most talented professionals to competitors or stalling growth resulting from a lack of experienced managers capable of taking on greater responsibility. Don't wait until the problem happens. Take by contrast a UK financial services firm we worked with over a four-year period. When its CEO was headhunted to lead a global financial services firm, his successor was announced immediately, reinforcing the continuity of strategic vision, an example of what the business media described as "smooth succession". Luck? Maybe. But this company had decided to take succession seriously as a strategic issue five years ago. Initially it undertook conventional replacement charting then shifted to more progressive ways of looking at the relationship between strategy, structure and leadership. More importantly it had varied the agenda and discussion to keep succession fresh and relevant and an ongoing theme on the corporate agenda.

FOCUS ON INTERPERSONAL RELATIONSHIPS MORE THAN FORMAL PROCESS

At its most fundamental, succession emerges, not from corporate announcements or the appearance of new policies, but from the momentum arising out of day-to-day conversations occurring throughout the organisation. Proactive succession arises out of:

- the priorities of the CEO in his or her discussions with the top team; what is said and not said and the tone of the discussion. A commitment to succession stems from strategic confidence and interpersonal trust. Destructive politics kill off any commitment to proactive resourcing. If the top team is divided, resolve this issue before attempting an ambitious programme of succession management.
- the meetings Directors have with their senior executives. Is the implicit message largely one of focusing on short-term delivery, to do whatever needs to be done to see results now? Or is long-term thinking encouraged? Is the mood of meetings one of "dog eat dog", and one senior executive's gain another's loss? Or is there a climate of cooperation to support colleagues in their efforts to achieve business success?
- the conversations across the senior executive population and with each member of their teams. How important is the proactive management of talent; a "nice to do" if we have time or an important item on the management agenda?
- the dialogue between each line manager and their reports. How open is the conversation about current performance and future progression? Is there a management honesty to talk candidly about performance, an insight to identify the reasons and maturity to provide high-impact coaching and development?

FORCE YOURSELF INTO THE STRATEGIC AND BUSINESS PLANNING PROCESS

Is "HR planning little more than a postscript to the business planning process"?[10] Is HR on the sidelines, its role largely one of expedient execution of agreed strategy? Or is the HR function actively engaged in the debate about your organisation's strategy, its options for the future and the implications for resourcing and development?

If you operate within a human resources role, enter the debate with a meaningful contribution, with business intelligence about your current and emerging leadership population. Be proactive in highlighting business risks and vulnerabilities from the overview of succession coverage and exposure. Look closely at the pipeline of leadership talent to identify those outstanding individuals who might move the organisation forward in new directions.

If your role is within strategic planning or corporate development, work closely with your HR counterparts. Review the processes you use to guide executives through the business planning cycle. How is succession and talent management positioned in the preparation and finalisation of business plans? What questions about resourcing and development activity need to be asked to evaluate the robustness of your colleagues' proposals?

LOCATE THE KEY LEVERS AND TAKE DISCIPLINED ACTION

Accept the reality of the "good to great" trajectory. There are no quick fixes, consultancy-packaged solutions or off-the-shelf initiatives. Instead there is a willingness to ask the tough questions, the refusal to adopt the expedient solution and perseverance to stick with implementation to overcome obstacles.

Full-scale "big bang" succession is the stuff of textbooks and conference presentations, not of organisational reality. Waiting for all the "succession ducks" to line up in a neat row is unrealistic. But aligning changes in process and practice around business strategy is critical. You need to review your current people practices to identify those specific areas that will trigger further change. Typically in our consulting assignments, we find two priorities: *recognition and rewards* and the *appointments process*.

"Does your organisation recognise and reward line managers for their effectiveness in developing staff?" In our Strategic Resourcing Alignment Index survey[11] only a handful of organisations said yes. Eighty per cent of firms indicated they make either no or minimal use of rewards to drive succession management forward. "You can't always get what you want" but organisationally you will get what you reward. And if line management efforts at talent management are unrecognised then it is hardly surprising that organisations struggle in implementation. If you are serious about building future capability, then ensure that management activity in improving succession is reinforced and rewarded. "Put your money where your organisational mouth is."

Get on top of the appointments process, especially at senior levels to ensure that key roles are filled with individuals with the leadership outlook to work for the long term and who believe in the importance of people to drive the business forward. One bad resourcing decision will set your succession efforts back years. Put in place robust controls to anticipate vacancies, review role requirements, short-list candidates and improve selection decision-making.

STOP COUNTER-PRODUCTIVE ACTIVITY BEFORE YOU INTRODUCE NEW STUFF

Don't create new problems by introducing a solution that doesn't address the original fundamental problem. If, for example, you're not managing today via a robust performance management process you won't be able to plan "tomorrow's performance" through the introduction of a new succession system. Performance management is the business process at the heart of your organisation. If it's not working, fix it. If your managers are struggling in their role as "managers of talent" don't immediately commission an assessment centre to compensate for their limitations. Introducing assessment methodology can be a powerful way to enhance line management capability in the identification of the organisation's future leadership capability. But it is counter-productive if implemented as a substitute for line management talent management activity.

List out all the "stops" before you initiate the "starts".

SEE SUCCESSION THROUGH THE "EYES OF THE INDIVIDUAL"

Imagine you have recently joined your organisation. You are a talented individual keen to advance and progress your career. How do your organisation's policies and practices in succession management affect you? How does succession impact on you personally? If you find it difficult to respond to this challenge the chances are that succession is an organisational abstraction, a concept in the corporate ether which is making little practical difference to the realities of who is and isn't advancing and progressing and taking on greater leadership responsibility. How does succession management make a difference to:

- the way in which you are recruited and selected
- your induction process and how quickly you get "up to speed"
- your performance management review and the issues discussed in the evaluation of your contribution
- your career options and the realities of future progression and success
- your involvement in talent management processes, and the feedback you receive as a reviewed individual, or as a participant and the expectations of your contribution?

There is no shortage of concepts in succession management. The fascination of succession is that it encompasses such as a broad spectrum of ideas, from personal development, executive education, human resource practice and information technology to business planning and corporate strategy. The first step in implementation is to make sense of all the "stuff" out there in order to keep a clear focus on what matters and is real and will make a difference, and ignore the "frou-frou" and fashionable froth. Generating speculative plans for the design and implementation of succession is easy. Execution is tougher.

Implementation requires:

- A clear-headed *analysis of the causes* of the problem. Many attempts at implementation fail because the proposed solution doesn't address the fundamental cause of the problem. Driving succession forward, not as a vague principle, but as a business solution, requires an insightful assessment of the gap between where as an organisation you are now and where you need to be. Be clear about which problems you want succession to solve.

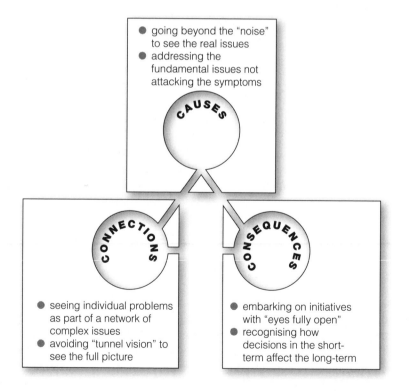

Figure 9.6   Implementation

- *Making the connections.* Implementation is the shrewd assessment of what has happened in the past, the current pressures and priorities of your organisation, and its ambitions for the future. Succession is the art of the possible to balance your corporate past, present and future. Of course, power from committed stake-holders makes it easier to overturn past failings and overhaul current processes. A lack of support from the top team constrains options to set a fresh agenda for the future. Implementation needs to accommodate organisational realities. Importantly, succession needs to join up the dots across different organisational processes and relationships. This doesn't imply full-scale change management but it does involve consistency of effort in recruitment and selection, performance management, training and development and career management. It also requires a dialogue across the functions of human resources, corporate development and IT to coordinate priorities and, at least, avoid management confusion and, at best, to formulate a coherent and credible organisational message.
- *Seeing the consequences.* A serious commitment to succession will drive action with implications to trigger further changes. If your efforts to move towards a more proactive stance to resourcing and development to advance your organisation's strategy do not create organisational ripples, then it may be that your game plan isn't working. Not every Board member will welcome succession. Be prepared for political gamesmanship. Some managers on the corporate fast track will be hostile to the idea of a greater emphasis on leadership character in talent assessment. One of your HR colleagues may be unhappy with your decision to jettison an inflexible succession software package they personally commissioned. Keep your focus on your end-point and be flexible about the means to get there. But don't compromise on the fundamentals that matter. Go into implementation with your eyes wide open.

Next steps

What overall game plan will maximise the chances of successful implementation?

- A top-down programme which issues new corporate policies and procedures and defines the detail of what and how succession should operate?
- A template from the centre to outline overall organisational aims but encourages different business units to formulate their own operating approach?
- A low-touch approach from the centre which coordinates innovative thinking throughout the business to share best practice?

What is the implementation plan to go from A to Z?

- Is Z a vague concept that we need to do something/anything to improve succession, or is it a clearly defined end-point vision of what needs to be achieved? What work needs to be done to tighten up Z and clarify succession success?
- Is there a reluctance to evaluate A? Will a candid assessment of A ignite difficult political tensions? Or is there a willingness to take stock of our current processes and practices?
- What is the scale of the challenge? A modest change agenda requiring no more than greater attention to existing processes? Or a gulf which will need substantial organisational effort to achieve Z?

- What does your initial review of your people policies and practices highlight as priorities? Which specific improvements will trigger more substantial change?

How much stake-holder power is there to support implementation?

- Are those who "know" those who "care", who "can" also deliver? Who are the few, the specific individuals who can make a real difference?
- Who is actively backing a more committed approach? Who is opposing this agenda? Who is on the sidelines awaiting others' reactions?
- What arguments do you need to use to engage the top team fully in the implementation of change and optimise their involvement?

How effective is current technology in providing "succession intelligence"?

- Poor.
- OK.
- Good? Why?
- What are your organisation's plans to improve succession technology? Does this represent an opportunity or a risk?
- How well are you exploiting the gains of on-line technology to reduce the "paper shuffle" and transform the speed and quality of information flows and decision-making?

Notes

1. "Who's Next", *HR magazine*, November 2003.
2. The concept of the "tipping point" was popularised by Malcolm Gladwell, who noted that rapid and dramatic change does not necessarily require significant causes. It is sometimes the small things that make the big difference.
3. Malcolm Gladwell, *The Tipping Point*, 2000.
4. S. Friedman, "Succession Systems in Large Corporations: Characteristics and Correlates of Performance", *Human Resource Management*, vol. 25 (1986).
5. Quoted in J. Collins, *Good to Great*, 2001.
6. Andrews Munro Ltd, "Best Practice Succession & Resourcing: Survey Results", 1999.
7. "Best Practice Succession & Resourcing: Survey Results", Andrews Munro Ltd, 1999; "Strategic Resourcing Alignment Index Survey", Andrews Munro Ltd, 2002.
8. Sun Tzu, *The Art of War*, Westview Press, 1994.
9. *The Times*, 23 April 2004.
10. D. Ulrich, *Human Resource Champions*, 1997.
11. Andrews Munro Ltd, "Strategic Resourcing Alignment Index Survey", 2002.

Bibliography

Andrews Munro Ltd, "Best Practice Succession & Resourcing: Survey Results", 1999; "Current Potential, Future Performance", 2001; "Measuring Organisational Resilience", 2001; "Is Talent Enough: A Survey of Career Tactics", 2002; "Strategic Resourcing Alignment Index Survey", 2002.

Azure Consulting International, "Leadership Dynamics Profile Survey", 2003.

Peter Bernstein, *Against the Gods: The Remarkable Story of Risk* (John Wiley & Sons, 1996).

Judi Bevan, *The Rise and Fall of Marks & Spencer* (Profile Books Ltd, 2001).

James Bolt, *The Leader of the Future* (Jossey-Bass, 1996).

Larry Bossidy, "The Job No CEO Should Delegate", *Harvard Business Review*, 2001.

R. Boyatzis, The Competent Manager: A Model for Effective Performance (Wiley, 1982).

Robert Bryce, *Pipe Dreams: Greed, Ego and the Death of Enron* (PublicAffairs, 2002).

Marcus Buckingham and Curt Coffman, *First, Break All the Rules* (Simon & Schuster UK Ltd, 1999).

Wayne F. Cascio, *Costing Human Resources: The Financial Impact of Behavior in Organisations* (South-Western College Publishing, 2000).

Ram Charan, Stephen Drotter and James Noel, *The Leadership Pipeline* (San Francisco: Jossey-Bass Publishers, 2001).

James C. Collins and Jerry I. Porras, *Built to Last* (UK, Century Ltd, 1993).

Jim Collins, *Good to Great* (UK Random House Business Books, 2001).

M. Cook, *Personnel Selection and Productivity* (John Wiley & Sons, 1998).

Mihaly Csikszentmihalyi, *Good Business, Leadership, Flow and the Making of Meaning* (UK Hodder and Stoughton, 2003)

Peter F. Drucker, *The Practice of Management* (William Heinemann Ltd, 1995).

L. Eastman, *Succession Planning* (Centre for Creative Leadership, 1995).

R. Eccles and N. Nohria, *Beyond the Hype* (Harvard Business School Press, 1992).

Gerard Egan, *Working the Shadow Side* (San Francisco: Jossey-Bass Publishers, 1994).

R. Farson, *Management of the Absurd: Paradoxes in Leadership* (New York: Simon & Schuster, 1996).

William G. Flanagan, *Dirty Rotten CEOs* (New York: Citadel Press Books, 2003).

Richard Foster and Sarah Kaplan, *Creative Destruction* (New York: Currency Books, Doubleday, 2001).

S. Friedman, "Succession Systems in Large Corporations: Characteristics and Correlates of Performance", *Human Resource Management*, vol. 25 (1986).

Adrian Furnham, *The Incompetent Manager: The Causes, Consequences and Cures of Management Failure* (Whurr Publishers Ltd, 2003).

Barry Gibbons, *Dream Merchants and How Boys* (John Wiley & Sons, 2002).

Malcolm Gladwell, *The Tipping Point* (Little, Brown and Company, 2000).

Daniel Goleman, *Emotional Intelligence* (Bantam, 1998).

David Greising, *I'd Like the World to Buy a Coke: The Life and Leadership of Roberto Goizueta* (John Wiley & Sons, 1997).

Andy Grove, *Only the Paranoid Survive* (Doubleday, 1996).

R. Giuliani, *Leadership* (Times Warner, 2002).

G. Hamel and C. K. Prahalad, *Competing for the Future* (Harvard Business School Press, 1994).

G. Hamel and L. Valikangas, "The Quest for Resilience", *Harvard Business Review*, September 2003.

Russell Hotten, *Formula 1: The Business of Winning* (Orion Business, 1998).

I. Kesner and T. Sebora, "Executive Succession: Past, Present and Future", *Journal of Management*, vol. 20, no. 2, (1994), pp. 327–72.

Manfred F. R. Kets De Vries, *Leaders, Fools and Impostors* (San Francisco: Jossey-Bass Publishers, 1993).

Rakesh Khurana, *In Search of the Corporate Savior* (Princeton University Press, 2002).

Richard Koch, *The Power Laws* (Nicholas Brealey Publishing, 2000).

F. Luthans, R. Hodgetts and S. Rosenkrantz, *Real Managers* (Cambridge, Mass: Ballinger, 1988).

M. McCall, M. Lombardo and A. Morrison, *The Lessons of Experience* (Lexington Books, 1988).

M. McCall, *High Flyers: Developing the Next Generation of Leaders* (Harvard Business School Press, 1998).

T. McEachen and C. O'Brien, *The New New Economy* (Amacam, 2002).

Ed Michaels, Helen Handfield-Jones and Beth Axelrod, *The War for Talent* (Harvard Business School Press, 2001).

Nigel Nicholson, *Managing the Human Animal* (UK Texere Publishing Ltd, 2000).

James O'Loughlin, *The Real Warren Buffet* (Nicholas Brealey Publishing, 2003).

J. Pfeffer, *The Human Equation* (Harvard Business School Press, 1998).

S. Pinker, *The Blank Slate* (Penguin Group, 2002).

C. Pollard, *The Soul of the Firm* (New York: HarperBusiness, 1996).

William Poundstone, *The Prisoner's Dilemma* (Oxford University Press, 1993).

Martin Seligman, *Authentic Happiness* (Random House, 2002).

Dave Ulrich and Bob Eichinger, *Human Resource Champions* (Harvard Business School Press, 1997).

Peter B. Vaill, *Managing as a Performing Art* (San Francisco: Jossey-Bass Publishers, 1989).

James Waldroop and Timothy Butler, *Maximum Success* (New York, Currency Books, Doubleday, 2000).

Index

About the Author

Andrew Munro (MA, C Psychol) is a Director of Azure Consulting International Ltd, a consulting practice focusing on the link between organisational effectiveness, succession management and leadership. Over the last 20 years he has worked with an array of organisations in the commercial and public sectors, implementing pragmatic solutions to help organisations build greater resilience and responsiveness through attention to strategic resourcing.

For further information about Azure Consulting's products, consultancy approach and research programmes, visit www.azureconsulting.com; e-mail him at andrew@azureconsulting.com or call on +44 (0) 1608 641160.

He is also a Director of Andrews Munro Ltd, a firm specialising in online systems for recruitment, professional and management assessment, performance management and career profiling (info@amltd.demon.co.uk).